The Mark of the Beast

New Directions in the Human-Animal Bond
Alan Beck, series editor

The Mark of The Beast

Animality and Human Oppression

Mark S. Roberts

Purdue University Press
West Lafayette, Indiana

ISBN 978-1-55753-474-3

Library of Congress Cataloging-in-Publication Data

The Mark of the Beast : animality and human oppression / Mark S. Roberts.
    p. cm.
  Includes bibliographical references and index.
  ISBN 978-1-55753-474-3
  1. Animality in Theory. 2. Philosophy and Science—Animality in Act.
3. Slavery and Holocaust—Restoring the Animal. 4. Modernity and
Postmodernity. I. Roberts, Mark S. II. Title.
  B105.A55R63   2008
  128—dc22   2007042131

Contents

Acknowledgments

I would like to thank Donald Pruden Jr., for the generous loan of works from his extensive collection of racist, pro-slavery, and anti-black literature, many items of which would otherwise have been extremely difficult to find. I would also like to thank him for reading the manuscript in its early stages, and for commenting on much of the section on slavery and on the literary work of the Reverend Thomas Dixon. In this regard, I would also like to express gratitude to David B. Allison for his comments and suggestions on the manuscript. Annie Rowland, researcher at the South Country Library in Bellport, New York, helped enormously in tracking down some of the more obscure volumes needed for the slavery section. Justus George Lawler, the initial editor of this book, smoothed out what were some pretty rough edges in the original manuscript, and in so doing made numerous important suggestions regarding revisions of the manuscript, in both form and content. In addition, I would like to thank the editorial and production staffs at Purdue University Press for their excellent work and assistance. I should also acknowledge the faith in and support of the book shown by the series editor Alan Beck.

Preface

And the smoke of their torment ascendeth up for ever
and ever: and they have no rest day nor night, who worship
the beast and his image, and *whosoever receiveth the mark of
his name.*

—Revelation 14:11

The over-animal.—The beast wants to be lied to; morality
is an official lie told so that it shall not tear us to pieces.
Without the errors that repose in the assumptions of
morality man would have remained animal. As it is, he
has taken himself for something higher and imposed
sterner laws upon himself. *That is why he feels a hatred for
the grades that have remained closer to animality: which is the
explanation of the contempt formerly felt for the slave as a
non-man, as a thing.*

—Friedrich Nietzsche, *Human, All Too Human*

The preceding quotations address the central focus of this book: the process of
consigning humans to the status of "beast"—a consignment that often subjects
them to mastery, domination, exploitation, and, in the worst cases, slaughter.
The process of animalization is, of course, an ancient one, assuming a multitude
of forms, many of which are intrinsic to early religious traditions, rites, rituals,
and customs. Clearly, just ritually transforming humans into animals or vice
versa is not in itself a pernicious act. Nor does the common mythopoeic and
literary practice of personification/anthropomorphism count exclusively as a
means of exploiting, mastering, or disparaging humans. Anthropomorphism
serves far too broad a range of functions in human cultures to be reduced simply to a means of repression. Rather, *animalization* here refers specifically to

the course of action that grew out of a number of theories aimed first at establishing human superiority over animals and then at the domination of certain classes and groups—a process that sought to ascribe, both "philosophically" and "scientifically," the presumed inferiority and brutality of various animals to these groups and classes. The present work, then, is primarily a historical and critical examination of those theories and practices that contributed to the peculiar contempt felt for what Nietzsche so colorfully described as the "grades that have remained closer to animality."

Apart from some foundational classical theory regarding animals, the first part of this book focuses on the modern era, beginning, appropriately enough, with Descartes. The emphasis here is on the Cartesian notion of the animal as machine, and, following this course, on the further implications of such a vision. Part 1 is largely devoted to those theoretical distinctions between humans and animals. Such distinctions lead logically to the various modes of animalization, or the rendering non-human of humans, employed during the long history of mastery and domination: biodeterminism, medico-psychiatric practices, punition, racism, sexism, colonization, genocide. Here what I explore is not so much the problem of distinguishing humans from animals, but rather the various ways in which the reasoning behind animalization is actually deployed—or, perhaps more to the point, the justifications for rendering humans as animal. This part particularly emphasizes the biodeterministic rationalization for the inferiority of certain groups or "races" of humans, particularly blacks, women, and other minorities, though other forms of mastery, domination, and exploitation are explored as well.

Beyond the theories of animalization lie the acts—arguably some of the most heinous acts imaginable. Although a virtually endless series of atrocities has been perpetrated during the modern era, the second part of this book centers on a detailed account of the practices of rendering animal so prominent in both slavery and the European Holocaust. The latter event was one in which the very nature of animalization/dehumanization leaps from virtually any literary or visual description of the depravities of this period. The early Nazi euthanasia projects, the "roundups," the "cattle cars," or, more pointedly, the slaughterhouse atmosphere of the death camps themselves, serve as striking examples. Even Martin Heidegger's one and only statement invoking Nazi atrocities brings this point home with chilling effect: "Agriculture is now a mechanized food industry; in essence, no different than the *production of corpses* in the gas chambers and death camps."[1]

The third part of the book is devoted to an account of how traditional theories, modes, and acts of animalization are interpolated and restored—often tacitly—in the discursive practices and actions of certain kinds of contemporary thinking. Consequently, the main point of part 3 is that the older conceptual frameworks for animalization are still being applied to contemporary modes of discrimination, racism, and sexism, but by far more sophisticated and subtle means: through film, media of various kinds, contemporary social and political theory, advanced medical technology, and so on. The end of this part focuses on the "future of animalization," that is, the continuing existence of what I am calling a "parallel dimension" of the human/animal controversy that still remains largely unrecognized. Special attention is thus paid to the human/machine controversy, which, to my thinking, owes (at least in part) its distinction between humans and non-humans, post-humans and cyborgs, to the concepts and practices of animalization.

The book closes on the affirmation that animals themselves are also fully exploited—perhaps themselves animalized—in the process of animalizing humans, and that they are in no way deserving of the negative views generated throughout both the ancient and modern eras. Effectively, there are no bad animals, just human conceptions of bad animals. To this I add the possibility of conceiving a continuum, a "unified field" as it were, of all species that in the end will be fully inclusive and thus render the largely specious, self-serving, exclusive arguments of the animalizers both empty and pointless.

PART I

ANIMALITY IN THEORY

"Philosophy" and "Science"

While Père Malebranche and his friends were walking along, a pregnant dog came fawning up to them. Père Malebranche knelt down to fondle her. Then, making sure his friends had their eyes upon him, he stood up, pulled back his cassock, and kicked the poor animal in the stomach as hard as he could. The dog went yelping down the street, and Père Malebranche hardened his voice, and this is the essence of what he said: Fie on ye! Restrain yourselves. That dog is nothing but a machine. Rub it there, it scratches. Whistle, it comes. Kick it, it yelps and runs away. There is a button to push and a mechanism for each of its actions. It is nothing but a machine.

— Richard Watson, *Cogito, Ergo Sum: The Life of Descartes*

There are monsters that are born with a form that is half-animal and half-human ... which are produced by sodomists and atheists who join together, and break out of their bounds contrary to nature, with animals, and from this are born several monsters that are hideous and very scandalous to look at or speak about.

— Ambroise Paré, *Des monstres et prodiges*

I

From Aristotle to Foucault

It is clear that perceiving and understanding are *not* the same. For while all animals have a share of the former, only a few have a share of the latter.

—Aristotle, *De Anima*, bk. III

Aristotle: Specifying the Animal

What are the characteristics that traditionally distinguish humans from animals? Big brains rather than small brains? Minds? Morals? An erect posture? Or, much more controversially, *are* there any distinguishing qualitative characteristics, outside of those imposed *by* humans *on* animals?

To a large degree, the last question posed seems most indicative of the method of the early Western scientific and philosophical traditions. Aristotle, arguably the most thoroughgoing naturalist of the classical Greek period, was also one of the first to make claims in the cognitive, anatomical, and physiological realms regarding differences and similarities between humans and animals. In what is referred to popularly as "The Zoology" (*Historia Animalium*), Aristotle advances several observations about distinguishing characteristics among animals, ranging from their simple and composite parts to a comparison of humans and animals. Animals, he argues initially, have parts that exhibit contrasting differences and qualities, particularly with regard to shape and color. Some have soft skin, others scaly skin; "some have a long beak or bill, others a short one; some have many feathers, others few."[1] Besides the physical characteristics of animals, they have "many differences of disposition [*êthos*]": "Some, like the ox, are gentle, sluggish, and not given to ferocity; others, like the boar,

3

are violent, ferocious, and untamable. Some are prudent and timid, like the stag and the hare, others are treacherous and crafty, like the snake; others are noble, courageous, and aristocratic, like the lion."[2] The terms used here—"noble," "aristocratic," "sluggish," and so forth—already indicate a transposition of human values and descriptions onto the animal world. Even the use of the term *éthos*, a clear reference in the Greek to disposition or (in terms of rhetoric) character, limits animal behavior to categories of strictly human evaluation. To further sunder animals from *Homo sapiens*, Aristotle adds: "But the only animal capable of deliberation is man. For although many other animals have the ability to remember and to learn through experience, no animal except man is able to recall the past at will."[3]

A more typical early Western conception of how humans stand vis-à-vis animals, though, is contained in section VI of *The Zoology*, where Aristotle distinguishes the two by analogy:

> While certain traits in men differ only in degree from those in animals—man exhibiting more of one trait and certain animals more of another—there are also traits in man to which the corresponding traits in animals are related only by the principle of analogy. For as men exhibit art and wisdom and intelligence, animals possess other kinds of natural ability which serve much the same purpose. This view of the matter is confirmed by considering human children: for in them can be seen the indications and seeds of their future dispositions, yet their psychic traits at that age are virtually the same as those of the lower animals.... Nature passes from lifeless things up to animal life by such gradual degrees that the continuity obscures boundaries and puzzles us how to classify intermediate forms.[4]

Although, to a certain degree, the die is cast here for the general Western view of the human/animal distinction, Aristotle gives considerable range and extension to this zoological relationship. Animals are not just dumb creatures, lacking human attributes and skills, and therefore totally outside the human realm, but, rather, equal players in a sort of bio-cosmological game of natural forms. Moreover, this close relationship most certainly reflects the kind of interactivity between natural species that Aristotle envisions in *De Anima* (*On the Soul*), in which the souls of animals, containing a universal tripartite division (rational, sensitive, appetitive/nutritive), are said to be integrated with those of humans in the larger picture of mutually fulfilling natural forms. In fact, in his treatise on the soul, Aristotle writes:

> The soul of animals is characterized by two faculties, (a) the faculty of discrimination which is the work of thought and sense, and (b) the faculty of originating local movement.... An animal is a body with a soul in it: every

body is tangible, i.e., perceptible to touch, hence necessarily, if an animal is to survive.... All other senses are necessary to animals, as we have said, not for their being, but for their well-being.[5]

Aristotle's sundering of the animal/human relation occurs most obviously and with the greatest force in his *Nicomachean Ethics*. Here the bio-cosmological unity of all living creatures is by and large unmade through one fateful characteristic: reflective moral conscience. Enter the "brute" and the "dumb beast": "The brutes do not share with man the power of deliberate choice, but like him they feel desire and passion."[6] Further on, the peculiarly human characteristics of "virtue" and moral "intelligence" are even more solidly erected as barriers between humans and lower animals:

> This means that we must reconsider the nature of virtue.... This is the relation between natural and true virtue; that is to say, between the good qualities we share with the lower animals and those which belong only to man. It is the universal belief that in some sense the moral qualities are each and all the gift of Nature; if we have a disposition to justice, to temperance, to courage, and the other virtues[,] we have it from birth. For all that we look to find that true goodness is something more than this, and that the good qualities that are in the full sense of the word good have their origin elsewhere. For the natural dispositions, which even children and wild animals possess, are demonstrably capable, if undirected by intelligence, of doing harm ... if we don't have a guide, we stumble. But if a man who possesses a natural disposition to goodness acquires good sense as well, then he behaves in the best way, and the disposition which *resembled* will now *be* goodness.[7]

So, even if we do share common traits and behaviors, the factor that divides us eternally from the animals is self-reflection or moral intelligence: not merely an application of intelligence to some specialized calculative function, but rather the ability to reflect upon and control our actions—not, as Aristotle fears, to trip and fall heavily as we wander about.[8] Distinctly human morality, then, consists in temperance; that is, the ability to know precisely what is good for us, what brings pleasure and avoids unpleasure. Children and animals do not employ this faculty: "Now what animals and children pursue are those pleasures which are not absolutely good, and it is freedom from the pain of being denied these pleasures that the prudent man seeks."[9]

For Aristotle, then, the human/animal distinction hinges not so much on individual characteristics or even on supposed inner states like intelligence, consciousness, sentience, cognition, and so on, but, rather, on moral reflection and intentional actions. In this sense animals and children could be categorized, in modern ethical terms, as amoral. They are neither fully aware of nor in control of their desires and drives; they do not have the capacity to effectively demonstrate virtue, that is, temperance. Thus, for Aristotle, the animal is separate from the human because it cannot achieve the highest value of human ethical life: the self-reflective fulfillment of pleasure and, ultimately, happiness. The animal, by its very nature, is incapable of achieving what humans ought to achieve. In certain respects, one could characterize the animal as a failed human.

This characterization of animals as amoral, and thus inferior, beings is often taken up in the scientific, philosophical, and popular literature of both the Hellenic-Roman and early and late medieval periods.[10] A striking example of this sort of depiction occurs, interestingly enough, with a thirteenth-century fictional account in Old French of Aristotle himself becoming animal, *Lai d'Aristote*. The *Lai* is based on a moral tale of Aristotle's hypocrisy regarding sexual passion. As Alexander the Great's mentor, he warns the young man to "bridle" his passions and to control his desires toward his lover Phyllis—but Aristotle is himself attracted sexually to Phyllis, to such an extent that he becomes her willing slave. As such, he is "animalized" by Phyllis, who forces him to prance around horselike on all fours, while she is mounted in a saddle on his back.[11] The horse, of course (particularly in Plato's *Phaedrus* and, much later, in Freud's *The Ego and the Id*[12]) represents a loss of control, the unrestrained rearing of sexual or libidinal desire, not to mention, in this case, a kind of bestial humiliation. The animal in him is, as Aristotle himself argues in his *Ethics*, an amoral beast that does the wrong thing without reflection, without self-control:

> In the tradition exemplified by the *Lai d'Aristote*, animality is an ethical failure. Aristotle knows what a perfect human should do, knows what is morally right, yet he is unable to act in accord with his knowledge. This is clear at the end of the *lai*, where Aristotle argues that the lesson to be drawn from his "becoming beast" is that the temptation to do wrong is so powerful that even the world's greatest philosopher cannot refrain, and hence Alexander should try even harder than ever to keep traveling on the right road to moral rectitude. Animality in this perspective is a failure of one's will to match the perfection of one's knowledge: Aristotle is knowledgeable, but not wise, since *wisdom* (and humanity, as opposed to animality) *is doing the right thing*.[13]

In Aristotle's philosophy, it should be noted, one can extend animal (and children's) amorality to a lack of reflective awareness in general, for, indeed, he stresses this both in *De Anima* and the *Ethics*. Failure to be aware of the ethical ramifications of one's behavior naturally extends to failure to be aware of the implications and meaning of behavior in general. This faculty, missing in animals, involves the ability to understand the unseen, the untouched, the universal, and the "disembodied truth behind sensations or appearance, to know the invisible causes of visible perceptions."[14]

The human/animal distinction was thus fixed quite early in Western thought. Aristotle began this rupture with the use of transposed valuations and terms to animals: They are "stubborn," "noble," "savage," "murderous," and so on. Even when they are "good" or "aristocratic," they do not really know or fully understand these actions and behaviors. Our relation to animals, though organically coherent, is, in contrast, strictly severed at the point of reflection, moral conscience, knowledge of the truth, and self-awareness in general. To be an animal, then, in the simplest terms, is to be inferior; to lack the capacity to know precisely the implications of one's actions, and, even more important, to be unaware of the goals of all positive ethical life: pleasure and the avoidance of unpleasure, of pain. This latter deficiency eventually proves deadly to the animal itself, as well as to "the animal in us."

Descartes and Cartesianism: Animal as Machine

One might say that Aristotle and the tradition that followed him gave animals a pretty fair shake regarding their comparison to humans. Descartes, in sharp contrast, relegates these creatures to the most inhuman level possible: machines, mere mechanical devices, automata: "And, doubtless, when swallows come in the spring, they act in that like a clock."[15] Also unlike Aristotle, who centered his objections to animals achieving human status on moral reflection, Descartes relegates the beasts to sheer automata because they are not animated by rational souls and therefore cannot demonstrate intentional, reasoned speech—indeed, could not speak at all in any human sense of the term.

Although consistent with his thought in general,[16] Descartes's objection to intelligent animal speech was specifically a response to Montaigne's rather generous definition of speech in his *Apology of Raymond Sebond*. Montaigne speculated in this work that animals may speak a language that we do not understand, and thus could be full participants in a larger sphere of inter-related though disparate voices and languages: an idea quite consistent with Montaigne's conception of universal humanism—and, I should add, with much modern research on animal communication. The principal reasoning behind Montaigne's speculation about animal speech was the fact that he could see no distinct dividing line between animal and human speech: where, in fact, did animal speech end and human speech begin? Indeed, Montaigne even went so far as to speculate, as did the ancients, that animals communicate with humans by their calls and gestures; they even feel and express love through their eyes, as do humans.[17]

This, of course, did not pose a problem for Descartes. Animals were not only incapable of rational speech, but were relegated to expressing only the simple motions of physical objects—were, indeed, nothing other than *materia*. The barking of a dog was really no different in kind from the grinding sound made by the gears of, say, a giant mechanical loom: both are expressions of reflex mechanical actions subject to the laws of physics.[18] Although this vision of animals as strictly physical objects was consistent with Descartes' philosophical conceptions in general, particularly those expressed in the *Discourse* and *Meditations*, it appears that much of Descartes' inspiration for this view came from actually seeing mechanical devices that simulated human and animal movement:

> In the *Treatise on Man*, the philosopher describes at length a fountain designed by de Caus for the royal gardens at Saint-Germain en Laye which contained an animated statue of Diana bathing. Visitors who entered the garden stepped on a hidden lever which caused the robotic Diana to retreat behind a rock. If they continued forward, they were surprised by a trident-waving Neptune or "a marine monster who vomited water in their face."[19]

Descartes' own description of this mechanical phenomenon is as follows:

> External objects which merely by their presence act on the organs of sense and by this means force them to move in several different ways, depending on how the parts of the brain are arranged, are like strangers who, entering some of the grottoes of these fountains, unwittingly cause the movements that then occur, since they cannot enter without stepping on certain tiles so arranged that, for example, if they approach a Diana bathing they will cause her to hide in the reeds; and if they pass farther to pursue her they will cause a Neptune to advance and menace them with a trident; or if they go in another direction they will make a marine monster come out and spew water into their faces or other such things according to the engineers who made them. And finally when there will be a rational soul in this machine, it will have its chief seat in the brain and will there reside like the turncock who must be in the main to which all the tubes of these machines repair when he wishes to excite, prevent, or in some manner alter their movements.[20]

Despite the charming little moral message inherent in the design of the fountain, Descartes seems most impressed with the way in which mechanical bodies can be animated. Clearly, the fountain designer, the master mover of the mechanical figures, operates much like Descartes' rational soul. Once it enters the body, it can control, adjust, and alter movement in a particular direction. It is precisely this power to control movement that indicates the existence of reason, the one element distinguishing humans from animals. All creatures are moved mechanically, but only humans can consciously manipulate their parts and, most importantly, their speech.

Having identified the factors that he believes distinguish humans from animals, Descartes is not satisfied to halt his inquiry at a purely scientifically descriptive and comparative level. He goes on to argue for the mastery of humans over animals, as if animals were some form of dependent slave/being that could only be tamed, used, and domesticated but never fully integrated into human life—in short, an "other," an outsider living in a parallel but "dumb" and inferior universe, that is, a material universe. This view is stridently presented in Descartes' letters to the Marquis of Newcastle (1646) and to Henry More (1649): in both instances he makes a case for the separation of animals from humans, even "the most stupid and the most foolish," on the grounds of reason and speech. These two human qualities represent absolute and insurmountable differences, which are readily demonstrable and at least not easily contradicted. Nevertheless, the reason for Descartes's conviction regarding the "dumb brutes" lies in the somewhat naïve supposition that because animals cannot communicate to us the fact that they can speak (i.e., we cannot experience animals speaking), they probably cannot speak to one another either:

> But the principal arguments, to my mind, which may convince us that the brutes are devoid of reason, is that, although among those of the same species, some are more perfect than others, as among men, which is particularly noticeable in horses and dogs, some of which have more capacity than others to retain what is taught them, and although all of them make us clearly understand their natural movements of anger, of fear, of hunger, and others of like kind, either by the voice or by other bodily motions, it has never yet been observed that any animal has arrived at such a degree of perfection as to make use of a true language; that is to say, as to be able to indicate to us by the voice, or by other signs, anything which could be referred to thought alone, rather [than] to a movement of mere nature; for the *word* is the sole sign and the only certain mark of the *presence of thought hidden and wrapped up in the body*; now all men, the most stupid and the most foolish, those even who are deprived of the organs of speech, make use of signs; whereas the brutes never do anything of the kind; which may be taken for the *true distinction* between man and brute.[21]

The behavioral validity of Descartes' observations aside, there is a tendency here to create a distinction based on mastery, one that parallels Descartes' larger view of the natural superiority of mind over matter. Here the animals are not only relegated to the status of "brutes" and "dumb beasts," but the very possibility of improvement, change, or rehabilitation in general is precluded. The reason given for this conspicuous inferiority is that animals can never achieve reason: no reason, no progress. Expressed in more positive but quite similar terms, Geneviève Rodis-Lewis proposes the following regarding Descartes' animal/human distinction:

> The animal's status is that of "all or nothing"; it either continues to exist or it perishes. Man sometimes envies its immediate reactions to the situation: an animal jumps into water and swims because its machine automatically establishes an equilibrium with the new environment. Man, on the contrary, "hesitates" and debates the issue; only those movements that he makes "without thinking" are perfectly appropriate.
>
> But his weakness is also his greatness. Because his knowledge is limited, it is capable of growing. For want of a perfect science, he trusts nature by exploiting the animal in him. But he is still able to know when the adaptive spontaneity begins to wear out. He then employs all his mental resources; he struggles and risks making mistakes. This is the ransom of his freedom.[22]

In a somewhat roundabout way, Rodis-Lewis's interpretation conveys the essence of the Cartesian notion regarding animal/human relations. Although humans are surely animals—and in certain ways, imperfect animals—the human is capable of "reforming" the instinctual functions so as to alter his patterns of adaptive behavior. In short, the human uses the animal in him to his advantage, exploiting what is beneficial and repressing or discarding what is not. The reason for this is simple—reason. Or, as Rodis-Lewis states, in referring to adaptation common to man and animal: "man invents his own language by mastering mechanical associations between physical elements (auditory or visual signs) and mental meanings."[23]

This exile of the animal, the automaton, to the outside, to the status of an extended object, is perhaps most strikingly expressed in the *Discourse on Method* (1637), in which Descartes not only relegates the animal to a machine but to a machine that fails even in view of its instinctual superiority. The animal is faster, stronger, more cunning, better able to instinctually cope with the environment, "shows more skill than we do," but it is precisely because of this superiority that it is inferior to humans. Why? According to Descartes, "that they do better does not prove that they have any intelligence, for if it did then they would have more intelligence than any of us and excel us in everything. It rather proves that they have no intelligence at all, and that it is nature that acts in them according to the disposition of their organs."

Although the analogy clearly fails, it is instructive to the extent that it demonstrates Descartes' use of reason as a weapon—a two-edged sword in the preceding case—to sunder the unity of species, and, most significantly, to ascribe inferior qualities to the animal. In a manner of speaking, the animal can't win for winning, because superiority is reduced to inferiority due to the absence of reason: If only the beast could reason, it would rule the world! Here there is also a subtle hint of competition and protectiveness. Earlier, in part V of the *Discourse*, Descartes sets up what amounts to a contest of reason, stated in terms of the ability to recognize automata, or what exists outside the realm of active reason:

> [I]f any such machines bore a resemblance to our bodies and imitated our actions as closely as possible for all practical purposes, we should still have two very certain means of recognizing that they were not real men.... Secondly, even though such machines might do some things as well as we do them, or perhaps even better, they would fail at others, which would reveal that they were acting not through understanding but only from the disposition of their organs ... hence it is for all practical purposes impossible for a machine to have enough different organs to make it act in all contingencies of life in the way in which our reason makes us act.[24]

Failure and lack—which I interpret as inferiority, as otherness—play a central role in Descartes' distinction between humans and animals. Lacking an immortal soul and therefore the vehicle of reason, animals neither converse intelligibly among themselves nor with us, nor are they in any way our equals. We cannot learn from them, because we cannot communicate with each other. We can observe their behavior, but this merely informs us of the complexity of their mechanical actions, which are by and large their only positive features. Thus, the animal mechanism reacts: "In the same way a clock, consisting only of wheels and springs, can count the hours and measure time more accurately than we can with all our wisdom."[25]

In the end, what is important about Descartes' theories for our purposes is not whether in fact animals are inferior to humans because they lack a soul and therefore rational thought and language, but, rather, that they have been excluded entirely from the human sphere; they fail to achieve either speech or intelligence, and are thus mere physical objects populating a material universe.[26] If we think about these "objects" in terms of relative status, position, standing, and so on—the terms commonly used to describe objects—we can quite easily envision the possibility of creating entire classifications of "others" who also lack or demonstrate inadequate human qualities such as reason, intelligence, souls, moral reflection, and so on, but who are still technically humans. These are the "flawed" others that the "madness and excesses of reason" have relegated to exteriority, and to the throes of animalization.

"The Rational Animal": Kant and the Increasing Divide

Kant's principal division between humans and animals lies in the distinctly human ability to exercise what he calls an "ego-concept," or, in more recognizable terms, self-consciousness. The key to mastery over all other creatures is this reflective state, and it provides humans with precisely that ability necessary to rule, both socially and politically. Indeed, it wholly removes humans (probably read: men) from the realm of things—a realm to which animals are irrevocably condemned: "He is a being who, by reason of his preeminence and dignity, is wholly different from *things*, such as the irrational animals whom he can master and rule at will."[27] In addition, like Descartes, Kant holds reason and language among the key functions of the distinction between human and animal. Both these faculties, moreover—as is not (at least explicitly) the case for Descartes—interact to create a condition of progress and evolution that is an inherent characteristic of human development but is entirely absent from animal evolution.

As Descartes tends to assign rationality to humans a priori, Kant sees the rational endowment as more or less the result of a process of perfection and development, that is, the necessity to make oneself into a rational being. Thus, for Kant, humans are not simply endowed with a fully developed rationality, but must undergo a series of transformations, which will in the end lead to the cultivation of the rational animal (*animal rationale*). The motivation for this evolutionary movement is that nature has uniquely planted in the human species a seed of discord, which, if not overcome, can lead to chaos and social imbalance. The human entelechy, then, is to "turn discord into concord or at least create a constant approximation of it."[28] According to Kant, this process can be divided into three parts: first, preserve the species; second, instruct and educate the species for social living; third, govern the species as a systematic whole.[29]

These three functions are accomplished through three essential human talents: the technical gift (mechanically connected with consciousness), the pragmatic gift (using others for one's own purposes), and the moral gift (the ability to act toward oneself and others according to freedom under the law). These, Kant argues, are enough in and of themselves to distinguish "man characteristically from other inhabitants of this earth."[30] By listing these various gifts in the *Anthropology*, Kant thus places a great deal of emphasis on their exclusively human character. Humans are in fact distanced from animals simply because they are capable of achieving the various ends of these social and rational processes. The technical gift, for example, is a uniquely human one because, unlike animals, humans can coordinate their prehensile movements and motor skills with the faculty of reason. Nature, Kant asserts, has given them the technological gift because they are a rational animal; this indicates, of course, that animals may stand on two legs, have prehensile digits, and so on, but lack the reasoning ability to apply these as technological gifts. The second of Kant's functions, the pragmatic gift, involves more or less the same anthropomorphic bias that Descartes demonstrates when he reduces the natural physical superiority of animals to a liability, by claiming that, because they are demonstrably physically superior, they should also be the most rational of beings.[31] In this regard Kant argues that even though humans are not capable of reaching their full destiny as individuals, as is the case with animals, they are prone to progress only as a species: "Above all, it must be noted that all other animals left to themselves reach as individuals their full destiny, but human beings reach their full destiny only as a species."[32] The implementation of this progress toward the fulfillment of his destiny requires that man invoke the third of Kant's gifts: the moral gift. In this respect humans must constantly fight off the innate evil that lurks in them, which, in turn, raises humans above all other animal species. Indeed, the very ability to struggle against the inclination to evil is, perhaps, the single most important human capacity that distinguishes the species from others.

With the threefold gifts and the processes they entail, Kant has effectively increased the divide between humans and animals. Now it is not primarily rationality nor even speech that separates humans from animals, but a group of peculiarly human endeavors as well. According to Kant, orangutans, chimpanzees, and other primates may stand erect, pick up things with prehensile hands and feet, and even interact socially, but they lack the technological skill to use these tools toward continuing progress; they thus accomplish all that is possible for them to accomplish within one generation—due, one presumes, to innate instincts for survival. Moreover, as animals are only "things," they also lack the capacity for moral reflection and probity, and are thus incapable of fending off the innate tendency (shared by both humans and animals) toward evil. In short, animals lack the ability to reflect on their place within space and time; they live in an atemporal and a-spatial domain, devoid of reason, morality, and law—that is, precisely Kant's fundamental building blocks of human civilization.[33] Lacking these vital characteristics of progress, so crucial to the development of human civilization, the animal simply stands well outside this process, assuming the position of usable "thing," a means by which to accomplish a higher and necessary human end.

Confining the "Animal"

The emphatic denial of animal rationality, speech, and progress in the Age of Reason tended to create increasingly negative categories for animals and, most importantly, any people or persons designated as animal-like: animals had become, as it were, the dross of the animal world, constituted by what they lack and what they fail to achieve of humanity. "Every attribute that it is claimed we uniquely have, the animal is consequently supposed to lack; thus, the generic concept of 'animal' is negatively constituted by the sum of these deficiencies."[34] In large part, these deficiencies became crucial to those who sought to victimize and lock up the animal-like in the name of reason, humanity, religion, morality, intellectual superiority, profit, normalcy, social progress, or just plain good etiquette.

In the post-Cartesian world, much of this repressive activity originated from a novel union between the emerging psychobiological, medical, and social sciences. As is well known, Michel Foucault, in his *Madness and Civilization*, characterizes these nascent sciences as functioning, among other things, to wholly direct and confine unreason. He asserts that, in both the Middle Ages and the Renaissance, madness was everywhere, absorbed into the patterns of everyday life, alive in the theater, art, and literature of the period.[35] To be mad was thus to be dangerously inspired, an onerous gift rather than a curse. In the Age of Reason, however, madness became an "embarrassment," and thus subject to severe but often subtle forms of repression:

> In the Renaissance, madness was present everywhere and mingled with every experience by its images and dangers. During the classical period, madness was shown, but on the other side of bars; if present, it was at a distance, under the eyes of reason that no longer felt any relation to it and that would not compromise itself by too close a resemblance. Madness became a thing to look at: no longer a monster inside oneself, but an animal with strange mechanisms, a bestiality from which man had long since suppressed.[36]

Thus, the Cartesian beast was cast in the image of the madman: the automaton, the brute, had now found a vehicle in the bestiality of madness. To stress even further this relation between madness and bestial automatism, Foucault cites Pascal's mechanistic description of what it takes to be human: "I can easily conceive of a man without hands, feet, head (for it is only experience which teaches us that the head is more necessary than the feet). But I cannot conceive of a man without thought; that would be a stone or a *brute*."[37]

The question that eventually arises regarding the treatment of madness is this: What is to be done with these unwieldy brutes? In effect, how can one save them from themselves and at the same time save society from utter embarrassment? The answers center on the question of confinement, of removing them from public sight, but yet keeping them under intense surveillance: the venue of the "cage," of the darkened, claustrophobic space, the cell. Whereas madness had "floundered about in broad daylight" in the Middle Ages and the Renaissance, it was now sequestered in what Foucault calls "the fortress of confinement."[38] Bound, isolated, and judged by reason itself, madness became not only an instance of Cartesian animality but also the total breakdown of Cartesian animality—a disordered, mechanical wildness, a lack of instinctual control that must be restrained at all costs; a clock, as it were, whose mechanism runs backwards.

In the latter part of the eighteenth and early nineteenth centuries, the confinement of the insane could only be described as an unmitigated horror. Mental institutions were generally no more than filthy holding pens, and those diagnosed as insane were handled in the most egregiously brutal manner, being treated literally like animals. Often they were placed twenty, thirty, and sometimes forty in an eight-foot-square room, packed in like rats in a hole. Those kept in the lower cells of the Salpêtrière, for example, lived in totally deplorable animal-like conditions, and "when the waters of the Seine rose, those cells situated at the level of the sewers became not only more unhealthy, but worse still, a refuge for a swarm of huge rats, which during the night attacked the unfortunates confined there and bit them whenever they could reach them; mad women have been found with feet, hands and faces torn by bites which are often dangerous and from which several have died."[39]

The most extreme animal-like treatment, however, was usually reserved for uncontrollable and violent patients. In a British hospital for the insane, a hysterical woman given to severe fits was chained in a pigsty and left to sleep on straw and her own excrement, just like the pigs themselves. Samuel Tuke, the famed reformer of British mental institutions, reported a case of a violent patient who was chained to a wall day and night, and who, during exercise periods, was walked around the cell attached to a long chain, much like the family dog. Foucault explains this gross inhumanity by the fact that "a certain image of animality . . . haunted the hospitals of the period. Madness borrowed its face from the mask of the beast."[40] Thus, those chained to the cell walls, or incarcerated in tiny cagelike structures, were no longer seen as human but as beasts in the throes of some primordial frenzy. It was precisely this equation of animality and madness that gave the asylum its menagerie-like look, its palpable feeling of a human zoo, replete with cages, catwalks, chains, neck collars, and feeding chutes:

Madwomen seized with fits of violence are chained like dogs at their cell doors, and separated from keepers and visitors alike by a long corridor protected by an iron grille; through this grille is passed their food and the straw on which they sleep; by means of rakes, part of the filth that surrounds them is cleaned out.[41]

Other descriptions of the period are frighteningly similar. At a hospital at Nantes, the "accommodations" were described as "individual cages for wild beasts." Each of the cages was elaborately constructed with a welter of bolts, locks, chains, and iron bars. Each cage was fitted with a chain fastened to the exterior wall, which contained a receptacle suited for delivering small amounts of food to the madman. Much like in the zoo, this sort of device protected the "keepers" from the dangerous rage of the animals. Like animals, many of the patients were left naked, allowed to sleep and take their meals on a little straw, where they could also deposit their excrement.[42]

The system of mental institutions in the Age of Reason was clearly in large part built to deter (or at least contain) the animalistic violence of the insane. The very architecture of these institutions was in many ways comparable to the sort of menageries that might fascinate the then-modern bourgeois strolling through a public park. Everything was arranged and organized so as to fascinate and protect those outside the confines of the asylum, in much the same way enclosures and gardens were intended to protect the populace from the fearful wilderness beyond medieval cities and towns. As Foucault suggests, "this inhuman indifference actually has an obsessional value: it is rooted in the old fears which since antiquity, and especially since the Middle Ages, have given the animal world its familiar strangeness, its menacing marvels, its entire weight of dumb anxiety."[43]

Even given its brutal treatment in the Age of Reason, though, animality had not yet become an irreversible sign of exclusion and inferiority. In fact, in some ways it served to protect the madman, giving insane persons something of an excuse for their behavior:

In the classical period . . . it manifested the very fact that *the madman was not a sick man*. Animality, in fact, protected the lunatic from whatever might be fragile, precarious, or sickly in man. The animal solidity of madness, and that density it borrows from the blind world of the beasts, inured the madman to hunger, heat, cold, pain. . . . Madness, insofar as it partook of animal ferocity, preserved man from the dangers of disease; it afforded him an invulnerability, similar to that which nature, in its foresight, had provided for animals. Curiously, the disturbance of his reason restored the madman to the immediate kindness of nature by a return to animality.[44]

II

From Gobineau to Freud

But it is precisely this development of the animal faculties that stamps the Negro with the mark of inferiority to other races. I said that his sense of taste was acute; it is by no means fastidious. Every sort of food is welcome to his palate; none disgusts him; there is no flesh or fowl too vile to find a place in his stomach. So it is with regard to odor. His sense of smell might rather be called greedy than acute. He easily accommodates himself to the most repulsive.

—Arthur Compte de Gobineau,
The Moral and Intellectual Diversity of Races

Race Theory and the "Sciences" of Animality

It was not until the end of what Foucault designates the classical era that animality became a clear sign of mental and social inferiority. By the beginning of the nineteenth century, its negative characteristics were employed as a means of separating racial groups, and animality became an important theoretical grounding for the nascent biodeterministic and hereditarian "sciences," particularly those dealing with race theory. In this regard, animality was viewed in its more historically traditional role as *lack*, as what failed to reach the level of the human. It was no longer associated with the ancient myths of animal savagery and instinct, which provided an explanation—and an excuse—for the excesses of madness. Now its various functions and effects served as the basis for inferiority, as a kind of calculus of otherness, separating those who bore strong resemblance to animals from those who were deemed to have fully human characteristics.

Theories of racial inferiority have a long and lamentable history in the West,[1] but one can arguably attribute their most systematic modern elaboration to the "Father of Racist Ideology," Arthur Compte de Gobineau. As a racist ideologue, Gobineau did not fall back on classic Aristotelian theory, nor was he overly concerned with finding a theory of racial difference in the philosophical tradition as a whole. Rather, he sought a new explanatory racist ideology in what he conceived to be a kind of collective natural, "internal" history. For Gobineau, the peoples composing a nation were pulsating with a certain "germ," which carried their destiny. This germ, though subject to certain types of invasive degeneration, was irreversible and inevitable, sheltered from outside change, coursing through the blood of a particular race or people. Gobineau also rejected the idea of applying external data—particularly, cases of individual achievement—to the explanation of racial inequality, basing inequality on purely physical and mental characteristics that could be determined empirically. In his view, the environment had virtually no effect on individual capacity. Each individual within a given racial strain had an innate ability to achieve certain levels of culture and civilization: "The true health of a people and the cause of life and death were to be found, as Kant and Lessing had observed, in 'inner constitution.'"[2]

According to his "empirical" method, what Gobineau referred to as "elements of civilization" could be classified and expressed in "objective" terms, such as relative proportions. In H. Hotz's detailed "Analytic Introduction" to the English translation of Gobineau's *Essai sur l'inégalité des races humains* (1853–1855), a chart appears that divides the races into three categories: intellect, animal propensities, and moral manifestations. The relative disproportion of these characteristics in the various races is instructive regarding the role of animality in Gobineau's general theory, as well as in early biodeterministic thought. The white race is classified as having a "vigorous intellect," "strong" animal propensities, and "highly cultivated moral manifestations," whereas the black race has a "feeble" intellect and "partially latent" moral manifestations, but "very strong" animal propensities." He used a purportedly objective, unilinear scale to determine the relative humanness of individual races; those judged lowest on the scale were subject to comparisons with the mindless, though instinctually proficient, brutes and beasts. Hotz continues: "If the animal propensities are strongly developed, and not tempered by intellectual faculties, the moral conceptions must be exceedingly low, because they necessarily depend on the clearness, refinement, and comprehensiveness of the ideas derived from the material world through the senses."[3] This kind of thinking, it should be noted, reflects both the Aristotelian and Cartesian distinctions between humans and animals, settling on the question of rectitude, particularly the necessity of intellect in reflective morality.

Nevertheless, Gobineau's conception of animality goes much further than the mere lack or the "partial latency" of moral reflection in certain races. For him, the presence of animality indicates a fundamental, unalterable nature that is markedly inferior and clearly demonstrable in terms of observable physical characteristics. For example:

> Let us suppose him now to examine another individual: a negro, from the western coast of Africa. This specimen is of large size, and vigorous appearance. The color is jetty black, the hair crisp, generally called *wooly*; the eyes are prominent, and the orbits large; the nose is thick, flat, and confounded with the prominent cheeks; the lips are very thick and everted; the jaws projecting, and the chin receding; the skull assuming the form called prognathous. The lower forehead and *muzzle-like* elongation of the jaws, give to the whole being an almost *animal appearance*, which is heightened by the large and powerful lower-jaw, the ample provision of muscular insertions, the greater size of cavities destined for the reception of the organs of smell and sight, the length of the forearm compared with the arm. . . . In contemplating a human being so formed, we are involuntarily reminded of *the structure of the ape*.[4]

One gets the distinct impression here that we are confronted with a "specimen" lying somewhere between a mountain gorilla and a human: a large, hulking creature, described in pronounced detail, that leans distinctly toward the non-human, and which even gives us the impression that it secretes some kind of mortal danger and savagery. The description purports to be accurate, cast as it is in purely anatomical terms. The animal in this African "negro" is not a matter of conjecture, but rather a "fact" established by strictly empirical observation. One need merely compare the gross skeletal characteristics of this "ape-like" creature to the subtle and delicate skeletal details of the white race to fully and immediately realize the exact difference between the two races. Particularly condemning is the existence of the immense "cavities destined for the reception of the organs of smell and sight," because animals are most dependent on these particular senses, whereas humans tend primarily to utilize cognitive and intellectual functions.

The ascription of animality here, however, is not limited to comparative anatomy alone. It indelibly marks the very possibility of a civilization's development—its culture, economics, and politics—because what appears without is indicative of what exists within. Those showing the proverbial "mark of the beast" are condemned to perpetual backwardness and inability to rise to higher levels of civilization: "Are we not, then, authorized to conclude that the diversity observable among them is constitutional, innate, and not the result of accident or circumstances—that there is an absolute inequality in their intellectual endowments?"[5] Thus, for Gobineau, one of the truest indicators of a civilization's decadence and inability to advance is its proximity to the animal, the observable "constitutional" trait of certain races:

> My opinion is, that the negroes, in respect to capacity for mental improvement, are far behind Europeans; and that considered in the aggregate, they will not, even with the advantages of careful education, attain a very high degree of cultivation. This is apparent from the structure of the skull, on which depends the development of the brain, and which, in the negro, approximates closely the animal form. The imitative faculty of the monkey is highly developed in the negro, who readily seizes anything merely mechanical, whilst things demanding intelligence are beyond his reach.[6]

What is interesting and disturbing about Gobineau's conception of animality is that the animal has now been placed squarely within the human, and is thus no longer just a standard for comparison. Rather, the degraded human *is* to some degree a lower animal, not only given to animal-like behavior, but also possessed of specific, identifiable animal characteristics: a sense of smell that accommodates itself to the repulsive, eating "raw viands," apelike jaws, animal pelvises, muzzlelike elongation of the jaws, and so on. These terms not only describe the various "races"—Negroes, "Andaman Islanders," Indians, and so on—but also invoke a new classificatory logic, a taxonomic construction that tends to incorporate both human and animal. Unlike Foucault's idea of an external societal obsession with animality, the animal has now invaded the body of the human, maintained by the Kantian ideas of innateness and inner constitution. If what is outside is an absolute indicator of what is within, the aesthetically based narratives of animality must give way to the precision of scientific observation, anatomical study, and purely descriptive physical science. The discovery of the truly non-human is now left to the craniometers, craniologists, and atavists—those who will attempt to prove that anatomy is surely destiny.

Measuring the Inner Animal: The Homologies of Animality

> Pity is not natural to man ... but acquired and improved by the cultivation of reason. Savages are always cruel. Natural affection is nothing: but affection from principle

and established duty is something wonderfully strong—so
savages have no more affection than do hens.
—Samuel Johnson, quoted in James Boswell,
Life of Samuel Johnson

Although the main thrust of Gobineau's work centered on the historical, political, and cultural implications of racial diversity, it also encompassed areas of
physical anthropology, particularly the then-voguish sciences of brain measurement: craniometry and craniology. In this regard Gobineau showed particular
interest in the work of Samuel George Morton, the American scientist and
physician who assembled what was at the time considered the *opus magnum* of
craniometry, *Crania Americana* (1839). Morton's scientific roots lay in the European tradition of comparative anatomy and racial studies begun, in large part,
by Carolus Linnaeus with his *Systema naturae* (1758) and further sustained by
the eminent naturalist and anatomist Georges Cuvier and his followers. This
school of thought took the position (among numerous others) that objectively
verifiable differences between races could be determined on the grounds of either physiological or behavioral similarities in animals. Linnaeus, for example,
attributed such things as excessive lactation in African women to animalistic
mothering tendencies. Cuvier, following the master, found native Africans
"the most degraded of human races, *whose form approaches that of the beast* and
whose intelligence is nowhere great enough to arrive at regular government."[7]
His postmortem remembrance of the famed "Hottentot Venus" contained even
more egregious animalistic comparisons:

> She had a way of pouting her lips exactly like what we have observed in the
> orang-utan. Her movements had something abrupt and fantastical about
> them, reminding one of those of the ape. Her lips were monstrously large.
> Her ear was like that of many apes, being small, the tragus weak, and the ex-
> ternal border almost obliterated behind. These are animal characters. I have
> never seen a human head more like an ape than that of the woman.[8]

Morton, pursuing this earlier comparative method, found what appeared
to be an even more objective set of standards than the largely approximative
and anecdotal Linnaean techniques. He collected hundreds of skulls of different
racial types, arranged them in categories, and measured them for cranial capacity. He then averaged out the cranial capacity of each specimen group, finding
some striking disparities among what he reckoned as the five races. In the end,
his supposedly carefully drawn-up comparative tables showed clearly that both
black Africans (what he referred to as "Ethiopians") and American Indians had

significantly lower cranial capacity than Caucasians, particularly those of the Teutonic family.[9] Although Morton did not draw explicit comparisons between Ethiopians, Indians, or Jews (another low-ranking group) and lower animals, the "irrefutable" brain-size data established what seemed to be a scientific grounding for the very real presence of animality in certain racial types. It did not take a great deal of imagination to decide, given Morton's ascending scale, that Ethiopians were much more closely linked to lower primates than to higher Teutons, for those with small brains were, by virtue of diminished cranial capacity, most certainly closer to animals than to higher humans who had significantly larger brains. Cranial capacity was thus not only an "objective" indication of intellectual differences between groups of humans, but it could also well serve to establish what appeared to be an irrefutable morphological connection between certain groups of these "tainted" humans and lower animals.

The finer details of this kind of morphological connection were not fully realized until the latter part of the nineteenth century, when more sophisticated, modern experimental methods like those of Paul Broca and his school were applied to craniological measurement. Broca, a distinguished surgeon and anthropologist, rejected virtually all forms of speculative science, placing his faith in a positivistic, data-based approach to scientific research. This fondness for objectivity was not, however, always present in his own research. Most of the results of his craniological experiments were simply disguised confirmations of one of the dominant prejudices of the time: namely, that white males—Teutonic types, in the vocabulary of racism—were at the very top of the intelligence pyramid and that the lower races occupied the bottom. His method, based on these prejudices, consisted of formulating a conclusion commensurate with this bias, and then manipulating the facts to fit that conclusion. After having reviewed Broca's research for an extended period of time, Stephen Jay Gould reached the following conclusion:

> I found a definite pattern in his methods. He traversed the gap between fact and conclusion by what may be the usual route—predominately in reverse. Conclusions came first and Broca's conclusions were the shared assumptions of most successful white males during this period—themselves on top by the good fortune of nature, and women, blacks, and the poor people below. His facts were reliable (unlike Morton's), but they were gathered selectively and then manipulated unconsciously in the service of prior conclusions. By this route, the conclusions achieved not only the blessings of science, but the prestige of numbers.[10]

Indeed, what Broca had really discovered was a method by which one could make just about any favored conclusion seem correct. Whether the results were produced by valid methods was of little significance; what counted was that the so-called facts were correctly derived, properly documented, and, most importantly, elaborately quantified. Numbers became a sort of underlying, unchallenged truth of the research, and if one could generate impressive enough statistics regarding the object of inquiry, the validity of the conclusions would inevitably follow. This, of course, represented a considerable advance beyond the work of Morton regarding morphological connections between humans and animals. Because, in theory, bodies can be measured in a virtually infinite number of ways, one could generate an endless flow of data, manipulate that data to fit a prior conclusion, and still maintain the appearance not only of scientific proof, but also of the soundness of the conclusion itself. Broca himself applied this method to an elaborate experiment based on the difference between the ratio of the radius (forearm bone) and the humerus (upper arm bone), assuming that a higher ratio marks a longer forearm—a distinct characteristic of apes.[11] He also made detailed statistical comparisons of the position of the foramen magnum (the hole in the base of the skull) in various races, reasoning that in the lower races the foramen magnum would be further back on the skull, indicating an apish trait: the further back the foramen magnum, the less upright the position. His preliminary conclusion in this experiment, though of course patently wrong, was: "In orang-utans, the posterior projection [the part of the skull behind the foramen magnum] is shorter. It is therefore incontestable ... that the conformation of the Negro, in this respect as in many others, tends to approach that of the monkey."[12]

Sliding Backward: Recapitulation and Atavism

> The idiot stands at an intermediate stage between ape and man.
>
> —Carl Vogt

Ironically, what amounted to perhaps the greatest scientific discovery of the nineteenth century served as a basis for some of the most egregious pseudoscientific claims regarding human animality. Darwin's theory of evolution, first introduced in his *The Origin of Species*, settled most of the arguments stemming from the two predominant forms of pre-Darwinian creationist evolutionism: monogenism and polygenism.

Before Darwin the two great questions in evolutionary theory were simply How precisely do species originate? How do they evolve? Darwin had a definite, though controversial, answer for these questions. Basically, he argued

that species originate and evolve because of chance variation and natural selection. Organisms are endowed with certain characteristic mechanisms that
allow them to survive in specific environments. Those better endowed tend to
produce genetic variations that increase chances for survival, whereas others
that fail to adapt either die off or leave fewer offspring—a tendency that usually leads to extinction. The theory also supposed that species as a whole evolve
along certain lines, developing adaptive skills that eventually lead to progressive
improvements. Subsequently, it was thought, a species like *Homo sapiens* would
advance through a series of stages from an apelike state to a fully human one,
all the time progressing in both outer appearance and inner qualities.

The latter concept was, of course, central to the hypothetical assignment
of animality, which centered on two evolution-based theories. On the one hand,
late-nineteenth-century evolutionary scientists, particularly Ernst Haeckel, the
German zoologist, introduced the idea of *recapitulation*, which assumed that
an individual, in its own growth, passes through a series of stages representing adult ancestral forms in a more or less precise order of progression.[13] On
the other hand, the idea of *atavism*, the search for signs of apish morphology
or neotenous features in contemporary humans, was introduced as a way of
discovering the sources and indicators of deviance (particularly criminality) in
certain undesirable groups.

Of the two means of assigning animality, the least directly relevant was
recapitulation, because recapitulation almost always involved human-to-human
comparisons. Such comparisons, as invidious as they may have been, concerned
a vast range of human activities and capacities, including such things as prehistoric and primitive art in relation to children's drawing, the propensity for
proper etiquette, higher suicide rates among women, and the child-like brains
of African natives.[14] The Reverend Josiah Strong, commenting on Henry Clay's
"naïve" defense of inferior peoples, provides a striking example of basic reca-
pitulationist thinking:

> Clay's conception was formed ... before modern science had shown that
> races develop in the course of centuries as individuals do in years, and that
> an undeveloped race, which is incapable of self-government, is no more a
> reflection of the Almighty than is an undeveloped child who is incapable
> of self-government. The opinions of men who in this enlightened day be-
> lieve that the Filipinos are capable of self-government because everybody
> is, are not worth considering.[15]

Strictly human-to-human comparisons, however, do not completely rule
out the use of recapitulation as a base theory for assigning animality. The fundamental structure of the theory consists of a linear ranking order: advanced

humans, the "Teutonic types" of the racist theoreticians, are placed on a much higher level than individuals that demonstrate characteristics of their children. Like craniometrics, recapitulation adds yet another dimension to the "science of inferiority": the lower types can be fully degraded—in, I should add, an acceptable scientific manner—by the very fact that they act, think, behave, and respond to their respective worlds like tiny white toddlers. Playful, spontaneous, naïve, they are "charming" but quite incapable of caring for themselves. This dependency could readily be translated into a kind of animal need, for even as early as the work of Aristotle, animals and children were seen as having quite similar traits: "for in them [children] can be seen the indications and seeds of their future dispositions, yet their psychic traits at that age are virtually the same as those of the lower animals."[16]

Atavism, in contrast, was a much more effective tool of animalization. The comparisons involved were largely human-to-animal ones, with apishness being the principal standard of inferiority. The general theory is simple, if not just simplistic. It is based on the notion that crime is hereditary, an evolutionary characteristic that can be discovered through anthropometric data.

Although a number of scientists applied the idea, the self-proclaimed discoverer and principal theorist of atavism was the famed Italian criminologist and physician, Cesare Lombroso. Presumably in the course of a long, frustrating attempt to discover some anatomical differences between criminals and the insane, he came upon the theory in a flash of inspiration:

> At last I found in the skull of a brigand a very long series of atavistic anomalies, above all an enormous middle occipital fossa and a hypertrophy of the vermis analogous to those that are found in the inferior vertebrates. At the sight of these strange anomalies the problem of the nature and the origin of the criminal seemed to be resolved; the characteristics of primitive men and of inferior animals must be reproduced in our times.[17]

Like most inspired visionaries, Lombroso went to extraordinary lengths to confirm his vision. The mere existence of apish or "inferior vertebrate" characteristics in criminal types was not, in itself, sufficient to fully confirm the moral obliquity of criminals, for, as Gould stresses, if "apes be kind, the argument fails."[18] To compensate, Lombroso went on to give what may be the most ludicrous account of animal behavior in the history of natural science. He attributed criminal qualities to all sorts of animals, including in his writings accounts of irate ants dismembering aphids; an adulterous stork, which, with her lover, murdered her husband; as well as a sort of criminal beaver Mafia.[19]

Oddly enough, in the introduction to the English translation of Lombroso's masterwork, *L'Uomo Delinquente* (1918), Maurice Parmalee, a noted sociologist of crime, added still more ludicrous evidence in support of animal depravity:

> But among animals are to be found veritable equivalents of crime in acts contrary to the general habits and welfare of a species by one of its members. Cannibalism, infanticide, and parricide frequently occur, while murder, maltreatment, and theft are used to procure food, to secure command, and for many other reasons.[20]

While Parmalee to a certain degree relieved animals of conscious wrong-doing, claiming that these so-called heinous acts are "natural and normal," he found, as did Lombroso himself, an equivalent, and less excusable, proclivity toward crime in savages. Savages, it seems, are really no different from animals in their criminal tendencies: "The same is true of many habits of savages. For example, homicide is frequently practiced under social sanction, such as infanticide, murder of the aged, of women, and of the sick, etc., while cannibalism is prevalent in many tribes. Theft also exists under social sanction."[21]

Interestingly, apparently realizing that Lombroso's log-extorting mafioso beavers were probably not the best possible scientific examples, Parmalee mitigated the patently unscientific, if not entirely absurd, Lombrosian animal examples by involving something of a middle term: savages. Now one could get to the criminal by a more circuitous but less scientifically unsound route. Although non-human animals could not be held responsible for their depraved actions, savages could. After all, they are human—barely human, but human nevertheless. The animal character built around savagery, immorality, dumbness, depravity, and so on could now travel an evolutionary path through the animal to the savage directly to the criminal type, the throwback. Thus, Lombroso and his followers tended to fulfill one of the most significant goals of racist theories of animality: to place the animal directly (morphologically) within the human, so as to render certain types of humans truly animalistic and therefore justify their maltreatment, confinement, and exploitation—even, in certain cases, their slaughter.

The Feline Factor: Breeders, Nurturers, and Vixens

> Even though [animal] mothers have their stomachs torn open. . . . [e]ven though their offspring have been the cause of all their woes, their first care makes them forget all they have suffered. . . . They forget themselves, little concerned

with their own happiness. . . . Woman like all animals is
under the sway of this instinct.

—Jean-Emmanuel Gilbert, quoted in
Sarah Blaffer Hrdy, *Mother Nature*

Animalizing theories were certainly not aimed at dark-hued and criminogenic
males alone. By the middle to latter part of the nineteenth century, a significant
store of "scientific" literature was being developed regarding the natural inferiority of women. Broca had already compared women's brains to those of savages
and white children, as well as proving, at least to his satisfaction, that there was
an increasing discrepancy between the cranial capacity of prehistoric women
and men and modern-day women and men. His principal disciple, Paul Topinard, attributed the small size of women's brains to innate sexual and gender
differences, arguing that "[t]he man who fights for two or more in the struggle
for existence . . . who is constantly active in combating the environment and
human rivals, needs more brain than the woman whom he must protect and
nourish, than the sedentary woman, lacking any interior occupations, whose
role is to raise children, love, and be passive."[22]

Direct comparison to animals was left, however, to the master misogynist
of Broca's school, Gustave Le Bon. Le Bon, one of the founders of social psychology, enjoys extraordinary eminence in the history of misogyny, standing,
perhaps, only a notch below Aristotle in this regard—which is no small feat.
He wrote numerous tracts against the rights of women, and, more importantly
for our purposes, often made casual comparisons between women and animals:
"[T]here are large numbers of women whose brains are closer in size to those
of *gorillas* than to the most developed male brains. . . . Without doubt there
exist some distinguished women, very superior to the average man, but they
are as exceptional as the birth of any monstrosity, as, for example, *a gorilla with
two heads*; consequently we can reject them entirely."[23] That Le Bon used the
image of a "gorilla with two heads" is, I think, significant. This image contains
two important components of the animalization of inferior types (in this case,
women). First, it implies that women share some direct physical, cognitive, and
psychological evolutionary link with animals, particularly with terrifying and
presumably violent ones like gorillas. Second, it lends an aleatoric, purely ac-
cidental quality to women's achievement, which is, of course, characteristic of
the lower animals: whatever animals may achieve of "civilization," of accom-
plishment in human terms, is achieved only as a result of the instinctual need
to survive, as pure happenstance.

The characterization of sexual difference in animal terms, however, was left largely to the evolutionary theorists spawned by Darwin. Broca, Le Bon, Lombroso, and their ilk had the basic idea (as well as the motivation), but they were not very active in applying Darwinian laws of inheritance and sexual and natural selection.[24] It was precisely with these laws that the neo-Darwinian sexists and antifeminists were able to reduce women to animality, for evolutionary theory had conveniently placed the human in a biological continuum with all other animal species:

> Women and savages, together with idiots, criminals, and pathological monstrosities, were a constant source of anxiety to male intellectuals in the late nineteenth century. (Children, though less than fully human, would eventually become so.) Man's place in nature so long established as a thing apart, separate and distinct from the rest of creation, had suffered a radical revaluation. The human species was now seen as sharing a common animality with the beasts that walked and flew and crept over the earth. Man differed in degree rather than kind from his nearest relatives, the anthropoid apes, and this was as true of the mind as of the body. . . . Rather than something distinctly human, "all our highest faculties and sentiments are differentiations and evolutions of instincts and desires which are represented in the lowliest organism by the most simple and most general vegetative instincts."[25]

This mortal fear of slippage, however, was transformed by certain thinkers into something of a weapon aimed against women. Darwin had argued that the existence of sexual characteristics, both primary and secondary, was the result of sexual selection. The male or female sexual paraphernalia—brilliant plumage in birds, scent glands, hairiness, etc.—were there because they contributed to reproductive success. However one interpreted sexual selection (and there were numerous views of the theory[26]), the irresistible, primitive force of reproduction always lay at the center of sexual difference. With an incontestable force like sexual reproduction guiding the form and function of the physiological and mental characteristics of the sexes, it was quite easy to assign distinct roles and features to the players in this primeval drama.

The animalization of women thus had a number of what appeared to be empirical sources in early evolutionary theory. On the one hand, it was argued that males demonstrated variability, whereas females were largely conservationist in nature. Although Darwin did not invent the variability/conservation theory, he did argue that males differed more—that is, were more varied—from the young and other males. The theory was adopted, in altered form, by several late-nineteenth-century evolution-dependent theorists, including W. K. Brooks and Havelock Ellis. In their hands, women were assigned social and

intellectual roles commensurate with their conservative function: unadventur-
ous and not given to nomadic roaming, females were by and large limited to
home and hearth, a life of reproduction and nurturing. To quote Patrick Ged-
des and Arthur Thompson's *Evolution of Sex*, woman was "an overgrown ovum
... the patience of the egg awaiting in joyful expectation the dynamic embrace
of the sperm."[27] This passive reproductive role was the perfect justification for
animalizing the female. Without curiosity, male intellect, wanderlust, or need
of education, the female was viewed not only as an "overgrown ovum," but also
as a kind of "animal in heat," whose primordial ancestry arose naturally at every
menstrual cycle, providing once again the "normal" course for survival of the
species. In this view, to suppress women—to keep them pregnant and at home,
deny them an education, and so on—was merely to act in accordance with the
natural course of things, the incontrovertible laws of sexual selection.

Female sexuality as the natural course of things served still another, quite
different, animalizing function. The free expression of female sexuality was an
underlying concern of much nineteenth-century male-dominated thinking, in
both the natural and the social sciences. If women were allowed to express their
reproductive desires by seeking sexual contact outside of the confines of the
home and family, the general order of social relations, it was thought, would be
seriously destabilized. One remedy for this presumed problem was to negatively
link female sexuality to animality, rendering it bestial, unspeakable, perverse,
and humanly unthinkable.

One example of such an attempt occurred at the beginning of the century
with the Hottentot Venus mentioned earlier.[28] The so-called Venus was in reality
a South African woman, Sarah Baartman, born in Capetown, who was carted
off to England as a circus exhibit. She was later sold to a French animal trainer
who took her to Paris, where she worked as a prostitute and died at the age of
26. The attraction of this woman was unmistakably sexual, not exotic. When
she was paraded naked outside her cage, the spectators were most fascinated,
and alarmed, by her extraordinarily large breasts, sexual organs, and outsized
buttocks. It was reported that English and French gentlemen, unaccustomed to
public shows of nudity, simply drooled over her "elongated genital flap." These
features were so coveted by interested spectators and serious scientists alike that
her sexual organs were dissected by the great Cuvier at her death and displayed
in several jars of formaldehyde at the Musée de l'Homme in Paris.

Anita Levy and Sander L. Gilman argue, respectively, that the reasoning behind the fascination and exposure of Sarah Baartman had to do with the
nineteenth-century desire to demonstrate the "maleness" of women's sexuality
(protuberant clitorises, well-developed prepuces, and the like) and to associate

female sexuality in general with African blacks.[29] Both are correct, but there is a third reason, connected with the animalization of female sexuality. In commenting on the Hottentot Venus, Gould makes the interesting observation that, to European audiences, she represented "a creature that straddled that dreaded boundary between human and animal."[30] Kept in a cage—she ate and slept there at intervals during her captivity—her animality controlled and regulated by her male keepers, her incarceration symbolized the dangers of female sexuality loosed. When she was caged, like the other animals in the circus or menagerie, or in Foucault's madhouse, she posed little danger. Outside the cage, however, in the socially ordered world, she could well represent the liberation of female sexuality, signs of "'primitive' sexual appetite and activity, in which the link established between the ill, the bestial and the freak was embodied."[31] The cage with all of its mechanisms of control stood between the orderly social world and the excesses of bestiality; the display of the Venus was not merely a spectacle but a spectacle carefully arranged so as to fascinate and frighten, like bestial, uncontrolled sexuality, but at the same time to assure the spectators of strict limits and distinct boundaries beyond which they were in perfect control.[32] After all, what could be more reassuring than eventually viewing the wild sexuality of the infamous Hottentot Venus decanted in formaldehyde?

Freud also used animality to negatively cast female sexuality, but in far more subtle ways than most of the nineteenth-century evolutionary biologists and psychologists, with their often pseudoscientific excesses. His writing on animality per se is sparse, appearing in only a few ancillary studies, the most notable of which is "Inhibitions, Symptoms and Anxiety" (1926 [1925]).[33] It is in this work that Freud gives us some indications, though preliminary ones, of his reduction of female sexuality to animality. In reviewing the famous case of "Analysis of a Phobia in a Five-Year-Old Boy" ("Little Hans") (1918), he suggests that "Little Hans's" fear of horses was not simply a phobia regarding animals, but, rather, an instinctual impulse directed against his father. "Little Hans" had apparently played horse games with his father, seen a horse collapse in the street, and witnessed his friend playing at being a horse and falling, as if he were dead, in the street. According to Freud, "Little Hans" had transferred this idea of a dying or wounded animal to his father, associating him with the "big animal":

> Children do not as yet recognize or, at any rate, lay such exaggerated
> stress upon the gulf that separates human beings from the animal world.
> In their eyes the grown man, the object of their fear and admiration, still
> belongs to the same category as the big animal who has so many enviable
> characteristics but against whom they have been warned because he may
> become dangerous.[34]

Following this, Freud goes on to cite two other minor cases of supposed animal phobias, which he claims, as with "Little Hans," had their source in destructive instinctual impulses aimed against the patients' fathers. Freud also mentions another famous animal-related case in the above text: "From the History of an Infantile Neurosis ('Wolfman')" (1918 [1914]). In the end, "Wolfman" suffers from symptoms not unlike those of "Little Hans." Apparently this "Russian patient," whom Freud did not analyze until the patient was in his twenties, had had a dream, after which he became terrified of being devoured by a wolf. In an analysis that purportedly revealed the meaning of the dream, Freud speculated that, like "Little Hans's" father who played "horsey" with him, the Wolfman's father played the wolf and threatened to eat him, once again invoking fantasies of the father as the "big animal" and providing grounds for directing destructive impulses at him.

But what does all this have to do with the bestial nature of female sexuality? It appears that both of the aforementioned signal cases, "Little Hans" and "Wolfman," have their point of departure in the Oedipus complex. In Little Hans's case, Freud suggests that he was disposing of "the two main impulses of the Oedipus complex," that is, his aggressiveness toward his father and his overfondness for his mother. Freud leaves the analysis at that point, as there seems to be little or no evidence of the patients' early Oedipal fantasies. In the case of "Wolfman," however, Freud goes further: this patient's deficiency lies elsewhere. "His attitude to female objects had been disturbed by an early seduction and his passive, feminine side was strongly developed. The analysis of his wolf-dream revealed very little intentional aggressiveness towards his father, but it brought forward unmistakable proof that what repression overtook was his passive tender attitude to his father."[35]

It is precisely in regard to femininity and the resolution of the Oedipus complex that the link between female sexuality and animality is established. Without going into extensive detail, Freud viewed the female's struggle to resolve the Oedipus complex as quite different from that of the male. The successful male deciphers the "riddle" by resolving his conflicts with both the mother and father figures—what Freud refers to as a "positive" Oedipus complex. Little girls are not so lucky. They must pass through a largely unconscious and amoral stage of father love, similar to that of "Wolfman," which takes on some of the characteristics of the wild beast, a state "totally without a sense of the implications of her acts, and thus beyond proscriptive morality."[36] In this view, the girl's sheer sexual attachment to what Freud had referred to as "the big animal" culminates in an unspeakable desire to have his child, which, in turn, leads to infantile masturbation, and, in the end, penis envy.[37]

Thus, the female, resisting her "tender feelings" toward her father, yet torn by the desire to "have his child," sets the father up as a figure who will—who must—at least in fantasy, impregnate her. Like a mindless beast, she is fatefully driven by the sexual need for impregnation, for sexual reproduction, even at the hands of her father. The irrepressible desire for reproduction involves a transformative stage as well. Locked into the fantasmatic desire for the father, the little girl becomes nothing less than a "little woman": "But now the girl's libido slips into a new position by means—there is no other way of putting it—of the equation 'penis = child.' She gives up the wish for the penis and puts in place of it a wish for a child: and *with this purpose in view* she takes her father as a love-object."[38] Thus, unlike the male of the species, the little woman is unable to raise herself to a level of true civilization and maturity, to positively resolve the Oedipus complex by mitigating her attachment to the father. Instead, she is embroiled in childhood struggle against her most bestial makeup, finally succumbing psychologically to the instinctual desire to mate with the amorphously conceived "big animal," to transform his envied penis into his child. Not unlike, I should add, the female subject's instinctual surrender to the incontrovertible evolutionary laws of sexual selection.

The animalization of women, then, counts as yet another largely artifactual, but historically consistent, "scientific" theory directed, once again, at human repression. To render someone animal-like is also to subjugate that person to some form of mastery, to impose certain controls and limitations on that person and his or her physical and mental being. By and large, these controls—whether they be Sarah Baartman's cage or Emma's sewing room—served to suppress women's achievement in a variety of spheres. Keeping women home, breeding and nurturing, or fantasizing about their father's penis-child, kept them out of the workplace, out of the university, and remote from the possibility of financial, sexual, or personal power. Simply put, the pie did not have to be cut into too many slices. However, women and their modular equivalents—the poor, immigrant minorities, so-called inferior races, and so on—were to face much darker consequences, ones emerging from the modern sciences of medicine, psychiatry, and, most importantly, the newly rehabilitated science of eugenics.

III

From Tubal Ligation to Slaughterhouse

Excising the Animal: Eugenics

The "science" of eugenics, like racist thinking, goes far back in the history of Western thought. The theory itself is usually traced to Plato's *Republic* (v. 459), where the first systematic argument in favor of selective breeding appears:

> Clearly, then, we must have marriages, as sacred as we can make them; and this sanctity will attach to those which yield the best results.
>
> Certainly.
>
> How are we to get the best results? You must tell me, Glaucon, because I see you keep sport dogs and a great many game birds at your house; and there is something about their mating and breeding that you must have noticed.
>
> What is that?
>
> In the first place, though they may be of good stock, are there not some that turn out to be better than the rest?
>
> There are.
>
> And do you breed them all indiscriminately? Are you not careful to breed from the best so far as you can?
>
> Yes.
>
> And from those in their prime, rather than the very young or the very old?
>
> Yes.
>
> Otherwise, the stock of your birds and dogs would deteriorate very much, wouldn't it?
>
> It would.
>
> And the same is true of horses or of any animal?
>
> It would be very strange if it were not.
>
> Dear me, said I: we shall need consummate skill in our rulers, if it is also true of the human race.

The most chilling line of all, "if it is also true of the human race," had gone largely unnoticed for about 2,500 years until Sir Francis Galton revived it in the late 1860s. Galton, a natural scientist, biometrician, and a cousin of Darwin's, articulated the modern theory of eugenics in an extended article turned book, entitled *Hereditary Genius* (1869). The gist of the book is that genius, of course, is hereditary, and that those possessed of it should be encouraged to propagate among their peers.[1] Galton even encouraged a national examination to determine genius; high scorers would be brought together, married at Westminster Abbey, and sent off to breed new generations of British leaders, men of genius, and captains of industry.[2] This eugenicist trend led to the creation of various statistical procedures, most of which were intended to provide empirical data about the desirability of inbreeding the genetically superior.

With a simmering brew of quasi science, arcane statistics, and socially agreeable theory, Galton went on to establish entities like the Anthropometric Laboratory for the study of genetic variation. In the end, these entities and researchers simply contributed to a somewhat new, statistically oriented means of measuring inferiority, and thus reinforcing the perpetual myth of white male superiority. In this case, however, superiority was based not so much on the inner constitution of moral fiber, brainpower, or physical appearance as on the application of long-standing theories of animal husbandry (for the well-bred cow, sheep, horse, or chicken; the superior household pet; or, as Plato suggested, "the good stock") to human subjects.[3] Curiously, then, what had previously been an entirely pejorative comparison within the biodeterministic tradition—relegation to the level of the animal—now became a favored model for eugenic thinking. The thoroughbred racehorse, the prize-winning bull, and the like were seen as exemplary of the fruits of selective breeding—indeed, something that humans might even aspire to. In trying to recruit a prospective patron, Charles Davenport, an American follower of Galton, remarked that "the most progressive revolution in history" could be achieved if "human matings could be placed upon the same high plane as that of horse breeding."[4] Of course, there was also the dark side of animal mating and lineage: those creatures that failed to meet the high standards of the racehorse or prize bull. They too held a message regarding human breeding. It was to precisely these "abnormal" human births, these "monstrosities," that the science of eugenics turned its nearly undivided attention.

Although Galton largely devised the theoretical basis underlying the nascent science of eugenics, it was scientists like Charles Davenport who advanced it into a practical realm. Davenport conjectured that certain defects were unquestionably hereditary in character, particularly mental diseases. He also believed, following Lombroso, that criminality was an inherited trait and that much of it was being imported to the United States by European immigrants. He was no supporter of the indigenous unfit either: "Davenport deplored the fact that the government had to support tens of thousands of insane, mentally deficient, epileptic, and otherwise handicapped wards, not to mention the prisoners and paupers, at a cost he estimated to be about a hundred million a year."[5] In short, Davenport envisioned a future without those malevolent inherited traits (and their carriers) that, he felt, compromised the possibility of human perfection through selective breeding. The lean pigs, hobbled horses, and lame hunting dogs had to be culled rigorously from the gene pool.

Before the unfit could be removed from the gene pool, though, a body of scientific data had to be developed that proved beyond a doubt that genetic inferiority was both hereditary and reversible. Davenport himself opened the Cold Springs Harbor experimental station, where he devoted much time and gifted money—the Rockefellers, Carnegies, and Harrimans were especially generous in this regard—to the further search for heritable traits of inferiority. Oddly, eugenics, which had begun as a science of selective breeding that sought the perfect Mendelian combinations of genetic factors in the human animal, had by that time become a means of eliminating imperfections, finding ways to mark and remove those individuals who threatened the very foundation of normal human life.

One of the greatest threats to this sort of life was those suffering from feeblemindedness, or, as Davenport put it, "the feebly inhibited." Davenport tried to establish the palpable danger of the feebleminded by employing a kind of outreach program. Using the largesse of his generous donors and government grants, he organized an extensive study of what he considered the dross of human life; he sent hundreds of interns, trained in spotting genetic deficiencies, especially feeblemindedness, to virtually every institution on the eastern seaboard. As a result, he collected detailed reports on such "inherited" deficiencies as epilepsy, pellagra, multiple sclerosis, nomadism, tuberculosis, goiter, and so on, which in turn generated numerous bulletins, journals, and books recommending such eugenic cures as sterilization and exclusion from the United States of inferior germ plasm; that is, stopping the spread of tainted germ plasm at its point of entry (at that time, Ellis Island).[6] All this added impressive cachet to the pragmatics of selective breeding, but the theoretical bearings and the full force of the campaign to eliminate inferior germ plasm and its carriers were yet to come.

The eminent psychologist Henry H. Goddard was able to advance eugenics, both scientifically and popularly, by combining the tentative first steps of bioscientists like Galton, Karl Pearson, and Davenport with his refashioned version of the Binet scale. Alfred Binet, the French psychologist and education theorist, had developed a set of tests that were intended ostensibly to identify mildly retarded and learning-disabled children. This, Binet often proclaimed, was the one and only purpose of his testing procedure. However, once the tests reached the hands of Goddard, who had translated Binet's writings into English, they were totally dismantled and put into the service of American bio-determinism and eugenics:

> Binet refused to define his scores as "intelligence," and wished to identify in order to help. Goddard regarded the scores as measures of a single, innate entity. He wished to identify in order to recognize limits, segregate, and curtail breeding to prevent further deterioration of an endangered American stock, threatened by immigration from without and by prolific reproduction of its feeble-minded within.[7]

Armed with his numerical rating system, Goddard could document mental inferiority down to the smallest detail, arguing in some cases that a mere couple of quotient points on a Binet score could distinguish between a moron, imbecile, and idiot (technical terms used by Goddard to indicate low levels of intelligence). The scores, however, were not all that separated good American stock from bad. For Goddard, appearance also counted, and, applying some of the typical animalistic-trait strategies of the craniometers and atavists, he articulated a broad set of physical characteristics that accompanied mental deficiency. As an example of the appearance/performance hypothesis, Goddard chose a single family line that had been "ruined" by the mating of a relatively intelligent (i.e., nonmoronic) mountain man with a feebleminded woman. He called the family the Kallikaks, and wrote a book tracing their woeful lineage.[8] His general view of the Kallikaks, as well as of other so-called mental deficients, is central to the future application of eugenic principles and to the use of eugenics as an animalizing and thus dehumanizing function. For him, the feebleminded and such were largely undeveloped humans, "a vigorous animal organism of low intellect but strong physique—the wild man of today."[9]

The convergence of selective human breeding, atavistic/evolutionary thought, and hereditarian IQ theory plunged eugenics into its most dangerous and destructive phase. The mark of the beast was no longer indelible. It could be removed by careful planning, by breeding a selected line of human stock; or, failing that, it could be excluded from the population as a whole by any number of radical means, including sexual surgery (both castration and female sterilization), statutory exclusion, long-term imprisonment, and perhaps the darkest solution of all, euthanasia. In the period of atavism, craniometry, and early evolutionary theory, those determined to be animal-like were either excluded or hidden from society by means that were largely punitive. Although bestial madmen, oversexed and oversized black women, apish throwbacks, and the like were severely repressed socially, abused, and reproved in popular and scientific print for their drift into animality, they were seldom, if ever, subjected to any general, systematic program of control or elimination. Now, though, the eugenic solution, in large part because of the American stress on social deviance and national degeneration, had become a popular discourse, subject to its exigencies. Goddard, with the help of figures like Davenport and Harry Laughlin, head of the federally funded Eugenics Record Office, had created something of a national panic regarding the spread of moronity. Also, although both Goddard and Davenport were circumspect regarding large-scale sterilization, Laughlin was not: "[I]t ought to be a eugenic crime to turn a possible parent of defectives loose upon the population."[10] This intense fear of stock pollution, of the degeneration of the fragile American germ plasm, led to thousands of forced female sterilizations and perhaps an equal number of castrations of those alleged to be carriers of degenerate genotypes.[11] The fate of undesirables—the poor, immigrants, racial types, degenerates, perverts, criminals, and so on—was thus by and large sealed. By creating a program that reduced the human to sheer animality, with the institutionalized control of selective breeding and interbreeding, mastery over the very reproductive and sexual functions of large groups of individuals was achieved. Racial ideology in the form of sexual surgery, supplemented by political power, could now control and direct the destinies, the very lives of tens of thousands of defectives.

The American programs, however, were mild compared to the parallel application of eugenic theory and practice in Nazi Germany, where not only the so-called feebleminded were sterilized, but also an astounding range of other presumed degenerate types, including people who suffered from alleged hereditary disabilities like schizophrenia, epilepsy, blindness, drug and alcohol addiction, and deformities that interfered with locomotion or were grossly offensive.[12] In the three-year period from 1933 to 1936, the Nazis sterilized 225,000 people, almost ten times as many as were sterilized in a ten-year period in the United States—a fact that did not go unnoticed in America. Howard Hale, a staunch advocate of sterilization, issued a statement in 1934 ruing the fact that "[t]he Germans are beating us at our own game."[13]

However, the Nazi scientists and eugenicists were not interested only in eliminating the unfit. Like any good selective breeder, they were also concerned with producing high-quality, pure stock. This ideal required a breeding program of staggering proportions. Unfettered breeding between good and pure German *Volk* was encouraged on a national scale. Many cities gave special compensation to families that had third and fourth children. Heinrich Himmler, chief designer of the "final solution," encouraged his SS men to mate with as many racially preferred women as possible, even providing special homes for married or unmarried mothers so they could be given individual care during and after pregnancy. The imagery associated with this breeding project was also distinctively animalistic: the women were referred to as "cows" and the men "stud-bulls." Himmler even went so far as to demand reports on the milk production of nursing mothers, awarding prizes to top producers.[14] Indeed, this agricultural concern was integral to Himmler's entire vision of science. It was even noted that he had been advised earlier in his career to "transfer his attention from the breeding of herbs and the raising of chickens to human beings."[15] Thus, both ends of the husbandry/eugenics interface were burgeoning in the newly established Third Reich: the degenerates were being neutralized, and the so-called good stock was, presumably, on the rise.

This twofold breeding/elimination program, moreover, realized a youthful vision of the newly elected Reich-Chancellor, Adolf Hitler. He had argued, among myriad other things, in *Mein Kampf* (1924), that the state was coextensive with its people (*Volk*). The bond of the state was thus based on a culture of the "purity of blood and posited on the deepest longing of the triumph of the German spirit," rather than the Greco-Roman concepts of law, the reconciliation of opposition, politics, and so on.[16] As such, the roots of social organization, of civil society and its success, could be traced back to a primitive, animal-like state—a state predicated on the maintenance of aggressiveness and belligerence, of a kind of animal instinct for survival and conquest, a single, inevitable response to the fight-or-flight reaction: "Those who want to live, let them fight, and those who do not want to fight in this world of eternal struggle do not deserve to live."[17]

Natural animal tendencies were not, however, limited only to an individual's instinctual aggressiveness. Hitler also envisioned ironclad natural laws, applied intuitively by nature's creatures, that governed the whole process of propagation:

> Every animal mates only with a member of the same species. The titmouse seeks the titmouse, the finch the finch, the stork the stork, the field mouse the field mouse, the dormouse the dormouse, the wolf the she-wolf, etc. . . . This is only too natural. Any crossing of two beings not at exactly the same level produces a medium between the level of the two parents. This means: the offspring will probably stand higher than the racially lower parent, but not as high as the higher one. Consequently, it will later succumb in the struggle against the higher level. Such mating is contrary to the will of Nature for a higher breeding of all life.[18]

In incorporating a version of Herbert Spencer's notion of social Darwinism with current eugenic theory, Hitler drew upon "natural laws" that, when adhered to, effectively lead to self-preservation, protection, and, ultimately, the preservation of the species itself. But biological animal instincts go even further: they eventually express the very character of a race, by extending beyond the purely self-preservative (what Hitler calls "egoism") and attaining a state of altruism; that is, care and concern for others in the community. This, for Hitler, represents a definitive move from the animal to the human:

> In this condition the animal lives only for himself, seeks food only for his present hunger, and fights only for his own life. As long as the instinct of self-preservation expresses itself in this way, every basis is lacking for the formation of a group, even the most primitive form of family. Even a community between male and female beyond pure mating, demands an extension of the instinct of self-preservation, since concern and struggle for the ego are not directed toward a second party; the male sometimes seeks food for the female, too, but for the most part both seek nourishment for the young. Nearly always one comes to the defense of the other, and thus the first, though infinitely simple, forms of a sense of sacrifice result.[19]

So, in giving themselves to the community, humans break with their animal ancestry: "This state of mind, which subordinates the interests of the ego to conservation of the community, is really the first premise for any true culture."[20] Indeed, the entire conception of Aryan superiority is based on this "infinitely simple" action. For Hitler, it is precisely the sense of self-sacrifice that indicates that the Aryan has thrown off the atavistic characteristic of sheer self-preservation and is thus advancing toward the highest accomplishments of civilization. To divest oneself of sheer animalistic tendencies, to reach out to others and the community as a whole, is to reach a level of superiority and humanness—states that stand in sharp contrast to those still associated with the baser, self-preservative instinct.

Given this view, retention of the instinct for self-preservation becomes the basis for assigning animality to individuals and groups, a sort of atavistic principle applied much like Lombroso's signs of apishness. In short, if you cannot give to others, and tend to cling to your egoistic self-interests, you are still mired in the primordial ooze, in a bestial and primitive state. For Hitler, this single mark of civilization—of the human as opposed to the animal—is what distinguishes Aryans from the inferior races, particularly the Jews.

> The mightiest counterpart to the Aryan is represented by the Jew. In hardly any people of the world is the instinct of self-preservation developed more strongly than in the so-called "chosen." . . . In the Jewish people the will to self-sacrifice does not go beyond the individual's naked instinct of self-preservation. Their apparently great sense of solidarity is based on the very

primitive herd instinct that is seen in many other living creatures in this world. It is a noteworthy fact that the herd instinct leads to mutual support only as long as common danger makes this seem useful or inevitable. The same pack of wolves which has just fallen on its prey together disintegrates when hunger abates into its individual beasts. The same is true of horses which try to defend themselves against an assailant in a body, but scatter again as soon as the danger is past.[21]

Although there are many other well-documented causes of Nazi atrocities, the reduction of the "other," particularly the Jew, to animality and even subanimality had important consequences for the whole Nazi campaign against inferior races (consequences that are examined in much greater detail in part 2 of this book). As we have seen previously, to systematically attribute demeaning, animalistic tendencies to types or groups leads inevitably to maltreatment of those groups, ranging from exclusion to outright slaughter. The reason for this is simple: animals, generally speaking, do not have to be treated in the same way as humans.[22] Their entire natural history demonstrates their inferiority, and this inferiority, via theoretical tinkering, popular prejudices, and just plain bad science, can be transferred effortlessly from one species to another. This, in large part, is why a figure like Hitler, operating in the blinding glare of propaganda and public sentiment, could so easily attribute animality to certain types, races, or peoples—why, for example, the Jew could be presented as filthy, and the carrier of vermin and disease, like the common sewer rat.

Moreover, the imposition of inferiority invariably serves sociopolitical goals, as the animal comparison often functions as a means of achieving distinct practical ends. After all, Hitler was concerned not only with denigrating Jews as a "race," but also with eliminating them as a cultural and economic force in German society. Hence, "[i]n a short time I was made more thoughtful than ever by my slowly rising insight into the type of activity carried on by the Jew in certain fields. Was there any form of filth or profligacy, particularly in cultural life, without at least one Jew involved? If you cut even cautiously into such an abscess, you found, like a maggot in a rotting body, often dazzled by the sudden light—a kike!"[23]

Lessons from the Slaughterhouse: Medico-Psychiatric Forms of Animalization

> A patient should never be left alone while eating. . . .
> Patients must be taught to eat again. . . . Teaching them to
> eat again takes considerable patience. . . . We have stressed

the need of treating the patient as a child.... [A] spanking
is good for the patient though it may distress the family....
Usually when a stubborn streak develops, a "roughhouse" is
the best way of breaking it up. Pulling, pushing, grabbing
around the neck, tickling in the ribs, or wrestling in an
undignified way will bring the patient around panting and
laughing, and the resistance will drop from him.

—Suggestions for nursing post–frontal lobotomy patients,
from Vallenstein, *Great and Desperate Cures*

Ugo Cerletti began his illustrious career in electroconvulsive therapy (ECT)
by attempting to use an electroshock apparatus to induce repeatable, reliable
epileptic fits in dogs and other animals. Unfortunately, Cerletti did not have
much early success with the experiment, as he had placed one electrode in the
dog's mouth and the other in its anus; about half of his animal subjects died as
a result of the electric shock stopping their hearts. Persisting, though, Cerletti
was eventually able to induce epileptic fits in the dogs without instantly killing them. Nevertheless, the full utilization of ECT on humans did not dawn
upon him until he learned that pigs were being anesthetized with electroshock
before being butchered at a Roman slaughterhouse. Fascinated, he had his two
assistants visit the slaughterhouse to get a more precise and scientific reading
of the process:

> After the two had returned to Rome, Cerletti asked them to visit the city
> slaughterhouse, where, he had heard, pigs were being obtunded with electric
> current before being slaughtered. What could the researchers learn here
> about where to apply the electric shocks, and about the margin between the
> convulsive dose and lethal dose? Bini and Accornero then did systematic
> experiments at the slaughterhouse, discovering that placing the electrodes
> on the temples was practical, and that the margin between the convulsive
> and the lethal dose was very wide.[24]

The slaughterhouse seems an apt locale for the birthplace of a procedure
that initially killed hundreds of dogs (the dogcatcher made weekly deliveries
for more than a year to the Cerletti lab), and that had to be tested on doomed
pigs so as to eventually discover a nonlethal dose for humans. Indeed, it is precisely this process of blithely subjecting animals—which are generally regarded
as superfluous, entirely dispensable beings—to pain, suffering, and death that
often leads to the use on humans of patently dangerous and sometimes inef-
fective treatments and therapies, like electroshock.[25] In Cerletti's experimental
framework, the human subject is distinguished only by degree; that is, to what

extent an animal dose of electric current would kill or not kill a human subject, and so on. A general lack of caring, marked by a fusing of the human with the expendable animal, is thus already inherent in the design and structure of the animal experiment itself. The human subject, though absent in this particular case, becomes merely one of the many factors of the overall experiment; the subject takes on a certain abstract anonymity effected by the experimental situation. This phenomenon is the inevitable outcome of the constructed nature of the experimental process itself. This becomes quite clear in Kurt Danziger's examination of the structure of psychological experiments:

> Another necessary conceptual distinction is that between the identity that participants have outside the experimental situation and the identity they have within it. As noted, the former involves the unique personal identity of the individual and identity conferred by membership of various social categories like those of age, profession, and educational status. But because experimental situations involve a division of functions, the published reports are also likely to identify the participants in terms of these functions. . . . These temporary identities, which begin and end with the experimental situation, are deliberately created in order to construct such a situation.[26]

The morally indifferent and callous nature of these animal-based experiments transposed onto human subjects is also evident in one of the experimenter's view of the procedure's eventual implications. Cerletti's assistant, Accornero, pondered: "If the experiment on the human, for whatever unforeseen reason, had ended with the death of the subject, all responsibility would have fallen on Cerletti. Our school, already considered to be highly interventionist, would have fallen into enormous discredit and its director would have suffered the consequences."[27] Given this statement, what, then, distinguishes the human from the animal? Effectively, nothing, other than the fact that a human subject's death would scandalize the scientific work of the school and ultimately imperil further research. The human subject becomes indispensable, not as a living, feeling human being, but as a risk factor in and an essential component for the continuation of future research. If the animal dies, one can always pull the electrode from its anus, reposition it on another's testicles or, perhaps, in its vagina, and restart the torturous course of further testing; if the human dies, everything may be lost—though not for the human, but for the program.

After applying the knowledge gained from animal experiments (particularly the breakthroughs in dosage and electrode placement inspired by the to-be-butchered pigs), ECT emerged as a minimally functional, though still controversial, therapy for depression and certain other forms of mental illness.

But ECT was not by any means problem free. For example, during the electrically induced convulsions, many patients would thrash about on the table, sometimes incurring severe limb and vertebrae fractures. To mitigate the danger, several remedies were tested directly on human subjects. At the Horton Hospital in England, a team of nurses would form something of a rugby scrum around the patient, holding down his or her extremities, chest, abdomen, neck, and head. Curare was also tested as a muscle relaxant, but curare was dangerous—another potential heart-stopper. Metrazol-convulsion therapy was used as a replacement for electroshock, but metrazol had toxic side effects. Interestingly, at this more advanced stage of ECT evolution, human subjects began to take the place of laboratory animals. Because the injuries caused by the convulsions were peculiar to human anatomy, humans were really the only reliable source of experimental data. The transference from the animal to human thus came full circle: whereas humans were positioned abstractly in the experimental model in the early development of ECT, they now occupied a very real, tangible place in the evolution of the ECT procedure. They had, in a very genuine sense, replaced the stray dogs, to-be-slaughtered pigs, lab rats, guinea pigs, and so on.

The influence of this interchangeability of humans and animals—the reduction to animality—can still, even today, be seen as a repressive factor in ECT treatment and its application. The fullest force of modern forms of repression, though, does not lie directly in the careless and casual transference of procedures from human to animal, and vice versa. Rather, it lies more in the full mastery of the practitioner and the medico-psychiatric establishment itself over certain traditionally demeaned and repressed groups, such as females, the elderly, minority and poor mental patients—a mastery that often subjects these groups to disproportionate, and sometimes unwarranted and unwanted, use of ECT procedures.

In a California survey of electroshock patients, it was discovered that more than two-thirds of those receiving the treatment were women. Because mental patients in California are more or less divided evenly between the sexes, this indicates at the very least a strong bias toward subjecting women to this particular treatment. Another target audience of electroshock is the elderly, particularly, again, females. By 1988, 53.1 percent of all patients receiving shock treatment in California were elderly, which represents nearly a 50 percent increase in the eleven-year period dating from the beginning of the California survey.[28] If the two-thirds majority of female electroshock patients holds for this group, then elderly women are being shocked at a disproportionate rate.

Much the same could be said for minority and poor mental patients. Without going into great detail, the case of Paul Henri Thomas, a Haitian immigrant, is exemplary.[29] Thomas had been confined to several mental institutions, with a diagnosis centered on the vague categories of schizoaffective disorder and bipolar mania. His former treatment, consisting of neuroleptic drug therapy, had caused several acute physical conditions, the most serious of which was liver damage. It was determined, upon his admittance to a New York area hospital, that he would have to receive electroshock therapy as an alternative to drug treatment. Apparently, Thomas initially signed a consent form to receive forty treatments, but when he was scheduled to receive another forty treatments he resisted, claiming that the procedure was a form of torture and that his constitutional rights were being violated. He and his attorneys brought suit to halt the treatments. His case was steamrolled in New York state court, and he was ordered, once again, to continue his treatments. Oddly enough, shortly after the court decision, and without having had any of the ordered shock treatments actually applied, Mr. Thomas was released from the psychiatric institution with a clean bill of mental health.

The answer as to the reason for the disparity in the use of ECT, of course, is multifactorial, involving numerous sociopolitical, cultural, and economic factors. Nevertheless, it is clear that the conflation of animality and humanness in the very developmental process of ECT, as well as the universal bias against animals, has at least something to do with it. Animals are simply held in much lower regard than humans, and those humans who have little or no status or power—the usual targets of repression—are, as I have shown, often associated with animals. This association makes these people susceptible to many of the indecencies piled upon animals, including torturous treatments like ECT. Animals are generally thought of as merely being there for us to do what we wish with; to be exploited for our own needs. Kant, perhaps more than any other thinker, consistently and powerfully stressed exactly this point. By claiming, "A man is not a thing," Kant surely implies that an animal is, and he further asserts that animals "are not self-conscious and are merely a means to an end."[30] That end, of course, is ours. With this long-standing, popularly accepted, debasing view of animals, mastery over groups and individuals deemed animalistic is easily achieved, on both a personal and an institutional level. Other than humane societies, some animal lovers, and animal rights activists, practically no one questions the inherent right of the master over his pet, the experimenter over his rats, or the "hungry man" over his Salisbury steak TV dinner. Given the right social conditions, the same license can easily be transferred to physician over patient; experimenter over subject; and, in the end, to powerful institutions over their largely powerless populations.[31]

Psychosurgery counts as yet another glaring and, in many ways, even more egregious example of the conflation of animals and humans within the medico-psychiatric establishment. The term *psychosurgery* is largely a synonym for lobotomy, the surgical removal or neutralization of the frontal lobes of the brain, though it also includes other forms of brain surgery purportedly involving mental illnesses. Egaz Moniz, a Portuguese clinical neurologist and politician, invented the actual surgical process of lobotomy in its modern form. The first operations, which involved drilling holes in the head of the patient and injecting absolute alcohol into the frontal lobes of the brain, were done in 1935. To justify this sort of operation, Moniz concocted what has to count as one of the most foolishly naïve scientific arguments ever in support of what he originally called *leucotomy*. He believed that the frontal lobes were the seat of human psychic activity and that thoughts and ideas are stored in the nerve-fiber connections of the brain. Taking all this literally, he then suggested that mental disturbances were the result of fixed ideas (Pierre Janet's *idée fixe*). If the fixed ideas were right there, stored in the nerve fibers of the frontal lobes, the elimination of the frontal lobes would also eliminate the mental illness.[32] This is, one could argue, a variation of Descartes' homunculus theory—or, more likely, Hippocrates' fatefully moving uterus.

Moniz, however, was not the originator of this odd procedure. Experiments that predated his concept of psychosurgery flourished during the latter part of the nineteenth century—and, by necessity, many of these experiments involved animal stand-ins for human subjects. It is precisely in the remarkably sadistic, patently inconsiderate treatment of these animal stand-ins that a sense of the total lack of caring for the human subjects they represent becomes manifest.

> A crowd of eager spectators attended the afternoon demonstrations. Goltz began by showing his dog to the audience, pointing to its deformed head and inserting his fingers into the holes in the skull. He explained that in five successive operations he had removed the greater part of the cerebral cortex on both sides. He then put his dog through the paces, demonstrating that it could run and jump, use its eyes to avoid objects, could hear (it cringed when a whip was snapped) and smell (it turned its head when Goltz had a physician in the audience blow cigar smoke at it).
>
> It all seemed convincing until Ferrier began his demonstration. He signaled for an attendant to bring a large monkey, which was obviously paralyzed on one side, to the platform. The monkey dragged one leg, and its arm hung helplessly. Charcot was reported to have uttered loudly, "Why, it's a patient."... The animal was alert and healthy in all other respects, rapidly taking food with its good hand. A second monkey was then brought out. This animal seemed unimpaired until the attendant, at Ferrier's signal, shot off a cap pistol. The second animal did not even flinch, while the first monkey, filled with terror, tried to escape but toppled onto the floor with

one foot and one arm flailing grotesquely. Ferrier explained that a precise lesion in the "motor cortex" on one side of the brain had been made in the first monkey; while in the second animal, a discrete lesion had been made bilaterally in the part of the temporal lobes that Ferrier had started calling the "auditory centers."[33]

What should certainly fill the reader with terror is the fact that these treatments and procedures were ultimately intended for human use. In his snide remark about the ape—"Why, it's a patient"—Charcot was thus not far from the truth. Interesting, too, is the fact that the animal/human comparisons implied in the experiments were limited to strictly instinctual animal behavior, the kinds of behavior that Descartes had construed as simple mechanical reactions. In effect, what both demonstrators had proved by the animal experiments was that brain lesions (that is, surgically altered parts of the brain itself) were functional if the effect on certain motor behaviors was minimal. The monkey that flapped around grotesquely was much better off than the one that had had its "auditory center" destroyed, in that it could react to danger signals. The dog with five holes drilled in its skull, however, seemed best off of all, as it could run through its paces without significant inconvenience.

In the end, this demonstrational reduction of the future human subject of psychosurgery to the level of basic animal instinct, once again, negatively affected the way humans were treated. Because having certain parts of their brains surgically removed only minimally inconvenienced animals, it was thought that the procedure could be applied successfully to humans as well. Of course, the emphasis on animal reaction (or lack of it) failed to account for more subtle human attributes, like emotion, sensation, personality traits, empathy, compassion, creativity—those various affective psychical states that are virtually impossible to measure.[34] The damage done to these delicate human qualities turned out to be immense, as witnessed by the following description of lobotomized patients:

> The changes in personality were generally serious. In five of the patients could be noticed an affective indifference, a loss of ethical and moral inhibitions, a loss of higher interests, both affective and intellectual, which causes the personalities of lobotomized patients to become much inferior to what they were before the lobotomy. . . . The therapeutic results obtained in our series are very slight, and the operation, by making the patients easier to manage, made them also, in a most definite way, very inferior personalities, to what they were before.[35]

IV

Exhibit and Punish

From Cages to Colonization

Ota Benga, the pygmy at the New York Zoological Gardens, the Bronx, made a desperate attempt to kill one of his keepers yesterday afternoon with a knife, and had to be overpowered before he was driven into his cage. Benga was in good spirits yesterday and allowed the children and other visitors to tease him as much as they pleased.
—*New York Daily Tribune*, September 29, 1906

Cages

By the turn of the nineteenth century, a specular alternative was added to the then-predominant form of discipline, which was "the discipline-blockade," a group of enclosed institutions, at the margins of society, turned inward toward negative functions.[1] With the addition of the panopticon—a form of penal architecture designed by the British political and social philosopher Jeremy Bentham—the inmate, the docile body, could now be kept under total observation. Briefly stated, panopticism was capable of literally making a spectacle of the prisoner or, for that matter, any other institutional inmate. It provided authoritarian power with a scopic "eye," in that the punitive subject became a specular instance in the gaze of power, an image continuously reflected in the panoptic mirror, always countable and accountable. Effectively, it brought discipline and punishment into the realm of pure spectacle:

All that is needed, then, is to place a supervisor in a central tower and to shut up in each cell a madman, a patient, a condemned man, a worker or a schoolboy. By the effect of backlighting, one can observe from the tower, standing out precisely against the light, the small captive shadows in the cells of the periphery. They are like so many *cages*, so many small theaters, in which each actor is alone, perfectly individualized and constantly visible. The panoptic mechanism arranges spatial unities that make it possible to see constantly and to recognize immediately. In short, it reverses the principle of the dungeon; or rather its three functions—to enclose, to deprive of light and to hide—it preserves only the first and eliminates the other two. Full lighting and the eye of a supervisor capture better than darkness, which ultimately protected. Visibility is a trap.[2]

Although the introduction of the panopticon in the nineteenth century was probably the first attempt to subject humans to scopic power, to render punishment a spectatorial phenomenon, there is a long history of this sort of treatment for animals. It began on a large scale in Roman times, when animals were routinely displayed at the popular games. These were not by any means ordinary zoological displays, intended to edify the audiences; rather, the animals were forced to act in theatrical and often violent and deadly ways. Placed on a giant stage, within the proto-panoptic viewpoint of the amphitheater, they killed and were killed to entertain as a sheer visual spectacle. Descriptions from classical authors indicate, for example, that the emperor Trajan had 11,000 animals theatrically slaughtered in the arena in celebration of his conquest of Dacia; this carnage included lions, tigers, elephants, rhinoceroses, hippopotamuses, giraffes, bulls, stags, and snakes.[3] The nineteenth-century historian W. E. H. Lecky stated that "[i]n a single day, at the dedication of the Colosseum by Titus, five thousand animals perished. . . . [C]riminals dressed in the skins of wild beasts were thrown to the bulls, which were maddened by red-hot irons, or by darts tipped with burning pitch."[4]

The visual display of animals, of course, did not decline along with the Roman Empire. If anything, animals became more popular as exhibition specimens. Like the punitive power that the panopticon brought to the evolving nineteenth-century states, the presence of vast menageries of animals, displayed openly in cages or parks, was a sign of power for rulers throughout antiquity. Indeed, animals were thought to be so valuable as displays of power that rulers would often have them all slaughtered just to demonstrate the extent of their authority, the extremes to which they were able to go and forgo. Even as late as 1719, the Elector of Dresden personally slaughtered his entire menagerie, which included lions, tigers, bulls, bears, and boars.[5]

This power function also includes the specular display of humans placed in animal-like situations as a means of demonstrating the supremacy of certain groups over others—in almost all cases, a powerful group over a much less pow-erful one. If one recalls, in Roman antiquity the lions, tigers, and bears were often killing and being killed alongside members of those groups considered dispens-able, eminently punishable, or, in some cases, politically dangerous: Christians, barbarians, criminals, captured enemy soldiers, condemned slaves, and so on. The unacceptable and abused minorities—those singled out for punishment—were placed within the same spectacular, theatrical space as the performing animals and subjected to precisely the same forms of abuse and denigration. Besides being outright murdered, these maligned groups and individuals were literally brought down to the level of the animal: to the aggression, savagery, stupidity, and dispensability thought to be characteristic of beasts. The interaction of hu-mans and animals in the planned spectacle thus represented a source of control and punishment and, most importantly, the expression of the superiority of the spectators and exhibitors over the exhibited.

What stands as one of the most remarkable modern-day examples of a human displayed like an animal and in the midst of animals is that of Ota Benga, the so-called pygmy in the zoo. Ota Benga, a pygmy Bushman, was brought from Africa to America to be exhibited at the 1904 World's Fair and Exposition in St. Louis, Missouri. The "Great Pygmy Hunter" transported him to America; that was the Reverend Dr. Samuel P. Verner, who, being something of a Buffalo Bill, concocted numerous fabulations about his hardships and ad-ventures, including fierce battles with man-eating savages in Central Africa. Ota Benga himself was described in an article in the *St. Louis Post-Dispatch* (Sunday, Sept 4, 1904) as

> the only genuine African cannibal in America today. He's also the only human chattel. He belongs to the Exposition company. Step right up. There's no charge except to see his teeth. He has the reputation of being a man eater and has on exhibition the identical molars and incisors with which it was done.
>
> His teeth are as sharp as those of any wild animal. They are pointed like the teeth of a saw. They have been filed that way.
>
> Otabenga himself looks playful and harmless enough. He is gentle and graceful, and the first impulse is to pet him and exclaim: "Poor little fellow; he looks so sad and lonely."[6]

Following his humiliating display at the World's Fair, Ota Benga was carted around the United States and shown at various expositions. Reports in-dicate that he created a huge sensation at the Mardi Gras in New Orleans. In 1906, Verner brought Ota Benga, along with a collection of chimpanzees and authentic native artifacts, to the recently opened Bronx Zoo. At first the pygmy, fitted out in a white suit and looking much like a Times Square pickpocket, was encouraged to mix with the crowd. After a period of wandering about the various animal exhibitions, he was drawn to the Monkey House, where he spent much time with a dancing, performing orangutan, which, incidentally, was also sometimes attired in a white suit. This caring friendship, however, led eventually to one of the most degrading, inhuman spectacles of modern times. The zoo directors decided that, rather than employing Ota Benga as a kind of exotic wandering guide, mixing with the crowd and creating a sense of untamed Africa moving among them, it would be better to integrate him with the caged animals, to turn his well-advertised savagery into a spectacle within the confined exhibition spaces of the zoo itself. The description of one of his performances in the monkey house is unsettling, to say the least:

> There was a more elaborate setting in the Monkey House than had been prepared the day before. Bones were now scattered around the cage to increase the impression of savagery and danger.
>
> Dohong [the orangutan] was admitted into the enclosure. The orangutan imitated the man. The man imitated the monkey. They hugged, let go, flopped into each other's arms. Dohong snatched the straw cap off Ota's head and placed it on his own. Ota snatched it back. He picked the monkey up and let him drop, then turned his back to walk away. Dohong jumped up on his shoulders to hold him back. Ota shrugged him off, turned again to walk away. Dohong grabbed an ankle with one arm. Ota took big, limping steps around the cage, shackled to the ape. The crowd hooted and applauded. Dohong and Ota hugged.... Children squealed with delight.[7]

The forty thousand or more viewers who passed in and out of the Bronx Zoo Monkey House on any Sunday were treated to a scene of savagery that was fully contained and ordered, and thus inscribed with the mark of "civilized" power. Ota Benga, as performer, interacted with the orangutan as if there were no distinct separation between the two. On occasion, they even lived in the same cage, ate the same food, and wore the same costumes, emulating each other's movements and actions in perfect symmetry. The ape had become the human; the human, the ape. Both were caught up in a continuous, perfectly smooth transference of roles. The lines of distinction between the "savage" and savagery, between what can be considered human and what cannot, were lost in the arranged spectacle.

This conflation of the human and animal, this total blurring of the boundaries between the two, represented the ultimate form of surveillance and punishment. Unlike the prisoner, schoolboy, madman, or other isolated by the gaze of power, by the panoptic machinery of control, the caged Ota Benga actually occupied a space of denigration, replete with slabs of raw meat and neatly arranged bones, acting out the drama of inferiority, the specular collapse of man into beast and vice versa. Indeed, Ota Benga and Dohong's staged dramatics were a perfect parallel to what had happened and was actually still happening in the world to which Ota Benga—who shot himself in the heart in 1916—would never return: the enslavement and ultimate destruction of the native populations of Africa, particularly those inhabiting the inaptly named Congo Free State.

Colonization

Colonialism, like racism, Nazism, and oppressive movements in general, has many well-documented causes, but animalization was clearly a factor in its development and proliferation. Colonialism, with all of its other despicable dimensions, was in one respect a form of absolute control: Colonized human beings were seen as mere objects, to be moved, transported, reformed, and redeployed in accordance with the needs of resource exploitation and commercial self-interest. Ota Benga, for example, was not alone when he arrived in St. Louis in 1904; a virtual traveling menagerie of native African "specimens" accompanied him. King Leopold of Belgium himself, the founder of the Congo Free State, authorized the seizure of the group, consisting of pygmies, tribal medicine doctors, chimps, exotic native birds, fabled "red Africans," and so on.[8] It was precisely this arrogance of control, the ability to willfully manage and manipulate other humans as one would direct a herd of animals—what Foucault in another context referred to as "docile bodies"—that led to some of the greatest indecencies of the colonial period.

The tactic of controlling, encircling, directing, marking, leading, transporting, and otherwise maneuvering humans in a herdlike manner was probably common to all forms of colonialist domination, but the method was used to particular advantage by King Leopold and the Belgian state in the takeover and long-term suppression of the Congo. By way of background, Leopold, the successor to his father, Leopold I, spent most of his childhood fretting about the unstateliness of the country he would eventually inherit. He looked upon tiny, unprepossessing, largely broke Belgium as a curse rather than a blessing. As king, however, he finally discovered a solution to his boyhood fears of having to run a third-rate country: buy a colony and become like Germany, Holland, France, or even England. He shopped around for years—even invested in a two-volume work on how to manage colonies—and came close to making deals for several small islands, including Fiji, but negotiations ultimately fell through. Finally, in 1879, Leopold settled on the idea of settling the Congo, then largely unexplored.

He established business ties with Henry Morton Stanley (of the famed Stanley-Livingstone encounter) and negotiated the sale and takeover of what he was to ironically call the "Free Congo State."[9]

Leopold's nearly thirty-year reign over the Congo was by any standards an unmitigated horror. Estimates of those killed by his mercenary interior security troops, exposed to fatal diseases, or just worked to death range from seven to ten million, not to mention the countless millions who were separated permanently from their tribes and families and forced into abject slave labor in the burgeoning rubber plantations. The ways in which many of these Congolese died, and the Belgian imposition of the types of discipline that Foucault calls "the military machine," provide, from our perspective, striking instances of the treatment of humans as animals or, perhaps more accurately, as sub-animals.[10]

The tactics of the Congo expeditionary forces were largely extensions of military thinking, but *military* not so much in the sense of fighting a war against an identifiable enemy, with its individual episodes of heroism, self-sacrifice, victory, and defeat; rather, *military* in terms of occupying and controlling a region or an area populated with usable bodies. Foucault, in describing this sort of new military vision, wrote: "[B]ut there was also a military dream of society; its fundamental reference was not to the state of nature, but to the meticulously subordinated cogs of a machine, not to the primal social contract, but to permanent coercions, not to fundamental rights, but to indefinitely progressive forms of training, not to the general will but to automatic docility."[11] Frantz Fanon described the discourse of colonization in similar terms: "Discipline, training, mastering, and today pacifying are the words most frequently used by the colonialists in occupied territories."[12]

Several animalizing/dehumanizing tactics were employed to achieve this military vision of docility and control. To begin with, although clearly a genocide of colossal proportions was carried out in the Congo (from Stanley's laying of the foundation for the Free State in 1879 to 1919, the population was cut in half), the self-installed Congo state was not concerned primarily with destroying any particular ethnic group; its one and only interest was in providing labor for the production of exportable raw materials, particularly rubber. In this regard, the military tactics were usually limited to maintaining a docile population of workers, a repository of interchangeable laboring bodies. This labor pool was usually sustained by instilling fear in the native populations, by selectively cutting off segments of the local inhabitants and making an example of them. To accomplish this, the Force Publique would choose a village, surround it, and routinely slaughter its entire population, leaving hanging, mutilated, and burned bodies encircling the village as a warning to the neighboring populations—in effect, the colonizers used humans as ritual signs of power, as sacrificial objects, in much the way ancient religious cults made animal sacrifices to propitiate the gods and organize the masses.

This concept of militaristic control extended to other means of punitive symbolism as well. One of the favored punishments and expressions of power employed by the Belgian state was to cut off the right hand of an uncooperative, condemned, or rebellious native. This indicated that the individual was for some reason ostracized, literally unable to further the pecuniary objectives of the Free State. Beyond this function, the removed hand itself also became a token indicating that a member of the Force Publique or the expeditionary forces had killed an outlaw. Eventually, however, rather than pursuing and actually killing presumed transgressors, soldiers often lopped the hands off random living natives just to collect bounties. The victim was, in this respect, no more than a source of ready cash, and his or her hand merely a trophy symbolic of the military's ability to dominate, exploit, and control native populations. Much like the mounted stag's head above the fireplace mantel, the human hand had become an object telling of triumph and domination. Unlike the trophy stag, though, the human continued to live on, unable to work, hunt, or contribute substantially to tribal or village life in general.

The Congo natives were also kept frightened and docile by the tactic of eliminating their most basic human needs: food and shelter, which in turn reduced them to what amounted to an animalistic way of life, as homeless, wandering jungle foragers.

> As news of the terror spread, hundreds of thousands of people fled their villages. In retaliation, soldiers took their animals and burned their huts and crops, leaving them no food. . . . As they fled these expeditions, villagers sometimes abandoned small children for fear that their cries would give away their hiding places. As a result, many children starved. . . . But for most people there was nowhere to flee except deep into the rain forest or the swamps, where there was no shelter and little food. The American soldier of fortune Edgar Canisius saw refugees from the scorched-earth policy "living like wild beasts in the forest, subsisting on roots, ants and other insects."[13]

As with the near destruction of the native American Indians—many more of whom were killed by disease than by maltreatment or direct massacre—diseases previously unknown in the region infected and killed huge portions of the native Congolese population. This spread of new disease, though multifactorial in nature, could at least in part be attributed to the controlling, militarized tactics of the colonialists. Local native populations were kept constantly on the move, for herdlike drives—population dislocations—were necessary to provide large work-forces for the various industries established by the Belgians. Conscripted workers were driven over immense distances, and thus made susceptible, by contagion, to a number of newly imported diseases, particularly smallpox and sleeping sickness: "Smallpox had been endemic in parts of coastal Africa for centuries, but the great population movements of the imperial age spread the illness throughout the interior, leaving village after village full of dead bodies."[14] The inhuman, nomadic, animal-like conditions caused by the destruction of the natives' sustenance base—that is, their food, shelter, family and village life—also contributed to the unimpeded spread of newly introduced diseases. As modern epidemiologists well know, infectious diseases like smallpox and sleeping sickness do not spread in a vacuum, nor are their fatal effects due strictly to the disease itself. An environment for disease must exist. And that is exactly what happened in most parts of the Congo, witnessed by the account of a presiding official at Stanley Falls: "Disease powerfully ravages an exhausted population, and it's to this cause, in my opinion, that we must attribute the unceasing growth of sleeping sickness in this region; along with porterage and the absence of food supplies, it will quickly decimate the country.... [M]en, like women and children, are thin, weak, without life, very sick, stretched out inert, and above all there's no food."[15]

The aforementioned native American Indians are yet another example of the tactics of colonization, but in their case the tactics centered on dislocation rather than outright exploitation. There was, however, a distinct similarity between the Congolese native and the Native American: Both were regarded as though they were mere beasts to be herded from place to place, treated no better than animals, thought of as comparable to animals—though in the case of the American Indian the herding and treatment were directed ultimately toward pressing the tribes into oblivion and toward total annihilation. In this spirit Francis Parkman, the American historian, commenting on the Oglala Sioux, wrote: "an impassable gulf lies between the white man and his red brethren.... [A]fter breathing the prairie air for a few months or weeks, he begins to look upon them as a troublesome and dangerous species of wild beast."[16] An excerpt from an article in *DeBow's Review*, a source journal for the American School, founded by Samuel George Morton of craniometry fame, fully confirms Parkman's assessment: "But the stern, proud Indian cannot be enslaved. The type of savage beasts among whom he lives, like them he will disappear before the new tide of human life now rolling from the East, and with the buffalo, will have vanished the red man of America."[17] Even worse, the witty American literary icon, Mark Twain, failing in this case to be very humorous, characterized the "real" Indian as "truly nothing but a poor, filthy, naked scurvy vagabond, whom to exterminate were a charity to the Creator's worthier insects and reptiles which he oppresses."[18]

This general, mainstream contempt for American Indians, and the desire, both in scientific and popular discourse,[19] to reduce them to brutishness and utter inferiority (e.g., "like their buffalo," "insects," "reptiles," "wild beasts") contributed significantly to their being driven, blindly and uncaringly, from one geographic point to another, from one desirable location to another far less desirable and often hostile one. Packed together in herdlike fashion, many whole tribes were held in what amounted to corral pens until they could be properly (read: legally) dispossessed of their lands, after which they were marched impossibly long distances to be relocated.

Exemplary of these kinds of forced marches is the infamous Trail of Tears, the passage of the southern tribes, particularly the Creeks, Cherokees, and Seminoles, to designated reservations in what was then termed Permanent Indian Territory. As with the Congolese conscripts, the inhuman treatment of these "herds" was very much a result of their socially imposed animalistic status. The large masses were pushed on at all costs, leaving the sick, young, and weak to die at the side of the trail, when in fact there was a trail: "agents left bodies by the side of the trail, barely covered with brush and certain lure to wolves and other wild animals."[20] Moreover, the emphasis on sheer removal—on enforcing the displacement of these supposedly onerous, unwanted peoples—had itself created an animal-like state of existence. Demoralized and depressed, many captive Indians turned to constant drinking; they were also unable to bathe or change clothing, and in some cases, had their clothing reduced to tattered rags; some marched naked, their bodies covered with welts, scrapes, scratches, cuts, and scars. An Arkansas newspaper, overlooking the fact that the Indian "herds" had already marched hundreds of miles, added to the image of brutishness by describing them as "the most dirty, naked and squalid."[21] All in all, the forced expulsions during the 1830s and 1840s took a devastating toll on the southern tribes, as described aptly in the following:

> Many thousands did not survive the trip. The eastern Cherokees lost an estimated one fourth of their population—some four thousand men, women and children. The Creeks and Seminoles had even greater losses—as much as one half the tribes when deaths during an initial adjustment period in the West are included. Epidemics and accidents contributed harrowingly to the losses; five or six hundred Choctaws died of smallpox in the journey across Arkansas, and more than three hundred Creeks drowned in the sinking of the steamboat *Monmouth*. (This incident provoked some public outcry against contractor cupidity in jamming the unwilling emigrants on unseaworthy vessels.)[22]

As is the case with most brutalizations of humans, the expulsions were ultimately successful. By the end of the Civil War, most Indian tribes had either been contained in reservations or driven into remote regions. The "drovers" were not fully satisfied, though. Indians constrained by punitive boundaries were, after all, still savages: like the irate Ota Benga, brutes apt to break out of their cages and attack their keepers. And they did. Heroic figures like Black Kettle, Sitting Bull, Crazy Horse, and Geronimo rose up in the Western territories, rallying the shrinking Indian forces against the white man. Unfortunately, this only delayed the inevitable. As non-humans, as comparable to "filthy," "reptilian" "sub-insectivores" (Mark Twain), the native American Indian was driven further and further, kept in constant motion or in a state of tragic stasis, grazing on barren land. Occasionally, like the hapless buffalo, they were slaughtered for convenience or the expansion of enterprise and capital (buffalo hunters took the valuable skins of the buffalo and left the meat to rot). This kind of slaughter is precisely what happened at Wounded Knee (December 29, 1890), where 120 men and 230 women and children were encamped in a military controlled area and then strafed by carbines and shrapnel cannons. The descriptions speak for themselves:

> [T]hen the big Hotchkiss guns on the hill opened up on them, firing almost a shell a second, raking the Indian camp, shredding the tepees with flying shrapnel, killing men, women, and children.
>
> "We tried to run," Louise Weasel Bear said, "but they shot us like we were *buffalo*. I know there are some good white people, but the soldiers must be mean to shoot children and women. Indian soldiers would not do that to white children."
>
> When the madness ended, Big Foot and more than half of his people were dead or seriously wounded; 153 were known dead, but many of the wounded crawled away to die afterward. One estimate placed the final total of dead at very nearly three hundred of the original 350 men, women and children.[23]

With so many "shot like buffalo," Wounded Knee effectively ended the several-thousand-year boundless residence of the Indian in America. Their fate was no different from that of the African, Asian, Australian, Caribbean, or South American natives. Colonizers up until and well into the twentieth century had devastated most tribal cultures, in search of convertible natural resources and "docile bodies" to deliver them. The caged Ota Benga—though in reality driven to suicide—was symbolic of the acts of animalization entailed in this massive exploitive project. He was not directly brutalized or beaten, but rather contained, kept in a specular space so as to be observed in his presumed savagery and bestiality. This project of containment and spectacle, though often accompanied by violent death or dislocation, in the end served largely the same purpose for the colonizers: Native populations were restrained, kept under observation, and made moveable and usable. Thus, for the caged Hottentot Venus, the pygmy in the zoo, and all those carefully contained and watched spectacles of colonizing control, visibility, as Foucault contends, surely was a trap.

Conclusions

The main point I wish to make in this first part of the book is that attribution of animality to certain groups is intended primarily to achieve power and mastery over those groups. As such, animalization operates on the periphery of science and philosophical thought, using specious argumentation, pseudoscientific methods, political propaganda, and culturally formed biases as justifications for this ideological imposition of power. Aristotle, for example, had no difficulty in accepting the fact that humans and animals share a common nature and constitution; indeed, he saw this as part of the natural order of things. However, he then proceeded to exploit this biological unity by attributing animal-like inferiority to the slave, because the slave is presumed inferior to the freeman in his reasoning powers: the slave is "a living instrument," and "though remaining a human being, is also an article of property."[24] Descartes, moreover, had no compelling empirical basis on which to assign purely mechanical qualities to animals. His "experiments" with animal behavior were largely without rigor or control, based almost entirely on anecdotal evidence, casual observation, and religious belief—and, of course, the fact that the automata theory corresponded to his philosophical vision.[25] Thus, assigning animals to the status of simple machines served, in the end, as a means of creating absolute mastery over them and their world[26]—a mastery that, without much of an imaginative leap, could be extended to those humans who might bear a presumed resemblance to animals.

Descartes' absolute division of worlds, and the utter degradation of one species in favor of another, did indeed inspire the unimaginative. By the late eighteenth and early nineteenth centuries, the "scientific" racists, like Cuvier and Gobineau, employed, among other things, the radical division of species to form a conception of inferiority: If an individual or racial group could be empirically determined to be in any way connected with animals, this would serve as an objective indication of their less-than-human standing. This inferiority, of course, was articulated and popularly validated through a virtually endless array of analogous terms: *apish, bestial, aggressive, mad, savage, uncontrollable, uncultured, unintelligent*, and so on.

By the mid to latter part of the nineteenth century, the racist ideologues gave way to the biodeterminists and physical anthropologists. So-called positivist thinkers, like Morton, Broca, Topinard, and Le Bon, shifted the scientific discourse from theory to practice, from observational and anecdotal evidence to what they thought to be statistical certainty. Certain humans were animal-like because their physical characteristics could be mathematically determined to correspond to those of higher primates. The "ape in the man" was no longer merely a theoretical construct, but rather the result of direct morphological measurement. If, for example, the radius bone of a chimpanzee's arm were found to be proportionately the same as that of a black human, and far out of proportion with that of a white Teuton, it seemed manifestly clear that the black individual was inferior to the Teuton. Natural inferiority had been reduced to a numerical ratio, an objective number impervious to falsification.

Once Darwin entered the picture, the correlation between humans and animals became easier. Darwin's evolutionary theory hypostatized a unity of species, an ongoing series of global evolutionary patterns that involved all types. Apishness was now no longer a designation, supported by measurement, but rather a fact of life itself. Furthermore, although what Daniel C. Dennett called "Darwin's dangerous idea"[27] was used to many positive biological ends, it also entered the social realm, where, in the hands of thinkers like Spencer, it became a condemning force used against the socially, economically, and educationally deprived. Women, the poor, the working class, racial minorities, and so on were cast low on the scale of human ascent, occupying a midpoint between the slouching fish and the fully acculturated Teuton. These middling types often paid dearly for their shortcomings, having their tubes tied, testicles removed, brains neatly sliced, or, in the worst cases, losing their lives.

To be sure, the myriad results of these theories of mastery are far too numerous and extensive to record in any one place. Suffice it to say that the animalization of groups and individuals continued by and large unabated well into the twentieth century and beyond (an issue discussed in detail in part 3 of this book). The earlier theories had devastating results, though. Combined with other socioeconomic, historical, psychological, and political factors, these theories of mastery and repression contributed significantly to two great genocidal events of the modern era: slavery and the Holocaust—the principal subjects of the next part of this book.

PART II

ANIMALITY IN ACT

Slavery and Holocaust

And this creature, half-child, half-animal, the sport of impulse, whim and conceit, "pleased with a rattle, tickled with a straw," a being who, left to his will, roams at night and sleeps in the day, whose speech knows no word of love, whose passions, once aroused, are as the fury of the tiger— they have set this thing to rule over the Southern people.
—Thomas Dixon Jr., *The Clansman*

V

Aristotle Redux and the Slave Trade

Aristotle Redux: The Slave as Domestic Animal

As Aristotle's thought begins the first part of this book, so does it begin the second. Although human slavery had existed long before Aristotle, and chattel slavery (the ownership of human beings as a form of property) was common from at least 500 BCE, he was the first to develop a systematic philosophical position regarding the nature of the slave and the marketing of slaves.[1] Briefly stated, Aristotle's theory of slavery is derived largely from his political thought. For him, the Greek political paradigm was the ultimate indicator of civilization. Greek culture, he argued, had evolved to the point where laws, self-rule, and justice had replaced the chaotic barbarism of much of the rest of the ancient world. This idea of the capacity to rule politically extended to individuals and "elements" as well. Civil society was viewed as divided into those capable of ruling and those capable only of being ruled. This distinction also involves Aristotle's notion of intellect as opposed to physical strength. Some individuals have a preponderance of intellect, others of physical strength. Because intellect is supreme in political life, those having mere physical power will naturally fall under the sway of those who exercise intellect: "an element able 'by virtue of its intelligence to exercise fore-thought,' and an element 'able by virtue of its bodily power to do what the other element plans.'"[2]

Slavery, for Aristotle, is thus a more or less accurate reflection of the natural state of things. Some rise up in nature to rule, others are there but to serve. The difference is rooted politically in the natural ability to move from barbaric forms of governance to more sophisticated ones, particularly those like the Greek *polis*. Indeed, the Greek political and civil paradigm was the main indication of the difference between civilized and brutish regimes. Members of brutish regimes lack the faculty of intellect, and live in a primitive state based on natural affinity and sensuality:

> And of foolish people those who by nature are thoughtless and live their senses are brutish, like some races of the distant barbarians, while those who are so as a result of disease (e.g., epilepsy) or of madness are morbid. . . . It is plain that some incontinence is brutish and some morbid, while only that which corresponds to human self-indulgence is continence simply.[3]

This theory of brutishness leads inevitably to the comparison of slaves with lower animals, which, for Aristotle, have no power of choice or calculation. Lacking sufficient intellect and the power of choice, slaves, like lower animals, are compelled to serve those who are better endowed to rule. Aristotle also derives this idea of natural superiority and inferiority from his conception of the relationship between soul and body, as the soul has a natural superiority over the body, and that superiority translates into a principle of necessity: "And it is clear that the rule of the soul over the body, and of the mind and the rational element over the passionate, is natural and expedient."[4] What Aristotle is getting at is the "fact" that inferiority is the result of the natural and metaphysical state of things, and therefore irreversible. Those who are born superior will remain superior by virtue of an undeviating, inevitable natural order: "from the hour of their birth, some are marked out for subjection, others for rule."[5] Slaves, like women and lower animals, are thus no more than accurate reflections of their natural inferiority, their set place in the universal order of things:

> The same holds true of animals in relation to men; for tame animals have a better nature than wild and all tame animals are better off when they are ruled by man; for they are preserved. Again, the male is by nature superior, and the female inferior; and one rules, and the other is ruled; this principle, of necessity, extends to all mankind. Where then there is such a difference as that between soul and body, or between men and animals (as is the case of those whose business is to use their body, and who can do nothing better), the lower sort are by nature slaves, and it is better for them as for all inferiors that they should be under the rule of a master. For he who participates in rational principle enough to apprehend, but not to have, such a principle, is a slave by nature. Whereas the lower animals cannot even apprehend a principle; they obey their instincts. And indeed the use made of slaves and tame animals is not very different; for both with their bodies minister to the needs of life.[6]

What is set into motion by Aristotle's theory of slavery is the idea that the inferior slave may, in many respects, differ little from the domestic animal; Aristotle considers it a fact of nature that, to fulfill his or her potential, the slave must be cared for and dominated by his or her master, much like the household pet or the barnyard chickens. This idea, though clearly tendentious, persisted in the Western conception of the slave's status. It served not only as a means of justifying the enslavement of humans—that is, confirming their utter dependence on their superiors—but also as a way of mitigating the immemorial merciless treatment of slaves. As naturally inferior and dependent, the slave, like the household pet, benefits from whatever discipline might be imposed. Flogging, torture, or even the putting to death of a slave is not, in Aristotle's view, reprehensible, because the slave, like the lower animal, has no substantive human rights and is by nature subject to the absolute rule of a master: "It is clear, then, that some men are by nature free, and others slaves, and that for these latter slavery is both expedient and right."[7]

The Mistreatment of Slaves on the Middle Passage: Packing, Canning, and Coffins

> The captain called the officers and crew together and explained that every natural death of a slave would be a loss to owners (and themselves on commissions) while every slave thrown alive into the sea would be a loss to the underwriters. . . . In the next few days 133 sick Negroes were thrown into the sea.
>
> —F. George Kay, *The Shameful Trade*

Although there is some controversy as to exactly when the Atlantic slave trade began, most historians accept the period 1441 to 1444 as the approximate time of its inception. There is absolutely no controversy, however, as to what nation began the Atlantic slave trade: Portugal, with a major assist in ship design, slaving instruments, and methods from Great Britain. In fact, the first slaves snatched from the Atlantic coast of Africa were brought to Portugal as a gift to King Henry the Navigator. They were pursued and kidnapped by Portuguese sailors in an operation that was described by eyewitnesses as "being hunted down like wild animals."[8] However, little demand in other parts of Europe greatly diminished the flow of slaves in the latter half of the fifteenth century. Other than small shipments of slaves to maritime European countries, the Atlantic slave trade was not a very busy enterprise. Moreover, many of the Africans captured by the Portuguese during this initial period were baptized and educated, and, except for the indefensible, abrupt dislocation from family and village, the captives were treated in a relatively benign way. This changed rapidly, though. Once Columbus discovered the New World, numerous commercial settlers and explorers began to travel to the Americas, and over the next 350 years the sugar islands and the Americas consumed millions upon millions of slaves. "The Americas, and the sugar islands of the Caribbean, became as insatiable as the god Baal himself."[9]

With an almost exponential increase in slave demand, the slavers were primarily concerned with packaging their cargo in the most economical manner possible. In the same spirit of the modern design for cramming four debeaked, egg-laying chickens in a fifteen- by fifteen-inch cage, the slavers (particularly the British) began to devise the most functional holding pens possible, with the main design problem being how to store and preserve the most slaves in the least space. Given the need for crew and officer quarters to lie directly below the deck, the slave areas were almost always built on the lowest level of the ship, typically at or below the water line. Although "spoon packing"—slaves packed together spoonlike on top of one another—later became fashionable in the trade, the standard technique was similar to "book shelving," that is, cramming slaves, usually chained two-by-two, into very tight areas. The areas themselves had less than five feet of headroom, as the slaves were almost always positioned either sitting or crouching. John Newton, an adventurer, abolitionist, and friend of William Cowper's, described slave-quarter conditions in his posthumously published *Thoughts upon the African Slave Trade* (1808):

> laid in two rows one above the other, on each side of the ship, close to each other, like books on a shelf. I have known them so close that the shelf would not easily contain one more. And I have known a white man sent down among the men to lay them in these rows to the greatest advantage, so that as little spaces as possible be lost . . . and every morning perhaps more instances than one are found of the living and the dead, like the captives of Mezentius, fastened together.[10]

Other descriptions of the conditions within slave ships are equally harrowing. Olaudah Equiano, a freed slave, described the setting aboard a slaver as follows:

> The closeness of the place and heat of the climate, added to the number in the ship, which was so crowded that each had scarcely room to turn himself, almost suffocating us. This produced copious perspirations, so that the air soon became unfit for respiration from the variety of loathsome smells, and brought on the sickness among the slaves, of which many died.[11]

A ship's surgeon during the height of the Atlantic slave trade, James Barbot, lamented on the insufferable conditions faced by doctors who tried to administer remedies: "this they cannot do leisurely between decks, because of the great heat that is there continually, which is sometimes so excessive that the surgeons would faint away, and the candles would not burn."[12] Another narrative of a ship's doctor recounted the inhuman conditions afforded sick slaves: "The place allotted for sick Negroes is under the half deck, where they lie on the bare planks. By this means those who are emaciated frequently have their skin and even their flesh entirely rubbed off, by the motion of the ship, from the prominent parts of the shoulders, elbows and hips so as to render the bones quite bare."[13] Richard Drake, an American slave trader and chronicler of the slave trade, described similar horrors:

> On the eighth day [out to sea] I took my rounds of the half deck, holding a camphor bag in my teeth; for the stench was hideous. The sick and dying were chained together. I saw pregnant women give birth to babies whilst chained to corpses, which our drunken overseers had not removed. The blacks were literally jammed between decks as if in a coffin; and a coffin that dreadful hold became to nearly one half of our cargo before we reached Bahia.[14]

Hundreds, if not thousands, of similar stories are told about the intolerable conditions aboard slavers—ones involving the leaving of newborn babies on deck to "burn away" in the equatorial sun, the throwing of healthy slaves overboard to collect insurances, regular floggings, sexual assaults, and the outright murder of whole shiploads of slaves.[15]

These atrocities have, as one may sense, distinct comparisons to the shipping of livestock—a point made by Marjorie Spiegel. Her overall statement is quite simple: Slaves were treated like animals, both on their passage to the Americas and during the full course of their enforced visit. Her "dreaded comparison" with regard to human slaves and animals is most effective when she contrasts the shipping of livestock and that of slaves. Livestock—steers, cattle, pigs, and so on—is shipped great distances from auction, to feeding yards, to another auction, and finally to the slaughterhouse. Typically, livestock may travel as much as 2,000 miles, in cramped and abysmal conditions. The animals generally lose a great deal of body weight—as much as 9 percent—and are subject to what is commonly called "shipping fever," of which hundreds of thousands die annually.[16] The "livestock" cramped into the Atlantic slavers did not fare much better. Their living conditions were, as noted earlier, similarly deplorable. The tight packing, stress, and lack of nutritious food caused considerable weakening and weight loss during the crossings. Most slaves were fattened up again before the auctions in what were usually referred to as slave-yards, which is, of course, precisely what happens to feed cattle.[17] With no incentive to properly feed the cattle on the way to slaughter, the process of fattening is restricted to the feedlots attached to the slaughter facilities. Moreover, many slaves in transit died, like today's livestock, of contagious diseases exacerbated by poor nutrition, unsanitary conditions, and, perhaps above all, dire overcrowding.

Factory farming is another point of comparison between animal and human exploitation: "The horrors of the Middle Passage, with its cramped conditions, pools of excrement and urine, 'acceptable' mortality-rates, seemingly interminable length of duration, and finally insanity leading to violence and cannibalism, have been projected into modernity in the form of factory farming."[18] The factory farm carries on the paradigm of manipulation for profit so obvious in the cramming of slaves into slave ships. Sows, for example, are chained or clamped into narrow farrowing stalls, for months or years on end, so as to save caloric energy expenditure. Chickens and pigs are stacked in tiers three, four, or five high; the pigs' tails are cut off so as to prevent stress-induced tail biting.[19] All of these were, of course, the principal positions in which slaves were transported economically to the New World. Virtually every narrative description of slave-ship conditions entails some combination of chains, leg irons, stacking, handcuffs, cramped spaces, and penlike enclosures.

To be sure, this egregious abuse and exploitation of humans has spawned numerous and often disparate explanations and entreaties, including ones from such eminent figures as Marx, Bentham, and Mill. Most explanations of slavery, however, fail to fully account for the staggering disregard for human life in the initial stages of American slavery. Even given the incentive to deliver as many whole slaves as possible, there were still certain conditions created by humans for other humans that made torture, pain, disease, suffering, and in many cases the loss of life inevitable and, worse, acceptable. These conditions and acts, I suggest, can be fully understood only by considering the devaluation of the appropriated African slave to sheer animality. The aforementioned Aristotelian reduction of the slave to human property, and the subsequent equating of humans and domesticated animals, figure significantly in this notion. If the slave were naturally subordinate, like the animal fated to serve its master, then whatever improved his or her use-value would be seen as productive and necessary, regardless of the treatment any individual slave received. After all, as is the case with the domestic animal, the best results are not always achieved by kindness. As absolute subordinates, the African slaves could be treated in any way necessary to provide the best practical results, with economic interests (i.e., bringing in live rather than dead slaves) being the only mitigating concern. To ship cattle, pigs, chickens, or any other domestic animals in comfortable, spacious conditions, or to keep them in individual, well-ventilated pens would be patently absurd, as there is in this view absolutely no moral obligation to do so, and it would be economically impractical—what Aristotle, in his day, would probably have termed "unnatural."

Burdening the "Beasts": The Everyday Life of American Slaves

> A white man—a monster in human shape—a few months ago, at Charleston, compelled one of his negroes to cut off the head of another, while the master *superintended* the horrid deed.
>
> —Charles William Janson,
> *The Stranger in America 1793–1806*

To be sure, the animalistic treatment of slaves did not end with the unloading of slave-ship cargoes in the New World. In fact, one could argue that the boat voyages were among the least of the atrocious acts directed toward black Africans, who, upon arrival, were herded into slave markets, separated from family, and sent off to work under the harshest and often inhuman conditions. Slave markets and sales techniques usually varied from location to location, but all of them employed methods involving parallels to animal auctions and sales. Equiano reported that some slave dealers sold their slaves by the pound, with prices depending on the bulk or lack of it and the labor potential of the particular slave—which, of course, was at that time also the standard for animal auctions: "I have often seen slaves, particularly those who were meager, in different islands, put into scales and weighed; and then sold from three-pence to six-pence or nine-pence a pound."[20] Other slave dealers, however, sold their slaves "by the lump," that is, as a whole individual.

Perhaps the most astute observer of the social conditions of slavery, Frederick Douglass, indicated a similar animalistic pattern in the sale of the slave and the slave family. Slaves were not only traded in auction as laboring animals, but were even classified together with animals in presale evaluations. Douglass writes:

> We were all ranked together at the valuation. Men and women, old and young, married and single, were ranked with horses, sheep, and swine. There were horses and men, cattle and women, pigs and children, all holding the same rank in the scale of being, and were all subjected to the same narrow examination. Silvery-headed age and sprightly youth, maids and matrons, had to undergo the same indelicate inspection. At this moment, I saw more clearly than ever the brutalizing effects of slavery upon both slave and slaveholder.[21]

The separation and destruction of slave families is another indication of the slave's animal status. After all, livestock auctioneers have absolutely no concern about keeping piglets, or chicks, or calves with their original mothers. Indeed, within the factory-farm conception, the mothers serve merely as breeding stock to routinely turn out the best possible offspring. As Peter Singer poignantly notes, "neither farmers nor breeders of companion animals and research animals give any thought to the feelings of the non-human mothers and children whom they routinely separate as part of their business."[22] Slaves were rarely sold as family units either. In fact, the breakup of families was seen as a tactic with which to isolate and better control the individual slave, and thus increase his or her use-value. Equiano, again, offered a touching account of this sort of family separation:

> And at or after the sale, even those negroes born in the islands it is not uncommon to see taken from their wives, wives from their husbands, and children from their parents, and sent off to other islands, and wherever else their merciless lords choose; and probably never more, during life, see each other! Oftentimes my heart has bled at these partings; when the friends of the departed have been at the water-side, and, with sighs and tears, have kept their eyes fixed on the vessel till it went out of sight.[23]

The reduction of the slave to simple property, to a barely sentient human-animal, was thus so total that the average slaveholder or seller felt absolutely no compunction about completely destroying a family unit. What would have been unthinkable with regard to any other family was, for the slave family, a simple step in the commercial process, a way of improving the market value of profitable items. The whole question of family ties, love, support, dependence, sharing, and so on—those values emphasized by the prevailing Christian faith—was completely ignored in the drive to control and oversee the entire life of the slave. Any sign of normalcy—even the most primitive family structure—was seen as contravening the very basis of mastery, giving the object of domination a sense of human, rather than non-human or animal, social organization. On this phenomenon of absolute mastery, Douglass wrote: "After the valuation, then came the division. . . . We had no more voice in that decision than the *brutes among whom we were ranked*. A single word from a white man was enough—against our wishes, prayers, and entreaties—to sunder forever the dearest friends, dearest kindred, and strongest ties known to human beings."[24]

Like the move from slave ship to marketplace, the move from marketplace to plantation or individual owner usually held even greater horrors. Beatings were virtually a daily rite for many slaves, and excessive sadistic cruelty was a common means of teaching general lessons to slaves as a group. These beatings and various sadistic acts were intended largely to control and divert the energies of the slave into disciplined labor, and to impress upon the slave a sense of absolute submission to the needs of the master. Once again, one could argue that, in the disciplining of slaves, the measures were much like those imposed on domestic animals, particularly animals designated to serve the needs of humans. For a domestic animal to serve well, it must be controlled in virtually all its habits and behaviors: cattle must conform absolutely to the organized rules of ranching or farming; working dogs must be disciplined not to run freely, as is also the case with hunting dogs, and so on. The means of training, of course, include incontestably the use of punishment and reward, the master's edifying acts of power over his or her animals. Douglass illustrates just such an edification regarding his own discipline as a relocated slave: "and the thought of passing out of their hands into those of Master Andrew—a man who, but a few days before, to give me a sample of his bloody disposition, took my little brother by the throat, threw him on the ground, and with the heel of his boot stamped upon his head until the blood gushed from his nose and ears."[25]

From time to time, atrocities were committed on slaves that would not even have been imposed on domestic animals, largely because such acts would have been entirely debilitating—or fatal—and thus counterproductive to animal output. Cruelty of this sort went well beyond the discipline imposed by and for mastery. These acts can thus be consigned to the treatment of the slave as a kind of under-animal, a being considered even below the status of animal— effectively, a mere living thing to be subjected to the darkest kinds of perversion and inhumanity. The behavior of Arthur Hodge, a planter on Tortola, provides a devastating illustration of treatment going beyond (or below) even the cold pragmatics of exploiting the "animal-in-the-slave":

> Slaves' children had been picked up by Hodge and lowered into tubs of water till they nearly drowned. He then suspended them by their wrists and horsewhipped them. One ten year old boy had been dipped into a cauldron of boiling water. The motive was purely sadistic; no offences by the children were known. . . . Real or imagined offences by adult slaves were punished with appalling cruelty. Two Negroes who had annoyed Hodge were pinioned to the ground face downwards and flogged for more than an hour; both died. . . . A slave freed from another plantation, and employed by Hodge as a cooper, was clubbed to death when he grumbled about having to do unskilled field work. A household slave had a hot iron rammed into his mouth; he died from the injuries. Two women slaves, accused by Hodge of putting poison in his food, were held motionless while boiling water was poured down their throats. They died in agony. Altogether Hodge had been responsible for the murders of nearly a hundred Negro men, women and children.[26]

In many respects Hodge's acts entail a distinct regression from mastery to unreflective sadistic, violent, and total domination over the other. In the case of mastery, the acts of the slaveowner were usually motivated by both the economic benefits and the need to control others. In Hodge's case, neither of these factors seemed to be of much interest. His acts totally disregarded even the most fundamental sense of human existence and ignored the point that slaves even felt pain—a necessary condition for punishment. In fact, one could say that he reduced the body of the slave to that of the insensate Cartesian machine, the automaton that was there simply to be used. Just as Père Malebranche had kicked the pregnant dog to demonstrate that it was merely a reactive machine, Hodge tortured and murdered his slaves to inscribe his own sadistic signature on their presumably unfeeling bodies. In this, he did not only disregard the feelings and pain of the African slaves he abused, but reduced them to the most primitive form of living matter, to a surface upon which to inflict pain, suffering, and death—in short, to an under-animal, an amorphous body without form, design, feeling, or the least bit of sentience. Moreover, one could argue that this sort of action is not even sadistic in the Sadean sense, as Sade himself viewed the infliction of pain as a reciprocal erotic act, requiring the relationship of two equally feeling bodies: that of the inflictor and that of the receiver. There is, in Sade, almost always a consensual mutual use or abuse of one by the other, as is witnessed in Juliette's initiation into the Society of the Friends of Crime: "What think you of the lash? I like to use it and have it used upon me."[27] Conversely, in the slaveholder Hodge's acts there is only the one-sided desire to injure, to inflict pain and death—a desire that has little, if anything, to do with discipline.

Not all slave life was as miserable and unsettling as that under the slaveholder Hodge. There were even reports of kind slaveholders—if one can allow the oxymoron—and slaves had to be adapted necessarily to the conditions of their captivity. These conditions included home life, working the fields, and a variety of other activities surrounding their daily lives. These various activities, too, serve as indicators of the slaves' reduction to animality. Although conditions varied from one locale to the other, most field slaves ate and slept in routine with animals on the plantation or farm. Animals were usually fed quickly, so as to get them out to work a full day. Little decorum surrounded the meals of oxen or draft horses, and so was it with slaves. Douglass related a typical meal during his day as a field worker: "Mr. Covey gave us enough to eat, but scarce time to eat it. We were often less than five minutes taking our meals."[28]

Fieldwork also had its elements of animal labor. Most field workers toiled from sunrise to sunset, and in the busy seasons—planting, harvesting, fodder-saving, and so on—the work often lasted until midnight, or sometimes later. Indeed, the requirements imposed on field-working slaves were frequently far more stringent than those imposed on work animals; animals were often rested and watered down in the blazing afternoon sun of the South, whereas slaves were required to work under almost all conditions. Pregnant mares and cows were stalled and pampered when they were about to give birth; pregnant slaves were usually worked a full day right up till birth, and there are numerous accounts of the flogging of pregnant slaves to extract a few last hours of labor. Sick work animals were usually removed from the fields and tended to by veterinarians; sick slaves were usually whipped into line, as they were routinely seen as malingering, not to mention wasting valuable labor time. Douglass related an episode of his own sickness and the treatment that followed:

> About three o'clock of that day, I broke down; my strength failed me; I was seized with a violent aching of the head, attended by extreme dizziness; I trembled in every limb. . . . When I could stand no longer, I fell, and felt as if held down by an immense weight. . . . Mr. Covey was in the house, about one hundred yards from the treading-yard where we were fanning. . . . He hastily inquired what the matter was. Bill answered that I was sick. He then asked where I was. He was told by one of the hands. He came to the spot, and, after looking at me awhile, asked me what was the matter. I told him as well as I could, for I scarce had enough strength to speak. He then gave me a savage kick in the side, and told me to get up. I tried to do so, but fell back in the attempt. He gave me another kick, and again told me to rise. . . . Covey took up the hickory slat with which Hughes had been striking off the half-bushel measure, and with it gave me a heavy blow upon the head, making a large wound, and the blood ran freely.[29]

Accommodations for slaves also bordered on the animalistic. Although housing differed from plantation to plantation, most slaves were crowded into ramshackle cabins, and in many cases they lived in what was described as sheds. A slave narrator portrayed his shed as holding 29 other slaves. The floors of the housing were almost always dirt, spread with some straw. The walls were usually thin and cracked, allowing wind and cold to enter during the sometimes-bitter Southern U.S. winter. The crowding of cabins and sheds was legend: on one Southern plantation, 260 slaves shared 38 cabins, an average of 6.8 slaves per cabin; on another, 160 slaves were jammed into 18 cabins, the average being nearly 9 slaves per cabin. Austin Stewart, a freed slave narrator, described slave housing as "not as good as many of our stables in the north."[30] Housing, then, was merely a form of shelter to maintain, minimally protect, and, most importantly, hold in the working slave. They were provided with the absolute minimum to survive, so as to extract as much profitable labor as possible.

This is precisely the practical end of domestic animal use: the farm-work animal was valuable, and thus needed to be maintained and cared for, as was the case with most other domestic animals. Sheds, barns, and coops were thus constructed to shelter and to contain domestic animals; the chicken coop and yard served to house, protect, and hold the chickens; the horse barn both sheltered the horses and kept them from wandering off. The housing of slaves served all of these purposes, in a way not very different from that used for the common farm animals, though slaves were occasionally allowed a chair or lamp in their quarters.

Like deer, wild boar, turkey, raccoon, possum, and other traditional Southern game, slaves were also hunted. Indeed, escaped slaves were often viewed as nothing more than expensive game, and before 1863 hunting them down was officially sanctioned.[31] To pursue, capture, or kill a runaway slave was not in any way a punishable offense. What follows is a description of what the average runaway slave might face:

> Although his immediate purpose might be to escape the overseer's lash or to obtain a temporary respite from incessant labor, the black faced insu-perable odds. As he plunged into the nearby woods or swamps, the over-seer, gun in hand, was close on his heels. Almost immediately, or certainly in a few days, he would hear the hounds as they picked up the scent of his tracks. Reaching the woods unscathed, he had to fight off the pangs of hunger as well as blood-thirsty wild cats, wolves, and white men. Avid hunters, his master and overseer might know the woods as well, or better, than he did.... Capture would probably mean ... being handcuffed to heavy logs at night and to another slave during the day, or having a cow-bell hung around his neck or a tall instrument with several prongs covered with little bells attached to his head.[32]

Interestingly, not only is the description reminiscent of an animal hunt, but the treatment of the captured slave after the hunt appears to be precisely what one would do to restrain and stay constantly aware of unruly domestic animals: chain them up and attach cowbells or noisy headgear.

VI

Narratives of Oppression

> The Negro, being an ape, entered the ark with the rest
> of the animals; and as the descendants of Noah spread
> out over the earth they carried with them their negroes
> and other domestic animals, domestic plants, metallic
> instruments, etc., and developed those superb civilizations
> the remains of which are found on every continent of
> the earth.
>
> —Charles Carroll, *The Negro a Beast*

One can generate virtually endless examples of the animalistic treatment of African slaves in the Americas. Each day was experienced in much the way an animal would experience its own captivity and use. Incarcerated, restrained, beaten, overworked, the slave was totally subjected to the will of the master, to mastery in general. This animalistic relationship of master and slave-beast was not, however, casual or unmotivated; rather, it was the result of a long-standing attitude and moral position regarding inferiority, and it was sustained by contemporary popular scientific, religious, literary, and philosophical discourses. These discourses usually took the form of written material, both fictional and nonfictional, and these texts were widely distributed and read throughout the United States both before the Civil War and well after it.[1]

Although the mass of writings supportive of slavery and opposed to blacks in general was diverse and multifaceted, the writing of animality can be divided into three typical narrative categories: fear of emancipation and assimilation, fear of miscegenation, and "scientific" racism. Fear of emancipation and assimilation is in large part rooted in the potential loss of slave labor, and in this regard it is based on economic considerations. It is also involved, however, on a subliminal

73

level, with the fear of the loss of superiority, of control over those who had traditionally been reduced to an inferior, animal-like status; it is in effect an expression of the fear of losing control. Fear of miscegenation, related to fear of emancipation and assimilation, is perhaps the most deeply psychologically rooted of all the narratives of animality. Here the writers express a profound terror of and a strange fascination with black sexuality and articulate these concerns in terms of animal strength, potency, promiscuity, and savagery, with the "final solution" to this problem centered on expulsion or harsh punitive measures. The last category, scientific racism, has connections to both of the first two categories, as the strategy is to use the so-called sciences of race to entirely reduce the slave and, later, the freed slave to the kinds of animalistic (i.e., dependent and manipulable) types examined in the first part of this book.

The pre–Civil War works in support of slavery were usually tinged with a sense of urgency. Slavery as a Southern institution was on the wane, threatened mostly by the failing Southern economy, widespread abolitionist activism, and the reluctance of slaves to contribute to their own suppression.[2] In this regard the pre–Civil War pro-slavery texts generally conjured as negative a picture of slaves as possible, relegating them to a state of absolute dependency on the white man. In doing so, comparisons to lower animals served an important function. The portrayal of the black as more or less a separate creature falling outside the family of man was the perfect pretense for keeping the slave in his or her position of dependence and inferiority—that is, as a justification for the continuation of slavery.

The best-known and most widely read of the pre–Civil War pro-slavery, anti-black writers is J. H. Van Evrie, a southern physician, publisher, and popular science writer. His "classic" work, *White Supremacy and Negro Subordination or, Negroes a Subordinate Race and (so-called) Slavery Its Normal Condition*, originally published in 1859, stressed the various differences between whites and blacks, settling in many places on the kind of discredited strain of comparative physical anthropology and anatomy touched upon in part 1 of this book. For Van Evrie, blacks are not exactly animals, but they seem to have much in common with the lower animals, or, at the very best, the lowest sort of human strain. A number of chapters in *Slavery Its Normal Condition* are devoted, among numerous other things, to exposing these animal similarities.

In the first chapter dealing with this comparison, "Color," Van Evrie stresses the scientific "fact" that skin color is inevitable, the divine work of the Creator and therefore quite irreversible. He is here not just discussing celestial causality, though he does stress the causal necessity entailed in human coloration; rather, his foremost point is the fact that the black has been created that way because of some ineluctable divine plan. This revelation is, in turn, used to characterize the black as forever incapable of expressing emotion in the same way as the white. Van Evrie noted:

> The face of the Caucasian reflects the character, the emotions, the instincts, to a certain extent the intellectual forces, and even the acquired habits, the virtues and vices of the individual. This, to a certain extent, depends on the mobility of the facial muscles, and the general anatomical structure and outline of the features; but without our color, the expression would be very imperfect, and the face wholly incapable of expressing the inner nature and the specific character of the race. For example: What is there at the same time so charming and so indicative of inner purity and innocence as the blush of a modest maiden? . . . Can anyone suppose such a thing possible of a black face? That these sudden and startling alterations of color, which reflect the moral perceptions of the white woman, are possible to the negress? And if the latter cannot reflect these things in her face—if her features are utterly incapable of expressing emotions so elevated and beautiful, is it not certain that she is without them—that they have no existence in her inner being, are no portion of her moral nature?[3]

The incapacity to express emotions has even deeper sociocultural consequences. This fundamental difference between white skin and black skin is also taken as indicative of the constitutional incapacity of the black to achieve the level of moral and intellectual sensitivity realized by the white; blacks are doomed to remain inferior by the very composition of their physical bodies, to lack even the most fundamental ability to overcome their position of dependence. In short, outer appearance is fully indicative of what is inside, and blackness of the skin does not allow demonstration of the more genteel emotions. No sign, no existence. As constitutionally incapable of attaining civilization, blacks—as Van Evrie continually argues—must remain within their natural and God-given position: the "normal condition of slavery." To free the slaves, as desired by those "perverse creatures among us who clamor so loudly for Negro equality,"[4] would thrust a morally and emotionally bankrupt beast on the population of the South—one who, by the very color of his or her skin, is condemned irreversibly to these faults.

Whereas black skin indicates the absence of all finer emotion, the features of the black person indicate a far darker prospect: bestiality. Here Van Evrie uses the presumed uniformity of features in blacks initially to distinguish them from Caucasians. Whites have a vast variety of different features, including hair color, nose size, lip size, skull shape, and so on. But, Van Evrie stresses, they are all members of the white race, and this diversity indicates a certain depth of character, personality, and culture. Blacks, being quite uniform in their appearance, cannot rise to this level of human complexity. In support of this argument, Van Evrie reasons that the fact that all blacks have enormous lips, shallow eyes, flat noses, and protruding foreheads indicates that they are only capable of expressing the most limited emotional and moral qualities. In effect, these features serve primarily to express their most basic wants. The argument is, as was so often the case, supported by a comparison to animals: "The features of the animal are made to express its wants, to reflect the nature God has given it. We witness this every day among the domestic animals—the cat, the dog, the horse, all exhibit their qualities, their wants, their moods . . . all that their natures are capable of, are reflected in their faces, and we understand them."[5]

Van Evrie extends animal associations to black familial relations as well, especially to those between black children and their mothers. He points out that it is a known fact that black mothers tend to leave their children on their own much earlier than white mothers. In fact, he asserts, it is a rare occurrence to see a black child living with his or her mother past twelve years of age. White children, however, stay close to their parents until a much more advanced age. This, of course, gives one the impression of animal upbringing, in that it is generally assumed that animal mothers abandon their offspring at a much earlier age, and some, as was thought of reptiles, just deposit their offspring and make off to breed another batch. Moreover, according to Van Evrie, black mothers are not even capable of killing their young to save them from some imminent disaster. Unlike white European peasant women, who will kill their children at the first sign of disaster, the black mother is just too fatefully moved by her maternal instincts to do so. On this, he writes:

> Nevertheless, it is quite certain that, both living under equally favorable circumstances, the negress is less likely to destroy the life of her offspring than is the white woman. Her maternal instincts are more imperative, more closely approximate to the *animal*, while that sense of degradation which the higher nature and more elevated sensibilities of the white woman prompt to hiding of her shame by the destruction of her offspring, is entirely absent in the negress. She may possibly destroy her child in a paroxysm of rage, but her nature has guarded her too strongly by the imperative of *maternal instinct*, while those ten thousand chances in our higher habitudes and social complications which may involve the most exquisite suffering of the unhappy mother, and impel her, by one terrible and supreme crime, to destroy her own offspring, can never happen or influence the negro mother.[6]

The inability of blacks to demonstrate original vocal pitch and tone is another condemning animalistic feature. It appears as though blacks have no original sense of speech, and, like parrots and cockatoos, simply imitate the speech of others. Van Evrie explains this by the fact that the "vocal organs of the Negro differ widely from those of the white man, which leads to a corresponding difference in language. The specific or the most essential feature of the Negro nature is his imitative instincts, or his capacity for imitating the qualities and for acquiring the habitudes of the white man."[7] This tendency naturally leads to a total dependence on the linguistic behavior of the white man, and if the imitative model is lost (i.e., slaves are for some reason freed), the black will surely degenerate to incoherent "animal savagery." Van Evrie goes even further to attribute lack of original black vocality to the impossibility of blacks ever being able to make music. Blacks utter only simple tones, and thus are only capable of making mere sounds—not music: "Music is to the Negro an impossible art, and therefore such a thing as a Negro singer is unknown."[8]

Although, according to Van Evrie, blacks cannot sing, they seem to have more than their share of sensuality. Physiologically speaking, the black is, once again, just constitutionally different from the white:

> The large distribution of nervous matter to the organs of sense and consequent dominating sensualism (not mere animalism) is the direct cause of that extreme sloth and indolence universal with the race. The small brain and limited reasoning power of the Negro render him incapable of comprehending the wants of the future, while the sloth dependent on the dominating sensualism, together with strong animalistic appetites impelling him always to gross self-indulgence, render a master guide or protector essential to his own welfare.[9]

Fear of the loss of the slave as a key economic provider in the South is palpable in the preceding excerpt. Because of purely God-given, biologically and physiologically determined insults, the black must be led by a "master guide or protector" (read: slavemaster or overseer). Yet, there is a narrative of animality entailed here as well. Mastery is necessary not only because of the physical makeup of the black, but also because of his or her potential for animalistic savagery. The "dominating" sensualism combined with strong animalistic appetites might, unchecked, result in the possibility of bodily harm to the Caucasian—or worse, to the whole innocent being of the blushing, thrush-throated, blond-haired, tiny-nosed Southern belle.

In the second part of Van Evrie's text, he takes a slightly different path in associating Southern blacks with animals. Here he employs a mix of pre-Darwinian evolution theories and introduces what he calls the "laws of interunion and hybridism." His real intent here is to discourage miscegenation, which, given his objective, he aptly terms "mongrelism." Interestingly, what is essentially at stake in interunion or mongrelism is the loss of virility and potency; like the product of the union between donkeys and horses, Van Evrie believed that too much mongrelism leads to absolute sterility or "muleism." For some entirely unexplained reason, "muleism" is unavoidable after only five encounters between blacks and whites, with a precisely calculable loss of virility at each stage. For example, Van Evrie described the fourth stage as follows: "By still intermarrying with hybrids, and of a corresponding remove, virility is correspondingly decreased."[10] By the fifth stage, the physiological damage is already irreversible.[11]

Miscegenation is not only a mortal sin, but also turns out, according to Van Evrie, to be a gross perversion of both God's laws and those of nature. In fact, muleism counts as a kind of over-animal perversion, as fixed laws govern absolutely the instinct of reproduction in animals. Those who indulge their sexual appetites in this sort of folly are doomed not only to total sterility but also to some kind of damnable perversion. This perversion, in turn, leads inevitably to extreme, even satanic, forms of bestiality, and many of the products of mongrelism or muleism act accordingly: "But the mongrel leaders . . . were mere moral monsters, whose deeds of slaughter were alternated with scenes of beastly debauchery and unnatural and devilish revelry."[12]

Clearly, Van Evrie's text has no other compelling intention than to ward off the imminent end of slavery in the South. Every chapter is organized so as to demonstrate some indissoluble dependency of the black on his or her owners and masters. Many of these claims are "authenticated" by the use of the scientific or pseudoscientific literature of the mid-nineteenth century; craniometry, physical anthropology, comparative anatomy, and biodeterminism all play a significant role in degrading the black and elevating the white, as was precisely the intention of the scientific theories of inferiority touched upon in part 1 of this book. Unlike most mid-nineteenth-century science, religion was also used as a tool of denigration: specifically, to establish an absolute grounding for the place of the inferior slave in the God-given order of things. Inferiority was not only scientifically demonstrable, but also the result of the unquestionable word of the Almighty, a fixed part of the revealed celestial order.

Even though his main stress was on dissuading and discouraging the emancipation of slaves, the animal/black metaphor served as an important tool of degradation for Van Evrie, as an emotionally appealing supplement to the broader scientific and theological arguments. Blacks are incapable of fending for themselves not only because they are determined scientifically and theologically to be inferior, incompetent, and ill prepared to do so, but also because they have not achieved a level of full and complete humanity. As such, they remain dangerous and savage; much like escaped (emancipated) wild beasts, they pose a mortal danger to the very heart of Southern life and culture. Black women are sensuous and licentious, drawing the unsuspecting Caucasian into certain ruin and, in the end, like the barren mule, perhaps total sterility. Black men, in contrast, are prone to explosive violence, being dependent largely on their animalistic nature—violence that might be unleashed at any time if they were allowed their freedom. It was thus the remnants of the animal in blacks that in large part guaranteed their inability to function within a so-called civilized society, and, in the end, rendered them forever dependent on the superior Caucasian race—their "master guides or protectors."

Van Evrie's spate of parochialism and pseudoscience was not by any means an isolated phenomenon in pre–Civil War Southern writing. There were hundreds—if not thousands—of popular tracts, books, treatises, sermons, pamphlets, and so on that reviled the black and argued vehemently against emancipation. The patterns of mastery in these various texts pretty much follow those of Van Evrie, with the predominate concern centering on the standard evolutionary, physiological, cognitive, religious, and animalistic faults of blacks. With regard to the latter, the animalistic, there is often a tendency in pre–Civil War racist writing to amalgamate this trait with insufficient moral, cognitive, and religious character. This is clearly the case in another famous racist tract, *Bible Defense of Slavery or the Origin, History, and Fortunes of the Negro Race*, published in 1853. Its author, Josiah Priest, continually assails the entire black race for their animalistic savagery, which he attributes to their distinct lack of moral and mental endowments, and thus of a civilized religious and metaphysical sensibility. This, in turn, explains their repulsive acts of sexual and sensual excess, demonstrated by the fact that "they indulge almost universally in disgusting debauchery and sensuality, displaying every where gross indifference to the mental pains and pleasures of others."[13] The reasons for this behavior, according to Priest, can be found in blacks' native proximity to animals and their penchant for animal-like behavior: "There are districts of country in Africa, and especially along the Atlas Mountains, in which apes and baboons are so abundant, that in many of the mud hut towns of the Negro natives, these animals live altogether, as if they were members of the same community."[14] The assimilation of man and beast does not stop there, however. Priest goes on to quote the Greek historian, Herodotus, who, presumably, related a story of a tribe of Negroes in Africa who were so profoundly ignorant "that they had no names by which they could distinguish each other; their memories, respecting the looks of individuals, being their only guide when they met, the same as dogs after they get acquainted."[15]

Chancellor Harper, in his tract called *Harper's Memoir on Slavery* (1852), takes an approach remarkably similar to that of Priest. For Harper, the justification for slavery also lies in the ubiquitous uncivilized nature of the African native. Blacks fail miserably in meeting the standards of the Western Caucasian, demonstrating a lack of social tenderness, love of country, or even the ability to mount some concept of danger. They also lack an awareness of history, which situates them in some kind of eternal now, oblivious of past or future. In this sense, Harper argues, "they approach nearer to the nature of brute creation, than perhaps any other people on the face of the globe."[16] A dilemma to which Harper responds: "Let me ask if this people do not furnish the very material out of which slaves ought to be made, and whether it be not an improving of their condition to make them the slaves of civilized masters?"[17] The notion of slavery as salvation, obviously inserted in these arguments to strike a religious chord, is often stressed by Harper as means of reversing the inevitable course of African destiny. Without the intrusion of white civilization, Harper argues, the indigenous African is doomed to succumb to either his animal instincts or his enormous sloth, and thus to either grisly death or certain starvation: "The wild savage is the child of passion, unaided by one ray of religion or morality to direct his course, in consequence of which his existence is stained with every crime that can debase human nature to a level with the brute creation."[18] The solution to the problem is quite simple: redirect the wild energies of the black to constructive work. "It was a useful and beneficent work, approaching the heroic, to tame the wild horse, and subdue him to the use of man; how much more to tame the nobler animal that is capable of reason, and subdue him to usefulness?"[19]

This small sample of pre–Civil War racist writing is sufficient, I think, to establish the narrative patterns of mastery that are ingredients of virtually all this kind of writing. Blacks fail to have any real agency in these texts, and thus function as a kind of manipulable signifier in the various pro-slavery arguments; that is, their representations serve to substantiate the spurious arguments in some merely predicative way: they *are* slothful, animalistic, immoral, sensuous, savage, rapacious, unintelligent, and so on. This, of course, also extends to their animalistic representations—representations to which they are forever doomed because of their natural and spiritual, and therefore irreversible, place in the universal order of things. Driven by the fear of looming emancipation and thus massive economic dislocations, the pro-slavery writers attempt to depict as frightening a spectacle of the Southern black as possible. Their "incontrovertible" animalism served as the perfect tool with which to write the fearsome animal into Southern—and to some extent, Northern—life, society, and culture. Freedom would only mean the release of hordes of unruly, savage, immoral, sexually insatiable, potency-draining "beasts," who, without the sure guidance of Caucasian probity, would no doubt destroy everything created by the genteel culture of the Old South. Nevertheless, these justifications for domination and mastery largely faded after 1863. With slavery officially gone, urgency had to be transferred to the palpable dangers posed by the "free Negro," and these invented dangers were precisely what dominated post–Civil War anti-black writing.

Post–Civil War anti-black writing borrowed much from the earlier tradition, but was distinguished by narrative emphases on fear of miscegenation, and, unlike most of the early pro-slavery writing, on direct reference to black sexuality. Narrative techniques also involved the tried-and-true comparisons to animals, but this time not so much as a justification for dominance and mastery, but more as a *cri* to banish or tightly control the newly loosed "animal" in American society.

One of the most disturbing, brutal, and unintentionally comical of the post–Civil War texts is Charles Carroll's *The Negro a Beast* (1900). At first glance, the text appears much like the earlier popular literature supporting slavery. Lacking the existence of the institution of slavery, though, it tends to stress the absolute impossibility of culturally, intellectually, or, most importantly, religiously permitting black assimilation into American society. The author tried to accomplish this by producing a nearly 400-page thesis arguing that the black is not a person but, rather, an animal. What is especially interesting about this approach is that the claim of black animality is not metaphoric, symbolic, or comparative; rather, according to the author, it is based on a combination of biblical exegesis and objective scientific observation and empirical knowledge. For Carroll, then, the black is literally an animal that stands somewhere in the register of higher primates and thus distinctly apart from the human race itself.

Carroll's text, like the Old Testament, begins with the creation. After invoking Ernst Haeckel and Darwin as the principal proponents of "Atheistic School of Natural Development" (evolution) and their counterpart the "Scriptural School of Divine Creation," Carroll proceeds to make the argument that blacks, unlike humans, were part of God's separate creation of animals. Cleverly, he veers away from both the Aristotelian and Cartesian view of unreasoning animals and sides with Darwin who argued that animals possess some power of reasoning. This move allows him to place blacks in a creationist animal category without having to explain how a seeming human that is really an animal could have reasoning powers. At any rate, following an extensive examination of Scripture, Carroll is able to determine that in Samuel I there is a clear indication that God populated the earth with "wild beasts." From this point, he concludes, the phrase used by the Philistines to threaten King David, "beware of the man eating apes," indicates that "the Bible plainly teaches that there is a 'beast,' or an ape that is a man eater."[20] Now, because there is no ape on earth today that is a man-eater, Carroll concludes that the reference must have been to blacks, for, he asserts, "The Negro is not only a man eater, but he feeds upon the flesh of his own kindred, and even upon his own offspring, as well as on that of other apes."[21]

The reduction of blacks to mere animals in God's plan—specifically, to man-eating apes—does not, however, seem sufficiently degrading to Carroll. He is determined to prove further that the serpent in the Garden of Eden was not a snake after all, but, rather, a black person in the form of a "man eating ape" or "beast of the field." This is all confirmed by the fact that Adam himself chose the symbolic term *serpent* to describe the beast of the field, and this term had only a nominal relation to an actual snake. Carroll elaborates: "This was simply a name given it to distinguish it from others of its kind. Hence, the name serpent no more indicates that it was a snake than does the name of the late Indian chief, Sitting Bull indicates [sic] that he was a bull which habitually assumed the sitting position."[22] The snake, of course, in the form of a beast of the field, carries out its sinful plan, convincing Eve to eat of the apple of knowledge and thus initiating the fall from Paradise, the very decline of humanity. Indeed, Carroll construes the entire sin of Adam and Eve not to be simply that of eating from the tree of knowledge, but, rather, to be that of having taken the advice of the beast of the field.

> Their acceptance of this beast as their councilor necessarily preceded their acting upon his advice. Hence, their eating of the forbidden fruit was a second and later offense. This reveals the startling fact that it was man's social equality with the Negro which brought sin into the world; and it is man's social equality with the Negro and the evils which inevitably grow out of it that keeps sin in the world.[23]

Lacking the raw force inherent in the fear of emancipation, Carroll is compelled to direct his attack on blacks to the secular and spiritual dangers entailed in equality, assimilation, and a kind of spontaneous miscegenation (the title to an illustration in his book queries: "Will Your Next Child be Negro?"). However, his narrative strategy is not simply to malign the black with a spate of animalistic invective and disparaging "scientific facts"—though he is not entirely opposed to doing that as well. Instead, he focuses primarily on the entirely unbridgeable difference that separates blacks from every other racial type in the evolutionary scale: the fact that they are not even human. Not only are they incapable of reaching the most fundamental level of *Homo sapiens*, but also, in a religious context, they are the very source of all evil, the purveyors of the forbidden fruit. Carroll makes it manifestly clear that if blacks can destroy the bliss of Edenic innocence, create the prospect of a miraculously conceived Negro child in every white family, and cannibalize their own children, they surely cannot be treated as equals or in any way assimilated into the social order. If nothing else, one thing is clear from Carroll's text: new forms of narrative urgency must replace the now long-faded fear of emancipation.

The only popular post–Civil War racist text to substantially examine the presumed sexual threat posed by blacks is R. W. Shufeldt's *America's Greatest Problem: The Negro* (1915). In several ways, Shufeldt stands intellectually above many of the anti-black, pro-slavery writers of the pre– and post–Civil War periods. He was more than familiar with Darwinian theory, was a trained anatomist, did not depend heavily on religious rhetoric in his work, and was aware of Freud's work, particularly that on libido and the unconscious. His text centered on two principal concerns regarding the "Negro problem": equality and miscegenation. With regard to the former, Shufeldt tended to reiterate much of the theoretical material appearing in other pre– and post–Civil War writing. Descriptions of blacks as having inferior brain size, endless skeletal anomalies, prognathic jaws, lower intelligence, and so on are rife in most of the chapters. The question of miscegenation, however, necessitates the use of some unusual and revealing material—material that demonstrates a fascination both with the dangers and the hidden pleasures of "bestial" black sexuality.

Shufeldt, apparently uncomfortable with the whole issue, tended to shift the direct expression of the taboo subject of black sexuality to others. The most sustained account of the subject is therefore presented as a very long intratextual quote from a work by a supposedly preeminent physician and sexologist, William Lee Howard, who, we are told, also contributed "important articles" on sex to *The Ladies Home Journal.* The long excerpts are from Howard's work *The Basic Causes of the Negro's Sensuality.* His dissertation begins with what he believes to be a gross oversight in dealing with the "growing problem of the Negro in America." Apparently, no one had thought to look closely at the real cause, that is, unfettered black sensuality. The Negro, according to Howard, is fixed in his patterns of sexual desire, and these irreversible drives are aimed at one and only one objective: "sexual relations with the white girl."[24]

The fundamental difference between black and white sensuality lies, once again, in the very fact that, being black, blacks are different from whites: "if the man with black skin had been reproduced by germ cells containing the same elements as the white man ... But the fact that they contain elements which make him black, is suggestive of evidence that they also contained the

elements which made him vastly different in other traits."[25] The main difference, of course, lies in the fact that the black has been dealt a biologically perverse hand. Even worse, he cannot but transmit these genetic characteristics to
his offspring, "whether he is a college professor or laborer, just as he does the
color and odor of his skin, his kinky hair and anatomical features, especially
a large but flexible sex organ, which adapts itself to the peculiar sex organs of
the female Negro and their demands."[26]

Carrying an inherited and thus inevitable trait of sexual madness, the
American black is destined to act out this primal instinct. Doctor Howard relates stories of his own experience of this wildness, including one about having
never heard of a "Negro virgin over ten years of age." The anatomical locus of
this sexual madness is the brain. It seems that the sex centers in the black's brain
are subject to overstimulation, causing great amounts of glandular secretions.
The only way to properly direct these overwhelming instincts is to turn them
toward physical labor. Even then, though, the cure might not work, because the
native African was unused to labor in his indigenous environment, subsisting
primarily on animalistic sexual stimulation. Fortunately, constant tribal orgies
and initiation into sexual rites and excesses relieved this uncontrollable urge.
However, in America, free to roam the streets, it seems that nothing stands between the oversexed black and genteel white womanhood: "But once scattered,
free and non-segregated, his one overpowering desire was white women."[27] This
sexual madness can also be attributed to his "incessant determination to enjoy
all the rights of white men, and you see the real reason for the horrible raping
of white girls and women."[28]

In the end, Doctor Howard feels that these periods of sexual madness
lead to the release of a certain latent animalism in the black:

> During these periods of sexual madness, the Negro has all the active symp-
> toms of animalism. There is a loss of controlling power over what little
> higher centers of the brain he possesses. The power of inhibition given the
> white man, he does not possess—cannot as a Negro ever possess. This fact
> accounts for his skatalogic rites which last for days, his superstitions and
> lust ceremonies, his education from boyhood to death in matters purely
> sensual.[29]

The interface between animality and sexuality is employed often in the
text of Shufeldt's work. In his conditional defense of lynch law, for example, he
tries to establish the inevitability of black criminality on the grounds of their
constitutional animality. He does this, however, in a radically different way than
most of the contemporary nonfiction racist literature. He stresses the sensa-
tional and gory aspects of black criminality, creating a frightening mosaic of

bloodletting, mutilation, and white female terror, much like the kind of expressions that appear in the later traditions of pulp fiction and yellow journalism. The monstrous animal is now no longer confined to the laboratory, plantation, holding shed, or cabin. He is loosed on the public, free to exercise his sexual madness in the very midst of American city life. In fact, according to Shufeldt, sexual assaults and sexual murders are the only crimes for which the black is really qualified, as he is "lacking in courage, intelligence, forethought, and the necessary staying powers" to commit more sophisticated crimes, like embezzlement, theft, premeditated murder, and bank robbery. These, presumably, are left to the naturally more intelligent white criminals.

These graphic descriptions of alleged black sexual assaults and murders are almost always interlaced with animal references. This literary allusion is obviously aimed at underscoring the uncontrollable and involuntary urges forever set in the black psyche. Young white women, mere girls at times, are depicted as the "prey" of these uncontrollable beasts that freely roam the streets of Southern cities. A typical account goes as follows:

> The victim was a little girl not more than twelve or thirteen years of age. . . . Her mother had sent her on a little errand, and when on her way back a burly Negro accosted her. . . . Here he suddenly seized her arms, made a leap, and was instantly in some shrubbery that grew beneath the bridge. Out came his great clasp-knife. Some men overhead, hearing her cries, landed by her on the jump, but not, however, before the Negro had ripped her clothing with his knife and severely choked her. . . . Fortunately he did not have time to mutilate the child, a common practice among Negroes when they assault little white girls.[30]

A "well-known and highly cultured businessman" from Roanoke, Virginia, George J. Shields faced similar horrors when he returned home from a sprightly business luncheon only to find his three-year-old daughter "lying on the reception hall floor with two ugly wounds to the head. Following the bloodstains from the dining room to an upstairs chamber, he found his wife in a clothes closet with her throat cut from ear to ear and her head horribly hacked. Even so, Mrs. Shields managed to gasp: 'A large black Negro man came through the kitchen and attacked me in the dining room.'"[31]

If one overlooks the problem of how a woman who had been viciously attacked in the dining room was able to make her way up the stairs and into a chamber closet, and who, after having her "throat cut from ear to ear," was able to gasp that a big Negro did it, one can see that the narrative patterns of these descriptions are quite clear and preset. The "Negro" is always large, bulking, bestial, overwhelming. He carries an enormous knife or razor, and he always either slashes the throat of the innocents or mutilates them about the face and head. The victim is invariably a young white girl or woman, innocent, and usually a member of a typical hard-working, middle-class family. Descriptions often contain sexual innuendo, though some are quite graphic in their depictions of sexual assault. The conclusion drawn regarding the various incidents is almost always precisely the same:

> So great is their moral putridity, that it is no uncommon thing for step-fathers to have children by their step-daughters, with the consent of the wife and mother of the girl. Nor do other ties of relationship interpose moral barriers; for fathers, daughters, brothers and sisters, oblivious of decent social restrictions, abandon themselves without any attempt at self-restraint to sexual gratification whenever desire and opportunity arises. That such licentiousness is prevalent is not surprising, when we reflect that *animal impulse* is the sole master, to which both sexes yield unquestioned obedience.[32]

The graphic nature of Shufeldt's literary descriptions of black sexuality and animality may well have been inspired by the popular racist fiction of the era. Numerous novels, short stories, and long prose poems were written around the themes of black inferiority, miscegenation, and segregation during the period of reconstruction and the later Jim Crow era. Most of these fictions remain obscure today, relegated to complete oblivion or to titles in comparatively little-known reprint series. Perhaps the only works that have lasted and are relatively well known are the two novels by Thomas Dixon Jr., *The Clansman: An Historical Romance of the Ku Klux Klan* and *The Leopard's Spots: A Romance of the White Man's Burden—1865–1900*. Probably the only reason these abysmally written curiosities have survived is that they both served as the basis for the screenplay for D. W. Griffith's socially controversial but technically innovative film, *Birth of a Nation* (1915).

More important for our purposes is the fact that Dixon's writing is also a source of virtually endless associations between Southern blacks and animals—associations that convey a literary rather than a biological, theological, criminological, physiological, or sociological picture of the "animal impulse" in blacks. *The Leopard's Spots*, first published in 1902, is, as presaged by its title alone, a veritable storehouse of animalistic references and allusions to blacks. The novel begins by presenting, in a series of dramatic vignettes, the historical conditions that have created the "free Negro," stressing in particular the fact that slavery, and thus black obedience, is gone forever. With the loss of sociopolitical and economic control comes the threat of mass fraternization with those who were formerly underlings. In a terse conversation with a certain General Daniel Worth, a former

Confederate general, a supporter of the Old South accuses him of "organizing the Negroes, deserters and criminals into your secret oath-bound societies."[33] This paranoid sense of collusion between sympathetic white forces and the emerging free blacks constitutes an important narrative basis for the novel, as Dixon seeks to erect conflicts between sympathetic supporters of blacks, blacks themselves, and defenders of the traditions of the Old South. To accomplish this, he must continually denigrate blacks, which, in the end, he believes, will ennoble the forces of segregation and totally demean supporters of black equality and freedom.

Dixon articulates the battle between the heroes and villains in a kind of breathless counterpoint involving the heinous acts of the freed Negroes and the devout, deeply moral reactions to these acts by the good people of the South. For instance, a sympathetic protagonist, the Rev. John Durham, "on his rounds among the poor, discovered a little Negro boy whom the parents had abandoned to starve. . . . A few days later the child had disappeared. A search was instituted, and the charred bones were found in an old ash-heap in the woods near this cabin. The mother had knocked him in the head and burned the body, in a drunken orgy with dissolute companions."[34] The reaction to this bestial deed was to declare a day of prayer for the young victim, which was celebrated with much love, feeling, fear and trembling, and outright consternation: "The sense of impending disaster crushed the hearts of thoughtful and serious people. They felt that a pestilence worse than the Black Death of the Middle Ages threatened to extinguish civilization."[35]

In the novel, the scenes of panic, invasion, unprovoked attack, and just plain growing paranoia regarding the freed blacks continue to intensify. To punctuate the danger, Dixon employs animal imagery and metaphors, stressing the vague feeling of some dark, bestial force outside of Southern culture and life bearing down on it, ready to undermine its very social structure. A little vignette about a noble white woman who was about to lose her property to foreclosure is exemplary of this technique. Mrs. Gaston sat gazing at her parched lawn and dying flowers, praying that a northern contact would send her the money to save her little spread. This failed, and, in due course, the day of the sale of her property arrived. Suddenly, a crushing sight confronted her:

> When she saw the great herd of Negroes trampling down her flowers, laughing, cracking vulgar jokes, and swarming over the porches, she sank feebly into her chair, buried her face in her hands and gave way to the passionate flood of tears. She was roused by the thumping of heavy feet in the hall and the unmistakable odor of perspiring Negroes. They had begun to ransack the house on tours of inspection. The poor woman's head dropped and she fell to the floor in a dead swoon.[36]

But Mrs. Gaston is miraculously saved by the intervention of her hired hands and faithful black servants. Aunt Eve, Charlie, and Dick race to the rescue, wielding bullwhips and shovel handles. In their heroic defense of the set-upon white woman, Aunt Eve hurls the final animalistic epithets at the growing crowd: "Des put yo' big flat hoofs in dis house ergin! I'll split yo' heads wide open! You black cattle!"[37]

Dixon's *The Clansman*, published two years later in 1904, follows pretty much the same narrative pattern as *The Leopard's Spots*; it is just a bit more intense, vivid, and urgent in tracing the dangerous rise of freed blacks in the South. In *The Clansman*, Dixon develops probably the most fascinating character of the Klan series: Gus. Gus is interesting because he is portrayed as a kind of super-predator, an archetype, embodying virtually all of the negative characteristics of freed blacks that Dixon had been developing throughout the series. Gus's character poses an immediate danger because he has risen to the position of commander in the black militia, which Dixon characterizes as "Black hordes of former slaves, with the intelligence of children and the instincts of savages, armed with modern rifles."[38] This promotion in itself was an unspeakable horror, according to Dixon. The very fact that the noble white race was subject to the authority of freed blacks constituted a massive reversal of all history. Discussing the fall of Rome, he remarks: "The savages of the North blew out the light of Ancient Civilization, but in all the dark ages which followed they never dreamed of the leprous infamy of raising a black slave to rule over his former master."[39]

Dixon continues building the urgency against a black takeover through a dialogue between principal characters in the plot, using the by-then-customary animalistic rhetoric and imagery regarding black inferiority. One of these characters relates that the African black "lived as an ox, content to graze for an hour. . . . He lived as his fathers lived—stole his food, worked his wife, sold his children, ate his brother, content to drink, sing, dance, and sport as the ape." But all the time, the black troops led by Gus are marching in precision outside, swinging their rifles and making a fearful racket. The presence of impending danger becomes palpable.

After several pages of continually building Gus's image as a brute that wielded considerable social power, Dixon finally arrives at the culmination of the built-up action: a "depraved" rape of an innocent white child:

> The door flew open with a crash, and four black brutes leaped into the room, Gus in the lead, with revolver in his hand, his yellow teeth grinning through his thick lips.
> "Scream, now, an' I blow yer brains out," he growled.
> Blanched with horror, the mother sprang before Marion with a shivering cry: "What do you want?"

"Not you," said Gus, closing the blinds and handing the rope to another brute. "Tie de ole one ter de bedpost."

With the strength of despair she tore the cords, half rising to her feet, while in mortal anguish she gasped: "For God's sake, spare my baby! Do as you will to me, and kill me—do not touch her."

Marion staggered against the wall, her face white, her delicate lips trembling with the chill of a fear colder than death.

Gus stepped closer, with an ugly leer, his flat nose dilated, his sinister bead-eyes wide apart gleaming ape-like, as he laughed: "We ain't atter money!"

The girl uttered a cry, long, tremulous, heart-rending, piteous.

A single tiger-spring, and the black claws of the beast sank into the soft white throat and she was still.[40]

Dixon's racist post–Civil War fiction, then, does not vary much from the themes and imagery established in the earlier and contemporary nonfictional writing. Blacks are consistently depicted as potentially dangerous because of their being constitutionally and morally different from whites. The technique of apposition is also evident. Whites are chaste and ethereal, given only to goodness, kindness, purity, and light—the heading of the chapter containing Gus's rape of Marion the "innocent child" is "The Beat of the Sparrow's Wings." Blacks are represented as murderous, barbaric, savage, dangerous, and malodorous—characteristics perfectly aligned with their single most distinguishing feature, skin color. Animalistic references serve to further bifurcate black and white characters. Although Dixon occasionally depicted black or mulatto characters, like Gus or Lynch(!), in positions of power, their inherent animalism always negated their public standing. As beasts loosed upon society, they were doomed to failure and, worse, murderous destruction of the entire Southern social and political system.

In the end, Dixon's racist fictions served aims similar to those of the entire output of anti-black and pro-slavery literature. This literature tried to recreate a narrative condition by which mastery could be reinserted into a failed, slowly disappearing system. Blacks were overdetermined as fictional monsters, given to the most extreme negative traits possible. As such, at least in Dixon's mind, they would once again have to fall under the control of political and punitive white power. After all, how could one possibly integrate one's very opposite into society—a veritable animal into the register of civilized human beings?

Summary

The agony and genocidal destruction caused by slavery, like that of the European Holocaust, cannot be adequately written; it can only be pieced together in selective segments, in writings rather than writing. The preceding is thus a selective presentation of some of the effects of reducing slaves to animal-like beings. In retrospect, there seem to be two dominant modes of animalization associated with slavery: the treatment of slaves and the literary representation of slaves, particularly black Africans.

In the first instance, the treatment, though motivated largely by economic and social concerns, was very much a strategy of mastery and control. Slaves were reduced to animality so as to render them as domitable—controllable—as possible. Concerted efforts were made by the slavers to drastically limit the basic requisites of human existence, to treat the slaves in all facets of their captivity as though they were no more than animals, non-humans. On the Middle Passage, they were literally packed into small, uncomfortable, largely unlivable spaces; this limited the basic human necessity of free movement, even of breathing air with sufficient oxygen. Chained together, flogged, and ill fed, they were treated as human cargo, as livestock on the way to slaughter. By the time of arrival—if they did in fact arrive at all—they had already been rendered into "docile bodies." The neutralizing force of capture, captivity, domination, torture, and control had left the transported slaves compliant, so much so that they were peddled in lots in markets like so much livestock: weighed, numbered, branded, examined, physically exposed, tagged. Once sold, they met with similar treatment on plantations, in factories, and on farms. Housing was generally no better than barns or holding pens, and in some instances worse. Fieldwork and general working conditions corresponded almost exactly with those of working domestic animals, albeit with less respite than the animals in many cases. All considered, the treatment of American slaves was fully representative of the consequences of the strategies of animalization. Once rendered inferior and subjugated to socioeconomic exigencies, the slave became nothing more than a manipulable beast of burden, used to the ends of pecuniary exploitation and gain—treated as both a working "animal" and one that could be sold or bartered for profit.

The various discursive representations of slaves complemented their treatment. The primary concern of anti-black, pro-slavery writers was to textually supplement and popularly justify both the institution of slavery and the often reprehensible actions of slaveholders in general. To accomplish this, the majority of literature depicted African slaves in their most extreme and negative aspect. From Carroll's ridiculous "man eating ape" to Dixon's feral legislators, the African black was consistently portrayed as savage, dangerous, murderous, and incapable of conforming to any standard of Southern civilization—a perpetual outsider. The binaries of good and evil were also employed to this end: whiteness was always associated with sophistication, education, hard work, purity, vulnerability, virginity, goodness, and the like. These invented virtues were then routinely opposed to blackness, which always carried the stigma of savagery and bore the mark of the beast. Blacks were just that: pitch black, dark, bestial, sexually depraved, promiscuous, diseased, murderous, and so on. Every characteristic from body odor to maxillary angles was exploited as a device for separating the races, which separation in turn created an irremediable difference between master and slave, one sufficient to justify utter exploitation and mastery. One had no obligation whatsoever to treat the radically other in the same way as self. In this view, slavery and the segregationist policies that followed were merely necessary reactions to a primary invasiveness, acts aimed at warding off and controlling an inferior and potentially dangerous species.

VII

Humans as Sub-Animals

Whoever unnecessarily torments or roughly mishandles
an animal will be punished by up to two years in prison,
with a fine, or with both these penalties.
—Provision 1 of the *Law on Animal Protection* issued
by the Third Reich and signed by Adolf Hitler

Perhaps the best way to emphasize the unmitigated horror—the sheer reduction of humans to sub-animal abjection—of the European Holocaust is to begin with the full accumulation of its crimes at its culmination: the Nuremberg trials. One of the various sections of the Nuremberg trials was devoted to the "Doctors' trial." It began on December 9, 1946. Telford Taylor, one of the main prosecutors at Nuremberg, made an opening statement at the trial, addressing the crimes committed "in the guise of scientific research." Taylor's chief legal assertion was that the human experiments were not, as the Nazis had argued, intended exclusively to aid the German military in scientifically understanding the sorts of diseases and casualties they might encounter on the battlefield and in civilian areas subject to attack by the Allies. Instead, Taylor argued, the experiments were intended primarily to gather knowledge on how to efficiently slaughter large numbers of people, with the primary intention being the killing of undesirables rather than the advance of legitimate medical knowledge. His opening remarks went, in part, as follows:

> But our proof will show that a quite different and even more sinister objective runs like a red thread through these hideous researches. We will show that in some instances the true object of these experiments was not how to rescue or to cure, but how to destroy and kill. The sterilization experiments

were, it is clear, purely destructive in purpose. The prisoners at Buchenwald who were shot with poison bullets were not guinea pigs to test an antidote for the poison; their murderers really wanted to know how quickly the poison would kill. This destructive objective is not superficially as apparent in the other experiments, but we will show that it was often there.[1]

Following his opening statement, Taylor went on to specify and describe some of the human experiments. The first of these, high-altitude experiments, entailed locking the participants in an airtight, ball-like compartment, and then alternating the pressure in the chamber to simulate the atmospheric conditions at extremely high altitudes. The first report on the experiments indicated the effects of pressure changes in the chamber on a thirty-seven-year-old Jew: "After four minutes the experimental subject began to perspire, and wiggle his head. After 5 minutes cramps occurred; between 6 and 10 minutes breathing increased in speed and the experimental subject became unconscious; from 11 to 30 minutes breathing slowed down to three breaths per minute, finally stopping altogether." Dissection was then undertaken. The main reason given by the Nazi doctors for requesting human subjects was that "the tests theretofore made with monkeys had not been satisfactory."[2]

Freezing experiments were also detailed. These were used ostensibly to learn how best to treat German pilots who had to ditch in the North Sea, but they too were disguised attempts to persecute and murder undesirables. The experiments were even more dangerous than the high-altitude experiments, as the death rate was extraordinarily high. The victims were forced to remain outdoors without clothing in freezing weather from nine to fourteen hours. Others were forced to remain in a tank of iced water for three hours at a time. Rascher, one of the experimental doctors, related, "[T]he experimental subjects died invariably, despite the attempts at resuscitation."[3] This was not, however, viewed as a negative consequence, as the principal intent of the experiment was to dissect and draw blood from the subject—usually a full quart from the carotid artery.

The freezing subjects usually died within a day. Others were not so lucky. Most of the other human experiments involved long-term pain, usually induced by the external or internal application of infectious or toxic substances. Mustard-gas experiments involved deliberately inflicting wounds on the victims and then infecting the wounds with mustard gas. "Other subjects were forced to inhale the gas or to take it in liquid form, and still others were injected with the gas."[4] These applications naturally caused immense, continuing pain and suffering, due mostly to internal swelling. Bone, muscle, and nerve tissue regeneration experiments were equally brutal. Camp inmates were usually shot or hacked with blunt or sharp instruments to create wounds. Drugs were selectively used to treat the wounds; many of the wounded were not treated at all, so as to create a control group. Those not treated usually died. In many instances, those who were treated also died, because the drugs administered were experimental in nature and did not always work.

Sterilization experiments by and large followed the patterns established in the earlier eugenics programs, both American and German. By the early 1940s, though, the advances in the control of radioactive X-rays turned sterilization into a potential mass-production enterprise:

> One way to carry out these experiments in practice would be to have those people who are to be treated line up before a counter. The official attendant who sits behind the counter can operate the apparatus in such a manner that he works the switch which will start both tubes together (as the rays have to come from both sides). With one such installation with two tubes about 150 to 200 persons could be sterilized daily, while 20 installations would take care of 3,000 to 4,000 persons daily.[5]

Much of the data on infectious disease experiments came from the surviving journals of an infamous Dr. Ding, who committed suicide after the war. Most of Ding's experiments involved live typhus vaccines, but he also injected prisoners with yellow fever, smallpox, paratyphoid A and B, cholera, and diphtheria. The use of camp prisoners was justified by Ding in his statement: "since tests on animals are not of sufficient value, tests on human beings must be carried out." Regular entries in Ding's diary indicated the coldly horrific treatment of prisoners:

> 24 Apr. 43: Therapeutic experiments of Acridine-Granulate (A-GR2) and Rutinol (R-2) to carry out the therapeutic experiments Acridine Granulate and Rutinol, 30 persons (15 each) and 9 persons for control were infected by intravenous injection 2cc each of fresh blood of typhus sick person. All experimental persons got very serious typhus.[6]

The human experiments went on and on, ranging from those for poison testing to those involving seawater submersion, malaria, incendiary bombs, and bullet testing. At this point, one might reasonably ask: Notwithstanding the complaints of a handful of doctors, why did the Nazis substitute humans for animals, when animal experimentation with drugs and virtually any other untested substances and procedures had throughout history proven reasonably successful? One could certainly answer that the Nazis were especially perverse and uncaring in their sadistic treatment of undesirable humans—and this, of course, is patently true. Nevertheless, another, quite surprising, factor remains. According to Taylor, on the 24th of November 1933, the National Socialist government enacted one of the most stringent and comprehensive laws in Europe to protect animals. Taylor's summary of the law merits lengthy citation:

> The law states explicitly that it is designed to prevent cruelty and indifference of man towards animals and to awaken and develop sympathy and understanding for animals as one of the highest moral values of people. The soul of the German people should abhor the principle of mere utility without consideration of the moral aspects. The law states further that all operations or treatments which are associated with pain or injury, especially experiments involving the use of cold, heat, or infection, are prohibited, and can be permitted only under special exceptional circumstances.... Experiments for the purpose of teaching must be reduced to a minimum. Medico-legal tests, vaccinations, withdrawal of blood for diagnostic purposes, and trial vaccines prepared according to well-established scientific principles are permitted, but the animals have to be killed immediately and painlessly after such experiments. Individual physicians are not permitted to use dogs to increase their surgical skill by such practices. National Socialism regards it as a sacred duty of German science to keep ... the number of painful animal experiments to a minimum.[7]

One could thus assume that, apart from the practical advantages of using human subjects, the Germans substituted humans for animals because they were forbidden by statute and moral compunction to use animals in dangerous experiments. After 1933, reducing the number of painful experiments on animals was a "sacred duty" of German science.[8] The clear implication, then, is that by the time of the intensive eugenics programs of the mid-1930s and the acceleration of the euthanasia experiments, certain types of human life were considered not only non-human, but also less than animal; that is, sub-animal. Effectively, chimpanzees, monkeys, cats, rats, other domestic animals, and, particularly, dogs were treated with greater compassion, care, and respect than an immense number of humans, including mental patients, so-called mental defectives, the physically disabled, and (later) Gypsies, Jews, Poles, Russians, gays, Catholics, and many other undesirables. The result was that monkeys, dogs, cats, earthworms (they were anesthetized in experiments), and so on were considered "life worthy of life," while many millions of human beings were considered merely "life unworthy of life."

Killing the Sub-Beast: The Euthanasia Project

Hermann Pfannmüller of the hospital at Eglfing-Haar slowly starved the children entrusted to his care until they died of "natural causes." This method, he boasted, was least

likely to incur criticism from the foreign press and from
"those gentlemen in Switzerland" (the Red Cross).
—Robert N. Proctor, *Racial Hygiene*

A full understanding of the Nazis' implausible reversal of the general standard
of human/animal treatment (that is, holding animals in much lower regard than
humans) requires some knowledge of what has often been called the prelude to
the Holocaust, the euthanasia experiment. Euthanasia was by no means a new
prospect for Germany during the Nazi ascension in 1933. A serious debate on
the subject had been going on since the end of World War I, which produced
a spate of publications intended to confront the problems of death and suffering subsequent to the war. Karl Binding and Alfred Hoche wrote the pivotal
document of the debate, a tract published in 1920 under the title "Permission
for the Destruction of Life Unworthy to Live." The arguments presented were
described as "crassly materialistic," and tended to follow Binding's positivistic
legal thinking.[9] Binding's focus, like that of his American counterparts Goddard, Davenport et al., was on idiocy and its socioeconomic implications. He
argued that idiots were a tremendous burden on society and that their death
"would create not even the smallest gap—except perhaps in the feelings of their
mothers or loyal nurses."[10] He followed this callous assessment by stating that
idiots "were a travesty of real human beings, occasioning disgust in anyone who
encounters them," and assuring his readers that in more heroic times the state
would have had no qualms in doing away with them entirely. He also made the
morally derelict and largely absurd claim that euthanizing idiots would save them
the embarrassment of running "the gauntlet of cruel jokes and obloquy."[11] This
he added to the economic, pragmatic argument, which asserted that millions
of marks were being spent annually on incurable populations.

Binding's positivistic arguments were supplemented by his co-author, Alfred Hoche. Hoche in many ways was more extreme in his desire to euthanize
and far less sensitive than Binding. He centered his argument largely around the
economic liabilities posed by idiots, and in support of his argument he calculated
in a statistically complex manner the exact amounts of health care worker sala-
ries, medical costs, doctors' time and bills, and so on that would be saved by the
simple merciful killing of idiots. Besides, he adopted the view that idiots were
"mentally dead," "without human personality or self-consciousness, on the intellectual level which we only encounter way down in the animal kingdom."[12]

With idiots serving as a theoretical complement to the morons of Goddard, Laughlin, and Davenport, authors Binding, Hoche, and their supporters
were able to capitalize on the sense of urgency and economic disorder following

World War I in Germany. Saving marks was in many respects more important than saving unworthy lives. "Hoche claimed that 20–30 idiots with an average life expectancy of fifty represented 'a massive capital in the form of foodstuffs, clothing and heating, which is being subtracted from the national product for entirely unproductive reasons.'"[13] The economistic arguments, though they reduced humans to mere coinage, were effective. Why spend scarce money on those who were designated to be "without personality or self-consciousness," humans "way down in the animal kingdom"?

The economic factor was further reinforced by the confluence of euthanasia and eugenics. By the 1920s, the American work in eugenics was already influencing German racist and biodeterministic thought.[14] The fear of the generational spread of "bad stock," and the very presence of idiots on whom unnecessary sums of desperately needed national funds were being expended, created the conditions for a massive dehumanization of certain groups of individuals—a dehumanization that reduced these groups to sub-animal status. The thinking behind eugenic sterilization, combined, in certain cases, with the reasoning behind euthanasia, provided the perfect pretense for future racial exclusion, that is, mass killing. One could now argue not only that it was economically and scientifically necessary to exclude certain inferior types, but that it was morally acceptable as well. Without ethical considerations standing in the way, the proto-Nazi doctors and clinicians were largely free to determine a rough definition of human life itself—a definition rooted in a notion of the frightful, economically exhausting spread of inhuman or sub-animal characteristics and individuals. A former Stuttgart detective, Christian Wirth, who eventually became an inspector at one of the T-4 euthanasia centers and an especially vicious camp director, summed up perfectly the results of this definition:

> I have been assigned the task of running the castle from now on by the Reich Chancellory [sic]. As the boss I am in charge of everything. We must build a crematorium here, in order to burn mental patients from Austria. Five doctors have been chosen who will examine the patients to establish what cannot be saved. What can't be saved goes into the crematorium and will be burned. Mental patients are a burden upon Germany and we only want healthy people. Mental patients are a burden upon the State.[15]

Through the seemingly justified murder of thousands of defectives, the euthanasia projects opened a pathway for thinking the sub-animal. There were now people who were not only "way down in the animal kingdom," but who were determined by a set of presumably rational, carefully deliberated explanations to be entirely dispensable—the *what* "can't be saved," *what* must go into the crematorium. If someone is physically dispensable, merely flesh to be ignited and burned away, then that person certainly did not enjoy even the most basic animal rights—rights that, by official Reich statute, took into serious consideration the minutest incidents of animal suffering. Certain humans, then, could not even achieve the usually degraded status of animals, for they were determined to be entirely exterior to—the radical other of—healthy, strong, and desirable humans. Gerhard Wagner, Führer of the National Socialist physicians' organization, summed up this view perfectly when he chastised the Marxists for not recognizing the "inherently different value" between the sick and healthy. The doctrine of equality, generated by Soviet-influenced Marxists, Wagner argued, simply led to valuing "the sick, the dying, and unfit on a par with the healthy and strong."[16]

With the ethical and socioeconomic issues "settled" in the earlier phases of the euthanasia project, all that was left was to make the exclusion of the unfit fully systemic, and to select the general populations of sub-animal "invaders" who would be, justifiably, subjected to experimental torture and abuse, "merciful death," and ultimately total annihilation. In effect, the Nazis utilized bodies "only to the extent they contributed to a set of scientific protocols that had utterly no moral qualms about inducing intolerable suffering in those seen as 'life unworthy of life.' No moral principle or empathic responsiveness guided these experiments."[17] In commenting on the general nature of Nazi experiments, Robert Jay Lifton likewise stressed: "But all the other experiments as well reflect the Nazi image of 'life unworthy of life,' of creatures who, because less than human, can be studied, altered, manipulated, mutilated, or killed—in the service of the Nordic race, and ultimately of remaking humankind."[18]

Blood Trails: Identifying the Vermin, Parasites, Bacilli, and . . . Less

> There is a resemblance between the Jews and tubercle bacilli: nearly everyone harbors tubercle bacilli, and nearly every people of the earth harbors the Jews; furthermore, an infection can only be cured with difficulty.
> —B. Peltret, *Der Arzt als Führer und Erzieher*

One of the most powerful forms of exclusionary imagery for the Nazis was that of an invasive, infectious force: insects, locusts, sewer rats, or (in biomedical terms) blood pollutants, contagions, toxins, bacilli, biocontaminants, and so on. The core tactic of fascist propaganda regarding this sort of contagion was to make the outsider a carrier of disease and disorder, and then to erect an ethic based on resistance and asceticism. An excerpt from Ernst von Salomon's *Die Geaechteten* (*The Outlaws*) illustrates this basic apposition of good and evil, of German virtue and Jewish deception, which, in the end, turns out to be a kind of animal urge, an irresistible, unconscious need to spread "poison":

> During coitus the male semen is fully or partially absorbed into the lining of the female uterus, where it enters the bloodstream. A single act of intercourse between a Jew and an Aryan woman is enough to poison her blood forever. . . . It now becomes clear why the Jew employs every device of the seductive art in attempt[s] to dishonor German girls at the earliest possible age, or why the Jewish doctor violates female patients under anaesthetic.[19]

The spread of syphilitic microorganisms by Jews was only one of the presumed contaminations associated with undesirables. Jews were not only insidious spreaders of disease but themselves a thoroughly "diseased race"—in effect, the traditional carriers of dangerous contagions, much like vermin and particularly rats. The theory of disease-carrying peoples, of course, was integral to the broader Nazi concepts of anti-Semitism and racism. As early as World War I, Ernst Jünger, the single most important Friekorps novelist,[20] had described, in *The Storm of Steel*, rats as dark, loathsome creatures, carrying with them "a penetrating effluvium."[21] The carrying of rodentlike effluvium was advanced as a full-fledged characteristic of the Jewish race, which eventually found its way into Nazi propaganda—for instance, the film *Der Ewige Jude*. The film begins with scurrying rats filling the screen, after which the narrator utters: "Just as the rat is the lowest of animals, the Jew is the lowest of human beings."[22] Like rats, Jews were supposed to multiply at staggering rates, covering every corner of the world with their odious effluvium. In this respect it is not so much a matter of being equated with the animal itself (the rat, pig, weasel, etc.), but the very image that some form of invasive contagion can be carried by certain people and racial types which renders them sub-animal. This was supposedly merely the parasitic, inner biocomposition of the animal, the hidden filth and pollution carried by the animal—or, as Hitler so colorfully put it when referring to the Jew, "a maggot in a rotting body."

This sort of rendering was not limited to Jews alone. Gypsies were stereotyped and marked in similar ways. As nomads the Gypsies were constantly traveling from place to place, country to country, and subsequently were never rooted to the extent that they could establish ordinary residential lifestyles. Their habits, customs, and living conditions were also regarded as alien. For example, Gypsies believed in a kind of universal communal environmental order, involving the free use of all natural resources and property. They would thus trespass boundaries, and if, for example, they saw a farm animal running free, they would claim it. Their properties were conventionally unkempt, as they believed in keeping their caravans spotless, but were less concerned about the outdoors. They always evacuated in the nearby woods, because they were loath to keep excrement near food and food-preparation areas in their caravans. Bathing was not easy either, as the places they stayed usually were not equipped with canalized water. Besides, formal procedures of cleanliness were usually more related to ritual purity than to cleanliness in itself.[23] At any rate, these traditional lifestyles, customs, and traits were twisted and transformed by both the German public and governmental authorities into heinous and often illicit animal-like behaviors—in some cases, even sub-animal-like behaviors. The Gypsies were thus seen as spreaders of filth, disease, and excrement; as promiscuous sexual beasts, subject to uncontrollable drives; and as perpetrators of murder, theft, incest, and social crime in general.[24]

Indeed, in the full stigmatization of the Gypsies, they were eventually lowered to a category usually reserved for Jews: parasites. The chief of police in the Esslingen district in Wurttemberg argued that "[t]he Gypsy is and remains a parasite on the people.... For this reason it is necessary that the Gypsy tribe be exterminated by way of sterilization or castration."[25] This parasitic designation—the image of the lower-than-animal, the worm in the organism—was further emphasized in articles and tracts appearing in a wide variety of racist publications. In *Volk und Rasse*, published by the German Society for Racial Hygiene, Gypsies are referred to as "parasites spread among our people." Another article, appearing in *Deutsches Arzteblatt*, stated that Gypsies constituted a plague, and that wherever they go they "exploit nature and humans"—implying, of course, that they themselves were neither natural nor human.[26]

The unnatural, sub-animal character of Nazi outcasts was largely substantiated by what came to be called blood science, a fusion of racist ideology and history, propaganda, junk science, and biodeterministic thinking. What was central to blood science as a mode of mastery and repression was the absolute insistence on objectively demonstrable differences between the Aryan race and those who would pollute it. Jews, Gypsies, blacks, and virtually all non-Aryans were considered to be racially diametric to German Aryans—the difference, in effect, of one species from another, like mice from elephants, and earthworms from birds of paradise. "Non-Nordics" were viewed as occupying "an intermediate position between Nordic-man and the animal kingdom, in particular apes.... [W]e could also call non-Nordic Man a Neanderthal; however, the term 'sub-human' is better and more appropriate."[27]

Popular works that covered broad fields of history, culture, science, theology, and so on served to implement this radical distancing of the so-called races. Texts like Alfred Rosenberg's *Der Mythus des 20. Jahrhunderts* (*The Myths of the Twentieth Century*), for example, functioned to create a public vision of the Jew as nothing more than a historical aberration: a physically, mentally, and morally degenerate product of a depraved history and culture, or, to use Richard Wagner's phrase, a plastic demon.[28] Rosenberg offered the proof of Jewish degeneration by subtly tying the inside to the outside, by asserting that Jewish social and cultural endeavors were indicative of their debased inner constitution. In short, the Jew spread his "poison" by virtue of his divergence from, and his absolute opposition to, Germanic character, culture, and life in general:

> Left to itself, the German character would have achieved a balance. However, this was made impossible due to Jewish strength in the press, theatre, trade and sciences. We ourselves have been guilty—we should not have emancipated the Jews but, as Goethe, Fichte and Herder vainly demanded, should have created insurmountable exceptional laws for them. One does not allow a *poison* to drift about unobserved, nor grant it parity with medicine; rather one keeps it within careful limits.[29]

In part because of the influence of racist literature and theory, the outsiders could now be seen as carrying the most subtle and deeply hidden racial differences, because their humanity and culture, beliefs, and history (if they were granted possession of these at all) were completely unlike that of the German *Volk*. As radically different in mind, culture, and status, the outsiders'—that is, the non-Nordics'—actual biological and physiological compositions were assumed to be different as well. The Jews, Poles, Czechs, Russians, Gypsies, gays, blacks, and so on were even presumed to emit a kind of noxious discharge; their very insides were seen as putrefied with foreign and unclean substances and odors, like dead and rotting animals. A Stuttgart physician, Dr. Eügen Stahle, commented on precisely this subject:

> In describing the various races, we must not stop with the external shape of the body, nor even the mental characteristics in the classical manner of [Hans F. K.] Gunther and Ludwig Ferdinand Clauss. We must go beyond this, to explore equally important differences in the inner organs of the body, differences that may reflect deeper, physiological differences among the races. Best known in this area is "racial smell." Europeans find the smell not only of Negroes but of East Asians to be repulsive, even when they are clean.[30]

By continually reducing undesirables to even less than animal status, to bodily excretions or oozing substances, the racial hygienists were able to eventually consign them to a level below that of a coherent living organism, below what John Locke referred to as "functional life," that is, something marginally more than a mere aggregate of living tissue.[31] As such, these marked groups were seen *only* as a kind of "living tissue," a random collection of bacilli, micro-organisms, and the like. As Glass noted, "it is far easier to kill sub-humans or non-humans than human beings."[32] The absolute disregard for human life so obvious in the heinous experiments in the camps and in the preceding eutha-nasia project can thus be at least partially explained by the reduction of humans to sub-animals, to nothing more than the most basic life forms, to a malodorous substance that could be manipulated in any way deemed necessary or pleasing. Without a face, in Emmanuel Levinas's sense of the term[33]—without even a form, a position in space, a culture, history, or body—the Jew or Gypsy or any other placeholder was subject to the most extreme form of mastery and control. They could be sliced, cut, electrocuted, shot, frozen, poisoned, fed to bears,[34] bisected, castrated, hunted, killed, burned, and then bulldozed into mass graves without the least compunction; for they were not even animal, nowhere near the level of the earthworm that was lovingly anesthetized in Nazi laboratories after 1933 so as to minimize its pain.

VIII

Emaciation and Slaughter

> Thus, in late 1944, pit burning became the chief method
> of corpse disposal. The pits had indentations at one end
> from which the human fat drained off. To keep the pits
> burning the stokers poured oil, alcohol, and large quantities
> of boiling human fat over the bodies.
>
> —Konnilyn G. Feig, *Hitler's Death Camps*

In the course of the most destructive phase of the European Holocaust, from 1941 to 1945, which saw the intensive building, filling, and maintenance of the concentration, labor, and death camps, the distinction between human, animal, and sub-animal became largely negligible. Unlike the earlier periods of proto-Nazi and Nazi terror, the eugenic and euthanasia phases, there was no longer any need to create a public image of "inferior" peoples to justify their exclusion and psychological and physical abuse: they were now subject to the Final Solution, doomed to slave labor, emaciation, or in most cases, utter annihilation. As Himmler put it in 1941, "The Jews are the sworn enemy of the German people and must be eradicated. Every Jew that we can lay our hands on is to be destroyed now during the war without exception."[1] Whether a person had an inferior culture, or was a member of a degenerate, small-brained, malodorous, disease-carrying, effluvium-discharging race, was of absolutely no interest to the Nazis—or, it seems, to the majority of the German people.[2] What was required at this point was practical means of transporting, incarcerating, slaughtering, and disposing of human subjects.

As a purely practical enterprise, the thinking behind the transportation of victims to the various camps was remarkably similar to that of the transportation of slaves on the Atlantic passage: get as many as possible from one point to another. Just as slaves were book-ended or spooned together in the holds of slave ships, Nazi victims were herded and crammed together in railway trains composed entirely of freight and cattle cars. The "necessary loss" assumption operative in both the Atlantic Passage and the modern shipping of livestock also came into play in the transportation of undesirables, but in an eerily different way:

> The special Final Solution trains, or *Sonderzüge*, made up of freight cars and cattle wagons, posed three areas of serious difficulty to Himmler and his staff, and to the Reichsbahn. . . . The Reichsbahn ameliorated the problem by lengthening the trains, packing more Jews in the cars, and using longer, more circuitous routes to destinations. The serious overloading and the long time period produced unimaginable horrors inside the airless, foodless, waterless, toiletless sealed cars. Many Jews did not survive the journey. But that was considered fine by the Nazis—it simply lessened the number of Jews they needed to exert energy to destroy in the camps.[3]

Ironically, practical necessity allowed the "sub-animals" to rise above the bacillus-like state attributed to them by the racial hygienists, but only to become subject to more traditional animalistic treatment, in that they were now being crowded together like cattle to be efficiently delivered to indefinite imprisonment, brutalizations, and finally to slaughter.

Arrival at the various camps was also analogous to the arrival of African slaves in the Americas. Like the slaves, the lives of each camp victim were carefully preplanned. Unlike the slaves, who were conditioned for endless toil and subjugation, the Nazi victims were to be taught, instructed, in the whole mechanism of death. Some went directly to the gas chambers, especially late in the war when the Allies were pressing toward the German and Austrian frontiers, but a significant majority were first exposed to the most dehumanizing treatment imaginable: "The Nazis planned it that way because it was important for them that their victims experience a life much worse than death. To die was not enough."[4] This life worse than death was unique to the concentration camp, which was set up as the ultimate operation of "absolute power." Absolute power differs from other forms of power, such as despotism, terror, and violence. It ranges over a far-reaching set of objectives, all of which are intended to engender absolute powerlessness in its victims[5]:

> Absolute power eradicates the line of demarcation between life and death. Before their deaths, persons were destroyed gradually, step by step. The production of "living skeletons" is one of the genuine inventions of the concentration camp. This indirect annihilation did not kill immediately; it allowed death time. Power creates an intermediate sphere, a state of

misery and sickness between life and death. In this limbo, the perpetrators could find countless victims when they desired to act. The mass dying transformed the camp into a field of the dead.[6]

Although the situations and agency are entirely different—it is quite impossible to directly equate the murder of a human being with the slaughter of livestock—there is nevertheless a structural resemblance between the killing in the camps and the slaughter of animals. Animals carried to, penned, and prepared for slaughter, though they cannot fully comprehend their own deaths, are placed in a similar situation of extended, indefinite annihilation. Just as the Nazi death camp guards saw their victims as doomed, as mere moving flesh to be destroyed over time, so it is with animals being readied for slaughter. In fact, rather than being starved or being denied the basics of life, they are treated in just the opposite way: that is, fattened, pampered, even massaged and force-fed beer (the famed Kobe beef). Nevertheless, the animals, as was the case with the death-camp prisoners, are trapped irreversibly in a technology of death, a practical means of killing that functions to produce the most carcasses possible in the most economical way, making room for the ever-flowing stream of potential corpses. This process has been called by some "the production of death." Food animals left alive, thriving and idly grazing, are of absolutely no use to their slaughterers; death-camp victims enjoying even a moment's respite from the threat of torture, starvation, and death were likewise abhorrent to their slaughterers. In both cases, the die is cast; there is no turning from death. Death, in both instances, is the one and only function and direction of the very place in which they are situated.

The slaughterhouse atmosphere is further underscored by the fact that slaughtered Nazi victims were often exploited for their lucrative byproducts. Virtually everything of value, novelty, or bizarre interest was salvaged from the death-camp corpses. In an exemplary incident, a camp physician demanded the skull of a living inmate, which was promptly placed on his desk the next day. Indeed, human skulls were of "kinky" interest to SS doctors, who collected them to use either in research or as mementos. One command from a medical officer read: "I need immediately 10 entire skeletons, 12 skulls, or individual parts of a body, or we need some interesting bullet wounds."[7] Tattooed prisoners invariably wound up on the dissection tables, as tattooed skin was at a premium, particularly for use in decorative materials like lampshades and belts. Indeed, the Nazi "scientists" even perfected a way of carefully flaying and tanning human skin so that it became tough like leather—one of the most valuable byproducts of cow, pig, and horse slaughter. Human bones were often recovered to use in decorative items as well: Frau Koch, the infamous wife of the infamous commandant of Buchenwald, "had a table lamp made of human bones and had a tattooed human-skin shade. Decorators pleaded for tattooed skin for their customers."[8] The trade in human hair was also a going concern. Prior to gassing, selected victims (usually females) were shorn, and the hair was ultimately used in a variety of products. The hair was woven into rugs, sweaters, and used in various textile products; outside of gold fillings, human hair was one of the most profitable items salvaged from the death camps. The liberators of Auschwitz discovered seven tons of human hair in the tannery. Even the fat rendered from burning bodies was considered a valuable byproduct; it was re-cycled to keep the bodies burning.

The manifestly incomprehensible sense of cooking human "meat" is fur-ther confirmed by detailed descriptions of the body-burning processes initiated in the death camps. Special units called "burning groups" were employed to arrange gassed bodies on a "roaster" (usually constructed of criss-crossed rail-way ties) in layers up to two meters in height. After neatly piling from 2,000 to 3,500 bodies on the roaster, huge piles of dry wood and branches were laid under it. The specifics of the process were recounted by a member of one "burn-ing group," who wrote:

> The SS "expert" on bodyburning ordered us to put women, particularly fat women, on the first layer on the grill, face down. The second layer could consist of whatever was brought—men, women, or children—and so on, layer on top of layer. . . . Then the "expert" ordered us to lay dry branches under the grill and to light them. . . . Liquid excretions from the corpses squirted all over the prison-workers.[9]

Stripping, "grilling," and selling the byproducts of corpses were far from the only inhuman absurdities at the camps. With thousands of prisoners being animalized—starved, blindly herded about, forced to march for days on end, dissected, whipped, stomped on, and then slaughtered—the commandant of Buchenwald, Karl Koch, built within this nightmarish human "menagerie" a full-scale hunting lodge and zoo. The hunting lodge was spectacular and ex-pensive, following precisely the design of old German falconries and hunting lodges. A performative equivalent of the animal-like existence of the prisoners, the hunting lodges housed falcons and caged wildcats; the prisoners themselves, along with SS guides, gathered deer, wild boar, foxes, pheasants, and other wild game animals for the adjacent preserve. The inmates were also forced to build the zoological garden, which contained monkeys, bears, and even a rhinoceros. To add to the absurdity, the zoo animals ate infinitely better than the inmates: "Although the camp suffered from a serious food shortage, the zoo animals received a daily meat ration from the prisoner mess. Bears ate honey and jam, monkeys consumed potatoes and milk, oat flakes, and other delicacies."[10] Thus, with imminent slaughter and walking death all around them, the inmates were obliged to capture, maintain, feed (sometimes be fed to), and care for the animals and game; the Jews were even forced to pay, through a "voluntary collection," for the replacement of animals that died.[11] Within the outer barbed-wire fences and machine-gun turrets of Buchenwald lay a cloistered, lovingly cared for game preserve and zoo—entities tragically representative of the state of animality to which the prisoners had been reduced.

Other dimensions of animality included the mass shootings at the camps, most of which were performed by firing squads, and done, as on slaughterhouse assembly lines, with chilling mechanical indifference. Assembly-line killings sometimes involved the particularly grisly technique of shooting victims in the nape of the neck—a technique borrowed from the military police.[12] But the method has another connection: it was used in a slightly different form to stun cattle and other animals prior to slaughter. Captive-bolt pistols would be fired from above the slaughter lines into the skulls of the animals, presumably rendering them unconscious and thus insensitive to pain.[13] Horses that are old, broken down, or have broken their legs—usually the case with racehorses—are also put down with a shot in the brain from the side or back of the head. Once again, even though the killing of human victims is profoundly different from the killing of animals, the same mechanical anonymity of killing is there, as is the same disregard for the value of life and sentient suffering.

Descriptions of human hunts, however, require little qualification regarding their similarity to animal hunts, because they were exactly like animal hunts—or, in certain respects, like animal predators hunting. The following account is of a prisoner hunt after a mass escape from Mauthausen:

> One of the best known massacres entered the chronicle of Mauthausen under the SS name of the "Mühlviertel rabbit hunt...." A total of 419 prisoners escaped from the camp area. But many only got few meters from the camp. They left a trail in the snow and were soon captured and beaten to death or shot. The SS then ordered a large-scale hunt with instructions "not to bring back prisoners captured to the camp alive."... The dynamics of a slaughter during a hunt differed substantially from that of an organized massacre.... In a hunt the victims are chased by the pack, ferreted out, and slaughtered on the spot.... Those who grab their prey most quickly have the right to strike first and kill it.... All are oriented totally to one aim: to kill their prey.... But the longer the hunt lasts, the more greedy the pack becomes, and the more bestial the atrocity once the pack seizes its hounded prey.[14]

There is an uncanny resemblance between this description and the slave hunt narrated earlier.[15] Both emphasize the viciousness of the pack and the sense of a wild presence invading the hunt scene. For the slave, it was the pursuing hounds, accompanied by whites who had joined the principal hunters—the overseers and masters. The camp escapees were not pursued by dogs, but (perhaps even worse) by local vigilantes who were encouraged by the SS command to join in. The vigilantes' viciousness, murderous enthusiasm, and determination to treat the escaped prisoners like hunted animals were described as follows: "[M]any civilians from the surrounding area took part in the search. . . . Everywhere people encountered them—in homes, car sheds, stables, up in the loft, down in the cellar—if they weren't dragged out and killed at the next house corner, they were shot right on the spot. . . . A few had their heads split open with an axe. . . . The bodies remained lying where they fell. . . . Intestines and genitals were exposed to open view."[16] Recaptured slaves, having at least some use as "beasts of burden," were typically returned relatively whole to the farm or plantation. Escaped camp prisoners, being deemed dangerous and thus fair game, were just killed on sight—the logical and desired consequence of an animal hunt.

What more can be said about the Holocaust? More, obviously—but nothing definitive enough to adequately represent it in its inconceivable inhumanity. In *Heidegger and "the jews,"* Lyotard makes the point that trying to represent the Holocaust in words, films, photographs, and so on is the best way to forget it. His thinking is that once the image or word is inscribed in the psyche, it can indeed be forgotten: memory functions as a repository of the lost, the beyond, and the repressed. Besides, as repressed material the Holocaust may be seen as no different from any of the other massacres down the centuries: the Stalin murders, slavery, the slaughter of the Armenian people at Smyrna, and so on. Instead, Lyotard, invoking the filmmaker Claude Lanzmann (*Shoah*), argues for the impossibility of a fully intelligible representation of the Holocaust. In his view, the faint sobbing, grunts, grimaces, incoherent utterances, silent stares, and pauses filling Lanzmann's *Shoah* are the only possible "representations" of the horrors of the Holocaust, expressions of a kind of indistinct surface upon which something unimaginable and unrepresentable had been inscribed. "[I]f one represents the extermination, it is also necessary to represent the exterminated. One represents men, women, children treated like 'dogs,' 'pigs,' 'rats,' 'vermin,' subjected to humiliation, constrained to abjection, driven to despair, thrown like filth into the ovens."[17] This also falls short of intelligible representation, because it is not as men, women, and children that these people were slaughtered, but, rather, as "the jews," that is, as an abstract conception of outsiders, defectives, undesirables, the world's and history's outcasts.

Nevertheless, Lyotard's reading raises some questions: Can the Nazis' long-term, multifaceted debasement of their victims to animality and sub-animality—to what Lyotard calls "pigs," "vermin," or "rats"—truly stand outside the representation of the Holocaust? Can one ever exclude that sub-human other to which all the victims of the Holocaust were calculably and irreversibly reduced? David Clark, in his deconstructive reading of Levinas's philosophical perspective on animality, proposed a somewhat different approach to the question of victimage and animality in the Holocaust.[18] Clark's reading is based on Levinas's "The Name of a Dog, or Natural Rights," in which Levinas reminiscences philosophically about a dog named Bobby that befriended him and other inmates while they were imprisoned in a Nazi slave-labor camp. Clark's point, briefly stated, is that Levinas ultimately refuses to accept that Bobby—and thus all animals—is a rational agent, or has sufficient reason and understanding to share the human world with some modicum of equality. Even so, Levinas does not reduce Bobby to an unfeeling beast, Descartes' vacant machine, nor does he argue that animals should in any way be intentionally mistreated. His problem is that he just cannot overcome the Kantian perspective on unreasoning animals. Thus, for Levinas, Bobby lacks both *logos* and *ethos*; the dog is, in simple terms, "brainless." He is, in effect, kept at arm's length by Levinas's inability to think beyond the dichotomy of human reason and animal instinct, articulated by Aristotle, by Descartes, and, most forcibly for him, by Kant. In other words, "the dog is granted the power to be more than itself only insofar as it rigorously remains itself—*dans l'animal*—vis-à-vis 'Man.'"[19]

It is precisely on the points of Bobby's brainlessness and muteness that Levinas's position is attacked, for the dog's so-called brainlessness is belied by his very presence to the camp inmates:

> Levinas says Bobby is brainless, as if he were absent from his own actions, yet this claim only throws into relief the forceful and articulate enigma of the dog's presence in the camp, the ways in which he obliges us to reconsider what we think we mean by *logos*, "animal" and of course we.[20]

Later on in the essay, this rethinking takes the form of a defense of animals as more or less equal functionaries in a kind of shared revelation of the unthinkable horror of the European Holocaust:

> For the Nazis a languageless human is nothing more than an animal; but what is animality that it not only names the incoherence to which the Nazis reduce the Jews but also represents the figure that comes most readily to hand to describe what it feels like to live and survive that degradation? Reading this bestial figure, I am thinking of Bobby's barking and of the

ancient assumption, against all intuitive evidence, that animal sounds are merely *phône asemos*, "signifiers without a signified." . . . For a disconcerting moment, the prisoners and the dog threaten to exchange their differently silenced spaces—a crossing made all the more troublesome in an essay that begins, as I have argued, by asking us to consider the butchery of animals against the backdrop of the extermination of the Jews.[21]

Thus, the specter of the animal in the Holocaust itself is embodied in Bobby's evocative presence outside the barbed-wire fences of the Nazi camp. Historically, the status of the animal haunts the Nazi vision of what constitutes the other, and thus serves, at least in part, as a justification for exclusion and eventually annihilation. As early as the turn of the century, proto-Nazi forces were at work distinguishing animality in the fields of eugenics and euthanasia, extensions of the nascent science of racial hygiene. By 1895, Alfred Ploetz, for example, had already calculated a Darwinian table of inferiority, a theory separating the strong from the weak. In doing so, he erected an evolutionary hierarchy of those who were above-animal, distinctly human, and those who must be regarded as animal; that is, the strong and healthy as opposed to the weak and sickly.[22] This conception grew exponentially—with an emphatic assist from American eugenics—to assume a central place in German racial science. By the 1920s, German racial science had formulated a theoretical basis for inferiority, which contained a significant component of animality. By the time the Nazis took charge in 1933, racial and blood science had become a dominant ideological and propagandistic tool. The excluded, the weak, the sickly, the racially inferior, the feebleminded could now be categorized at a level even below the animal, because animals had been given special protection and status by the Third Reich. This, among other things, set off a firestorm of gross dehumanization. The mechanism of comparison had largely disappeared; animals were raised above certain humans, proclaimed "life worthy of life," as opposed to "life unworthy of life." Jews, Gypsies, the disabled, Russians, gays, Socialists, Bolsheviks, and every other imagined "enemy of the Reich" could now be reduced to no more than a protoplasmic mass. The presumed enemy was no longer an inferior, a throwback downcast somewhere on the ladder of evolutionary progress. Instead, they were nothing: sub-animals, below-animals, merely parasites or maggots, or even just the faceless, formless source for the expression of inner contaminants, of deadly microorganisms. With the complete and utter destruction of any thread of humanity in the imagined enemies of the Third Reich, the killing could begin with abandon. Ironically, it was in precisely that cold, merciless killing process that the undesirables were returned to their animal status—herded, corralled, whipped, tortured, branded, slaughtered, and ritually burned.

Thus, in certain respects, both Lyotard and Clark are correct. On the one hand, those tossed into the crematoriums *like* pigs, *like* rats and vermin, form a conceptualized mass of inferiors, which Lyotard collects under the term "the jews." From the Nazi perspective, they were not throwing humans into the ovens like animals, but rather disposing of an abstract ideological concept: the jews. One cannot find an adequate representation for those reduced to nothing. In this particular sense the Holocaust *is* unrepresentable; the Nazis simply negated any specific material, discursive, or figural form that the jews might assume. As nothing, as not even animal, there is really nothing of substance to represent—only a psychical memory image, a phenomenon prone to fade and be forgotten. On the other hand, Clark allows for the possibility of representing the Holocaust through the charged silence of the animal, particularly that of Levinas's canine friend, Bobby. Even though Levinas, in his philosophical dogmatism, was unable to fully acknowledge Bobby as an equal presence—a face—as a communicative being bringing hope and a moment's respite from the terrors of the Nazi slave-labor camp, his rejection of Bobby illuminates the very question of humans reduced to the crudest form of animality, and thus the relationship between humans and animals in the Holocaust.

This relationship is, I propose, a complex and varied one. In virtually all of its aspects, though, it is used to master and oppress those who are in some way or other subject to animalization. The category of animal fits almost every designation of Nazi racist ideology and propaganda. When racial hygiene was in vogue, comparison with lower animals, especially apes, served to denigrate those targeted as inferiors; the idiots and feebleminded, as was the case in eugenics in general, were seen as "low on the animal scale" and therefore disposed for sterilization and, later, euthanasia. When racial hatred crystallized with the coming of the war and the specter of the camps, the imposition of mastery and outright oppression took the form of an utter reduction of human life to the level of putrid discharge, oozing microorganisms, contaminants, and vermin—to the sub-animal. With the advent of the death and concentration camps, in furtherance of the so-called Final Solution, the oozing mass of undesirables was converted, once again, to animal status: herded, crammed into stifling cattle cars, beaten, hunted, enslaved, slaughtered, burned on massive roasters and grills, and turned into human guinea pigs. It is precisely those guinea pigs, subjected to the cruelest human "medical" experiments possible, that the Nuremberg prosecutor Telford Taylor invoked when he mused on the sad irony of the 1933 Nazi Animal Protection Act:

> If the principles announced in this law had been followed for human beings as well, this indictment would never have been filed. It is perhaps the deepest shame of the defendants that it probably never occurred to them that human beings should be treated with at least equal humanity.[23]

PART III

RESTORING THE ANIMAL

Modernity and Postmodernity

IX

Cinema and Popular Culture

> This is the house of Tarzan, The Killer of beasts and many
> black men. Do not harm the things which are Tarzan's.
> Tarzan watches.
>
> —Sign on Tarzan's house, in Edgar Rice Burroughs,
> *Tarzan of the Apes*

Unfortunately, animality as a means of racial, ethnic, and sexual derision has
not disappeared entirely in the modern and postmodern era. It has just been
reformulated and placed in a variety of new and different contexts. With the
advent of technologically and electronically produced images, film—particularly the horror genre—has become a rich source of the depiction of animality.
Special effects and "Hollywood magic" have made it much easier to display the
characteristic kinds of transformations from human to animal that could earlier
only be described in literary and academic discourses. The apishness described
by Gobineau, Lombroso, and Cuvier is now writ large in the lovelorn, destructive, and murderous image of King Kong. The Nazi conception of "vermin" is
quite effortlessly represented as a chilling horde of rats sweeping off Dracula's
ghost ship in Murnau's *Nosferatu*, as is the "usurious" Jew taken up in the hook-
nosed, rodentlike image of Nosferatu himself.

   One of the most disturbing, yet largely unknown, images of animalization
in modern cinema appears in an obscure low-budget "B" film made in 1936,
Charlie Chan at the Race Track. In the early stages of the film, there is a scene set
in a makeshift horse stable in the hold of a steamship traveling from Australia
to California. The inscrutable detective and other principal characters gather
around the horse stall in which a horse-racing notable has presumably been

kicked to death by its occupant. In discussing the specifics of the crime scene, their attention turns to a possible witness, the stable boy. There is a cut to the stable boy, who is seen lying asleep at the rear of one of the horse stalls. He is young, slightly built, and black to the extent that one gets the impression that his face was even further blackened by makeup—which was sometimes done in movies to make blacks look blacker than they actually were (Griffith's *Birth of a Nation* is a primary example of this practice). Tucked in among the horses, lying with his legs stretched between two bags of animal feed, and cuddling a small pet monkey dressed in a sailor suit, the stable boy is the very essence of the human imaged as animal. He lives, eats, and sleeps among animals—it is manifestly clear that he does not occupy a luxury cabin aboard—and he is as deferential to the authority of the masters as any of the racehorses he tends. This deference is perhaps the one feature most indicative of his animal status. He is only spoken at; given directions, commands, and orders; treated with disdain as if he were the lowest of inferiors; less, even, than the pampered racehorses he tends. Indeed, he is even forced—actually pushed and prodded—to lie in a pile of hay at the back of stall to recreate the position of the murder victim, the prospect of which sets off his best "Step-n-Fetch-It" whine. Heightening the animalistic image of the black stable boy, there is a scene in which his pet monkey is shown leaping on the back of a prize racehorse, causing the creature to rear up and kick the sides of his stall. The stable boy is grabbed by the horse's owners and physically thrown toward the rearing horse, sternly instructed to remove his monkey and settle down the spooked horse. He does so, but only after tangling himself with the monkey and horse in a tragicomic scene reminiscent of Ota Benga's monkey-house burlesque.[1] By proximally inhabiting—actually living in—the space occupied by animals, by interacting with animals, and by his passivity before masterly authority, the stable boy is linked ineluctably to an image of animality, to an image of the black or any other "inferior" *as* animal—or at least no better than animal.

I invoke this particular scene because it is indicative of a certain pattern in the representation of animality in the modern and postmodern era. In image-centered technologies, particularly film, there is a tendency to visually connect individuals and types considered inferior with animals, or, in other instances, to associate them with animal savagery and iniquity through some form of magical transformation. In the first instance, a significant number of films, particularly those of the 1930s and 1940s, draw a distinct connection between human inferiority and proximity to animals. The depiction of African natives in the earlier Tarzan series is a glaring example. Loosely based on the original Tarzan stories, the movies generally follow the tendency of those stories to depict Tarzan as a controlling moral and intellectual influence on both animals and natives. By and large, the natives are impractical, savage, and manifestly incapable of running their own lives, particularly as regards moral standards and actions. In the Edgar Rice Burroughs stories, what he terms the "blacks" are often compared with Tarzan's tribe, that is, the Apes. Indeed, Tarzan stands as a kind of intermediary between the savagery of the blacks and the organized "civilization" he endeavors to create in the ape community. This is clearly illustrated when a scene of gross immorality and inhumanity in a native village confronts Tarzan:

> He had been sorely disappointed with the poor little village of the blacks, hidden away in his own jungle, and with not a single house as large as his own cabin upon the distant beach.
>
> He saw that these people were more wicked and violent than his own apes, and as savage and cruel as Sabor [the lioness] herself. Tarzan began to hold his own kind in low esteem.
>
> Now they had tied their poor victim to a great post near the center of the Village. . . . He wondered if they would spring upon their meat while it was still alive. The Apes did not do such things as that.[2]

Lower in character and habit than the apes, the natives stand at an intermediate stage between animal and human: they may, in the end, wind up eating raw, still-living human flesh, lacking the most basic civilized traits of killing and cooking their food, which of course highlights their irremediable animality. In the Tarzan movies, this transitional stage between human and animal is depicted in a series of images not dissimilar in structure to the portrayal of the stable boy in the Charlie Chan mystery. Natives, white or black,[3] are depicted as irremediably dumb, appearing to have no language other than continually repeated grunts, the occasional "Simba," and the ever-present "uga buga"—guttural sounds that are comparable to the whining, obsequious tones of the stable boy. They often react and run in herds or packs, gathering together in large numbers before the camera to attack some prey or enemy. The costuming of the natives is also intended to connect them with animals and animality. The chieftains are invariably arrayed in elaborate costumes consisting of loincloth-like lion, zebra, or leopard skins, with bones, feathers, bird beaks, and animal teeth used profusely as accessory decorations. In effect, the natives are virtually covered with animal parts, making them appear to be some hybrid species, dressed and behaving like animals but yet retaining human form. This does not differ much from the immersion of a figure like the stable boy in a setting that is dominated by animals and thus has the aura of animality.

The aura in popular images extends well beyond stereotypical racist representations of blacks and other lesser types. Transformation into an animal or animal-like state has been associated with evil and opprobrium since the beginning of film production. The several versions of Dr. Jekyll and Mr. Hyde, for example, invariably stressed his transformation into an animal-like being representative of his dark side, of the sinister and disturbing urges buried in the human psyche. Two of the most popular film icons, the werewolf and vampire, are also exemplary of this sort of transformation. The modern depiction of men turning into wolves carries its own dark meaning, as horror films from the World War II period employed one of the favorite Nazi animal symbols, the wolf,[4] to exemplify the epitome of evil: "Images of the devolved animalmen, often possessed of the wolfish traits so prized by the Nazis, were striking facets of horror pictures during the war years. . . . The Wolf Man himself was resurrected for three more films throughout the war, beating out both Dracula and the Frankenstein monster for screen time."[5]

The transformation of human to animal, however, goes further than just an Aristotelian purgation of fear and pity—particularly fear when it came to the Nazis. The Wolfman was not merely an embodiment of Nazi evil, but, even more, a striking image of the fearful state that lies beyond the line separating humans from wild beasts. The most popular of the Wolfman characters, Larry Talbot (played by Lon Chaney Jr.), is in human form a decent, sensitive, softspoken person, who demonstrates many of the characteristics of altruism and kindness. He is capable of love and caring, and is devoted to friends and family: a nearly perfect human being. After being bitten by a werewolf, though, his entire being is transformed. Not only does he become a wolf, but he also loses everything that made him human. As a werewolf, he kills savagely and unknowingly, tearing his victims apart in a furious bloodletting; he demonstrates the most uncontrollable bestiality possible, running on all fours, and even stalking his beloved.

Another popular film character imaged as animal is Dracula, the vampire. Unlike the Wolfman, whose animality is the result of an inopportune accident, the literary and movie vampire has presumably lived for more than 500 years as a soulless, godless embodiment of pure evil. The vampire myth, as is well documented, goes way back in history, probably issuing from the ancient world, but most emphatically embodied by Vlad the Impaler, a Romanian despot, who, incidentally, was considered somewhat of a liberal in his time. Bram Stoker used the legend built up around the Impaler to create the literary image of a demonic, blood-sucking count in his epistolary novel, *Dracula* (1897).

Several elements contribute to the image of animality in *Dracula*. To begin with, Stoker borrowed his image of the gruesome count from the criminal types developed by Lombroso, who was taken quite seriously as a criminologist at the time Stoker wrote his novel. As we have seen, Lombroso envisaged the criminal type as a throwback, marked by numerous signs of physical animality. David Skal, quoting Stoker's description of Dracula, points out this Lombrosian parallel: "A protuberance on the upper part of the ear, a relic of the pointed ear characteristics of apes; strongly developed canine teeth; the nose . . . often aquiline like the beak of a bird of prey; and bushy eyebrows that tend to meet across the nose." Following is Stoker's description of the count:

> His face was strong—a very strong—aquiline, with high bridge of the thin nose and peculiarly arched nostrils; with the lofty domed forehead, and hair growing scantily round the temples, but profusely elsewhere. His eyebrows were very massive, almost meeting over the nose, and with bushy hair that seemed to curl in its own profusion. The mouth, so far as I could see it under the heavy moustache, was fixed and rather cruel looking, with peculiarly sharp white teeth; these protruded over the lips. . . . [H]is ears were pale and at the tops extremely pointed.[6]

Dracula, then, was portrayed by Stoker as the epitome of evil, but not mystical or supernatural evil, that is, an evil falling distinctly outside of or transcending the human realm. He was, instead, a human type who was reduced to animality and criminality by virtue of a set of inherent physical characteristics—characteristics attributable more to Mendel and Darwin than to Satan. In both the novel and the later adaptations to the screen, Dracula thus became, at least in some respects, a compound figure representing certain kinds of degraded humans and racial and ethnic stereotypes. For Stoker, he represented the very image of Lombroso's criminal type, and thus a reflection of degenerative criminality and inherent animality.

In F. W. Murnau's early film adaptation of Stoker's novel *Nosferatu* (1921), the image of Dracula took on still another meaning. Murnau's emaciated, hunchbacked, hooked-nosed count was clearly a parodic representation of the Jew. His animality, consisting of long, pointed ears and elongated, ratlike fingers, tipped by sharp claws, was not directed to some general vision of evil itself, but rather to the presumed "blood-sucking" tendencies of the "usurious" Jew, the hated merchant, moneylender, and banker. One should recall that this was a period in which ideas of racial hygiene and eugenics were beginning to flourish in Germany. Furthermore, the bloodiest world conflict to date had inspired a deep curiosity as to the nature of blood and bloodlines. *Nosferatu* brought a great deal of blood to the screen, along with hordes of vermin pouring off his ghost ship, which clearly project the then-developing image of invasion, disease, and filth so readily associated in anti-Semitic artifacts with the Jew. The very process of transformation, which gained enormous verisimilitude through the medium of film, could be readily employed as a means of defamation and obloquy: the screen transformation into an animal already implied a state of inferiority.

The point here is that the technological generation of images, particularly what Walter Benjamin refers to as "technological reproduction" and Baudrillard calls "simulation," creates yet another, entirely new means of reproducing the relations of power and powerlessness that one finds in the more traditional discourses of mastery. As images inserted in a field occupied by similar images, they become effective by virtue of their mere resemblance, by their approximate place in a fully constructed reality. To a certain extent, then, modern film and other popular media tend to resurrect and extend the kinds of animalistic discourses that had preceded them—discourses couched in largely linguistic and thus more obviously notional terms.

X

The New Racism and Sexism

A possible definition of the real is: *that for which it is possible to provide an equivalent representation.*
— Jean Baudrillard, *Symbolic Exchange and Death*

Examine the contents of their [criminals'] hearts and minds and too much of what you'll find bears out this hypothesis: free-floating aggression, weak consciences, anarchic beliefs, detachment from the community and its highest values.... This is a predictable result of unimaginably weak families, headed by immature, irresponsible girls who are at the margin of the community, pathological in their own behavior, and too often lacking the knowledge, interest, and inner resources to be successful molders of strong character in children.
— Myron Magnet, *The Dream and the Nightmare*

The New Racism

In the modern and postmodern era, conceptions of inferiority associated traditionally with animality are given a new life of their own. As Baudrillard argues, in what he calls the "order of simulation,"[1] all images and discourses assume legitimacy because they are equivalent reproductions of a reality that has lost its grounding in the specificity of reference.[2] Whether images or ideas are true, real, or accurate, or have some basis in empirical reality is largely unimportant, as is the fact that they may have been scientifically discredited or discarded; as long as they continue to "orbit" in the trajectory of signs taken for reality, they are fully appropriable and assume a value by virtue of their semblance.

This is clearly the case with what I am calling the "new racism." After centuries of pseudoscience; cultural, racial, and sexual bias; miscalculation; misinterpretation; and so on, the racist theories that had reduced humans to animal or sub-animal status have been resurrected in the modern era in the form of politically and technically charged exchanges that appear to be feasible merely because they resemble other, more scientifically rigorous ones: "all possible [interpretations] are true, in the sense that their truth is exchangeable, in the image of the models from which they proceed, in a generalized cycle."[3] These counterfeit theories, moreover, do not overtly make the same sort of egregious claims as the earlier ones: no one directly compares blacks to apes, Jews to vermin, Indians to insects. Nor are blacks pictured explicitly as razor-wielding beasts, intent on slashing every white child they see. Instead, the animalistic comparisons are veiled in a dizzying array of euphemisms, epithets, and statistical, academic, political, and technical verbiage, which appear in both form and content to be much like any other contemporary scientific, psychological, sociological, or criminological discourse. However, these modern conceptions are in many ways even more dangerous than the obvious earlier attempts to demean and animalize certain groups, for much of this material is promulgated through popular vehicles, such as best-selling books, media commentary, television talk shows, and contemporary journals, magazines, and reviews. As Gould often points out, secondary and tertiary sources are often impervious to falsification.

There are numerous modern-day examples of these restorations and restatements of defunct and discredited theories of animality and inferiority, but two of the most obvious appear in Jared Taylor's *Paved with Good Intentions* (1992) and Dinesh D'Souza's *The End of Racism* (1995). Taylor's book—something of a right-wing cult classic—consists of an extended series of recriminations against racial liberalism that invoke unending accounts of liberal misdeeds, carefully culled from a long list (he has 1,139 footnotes) of mostly reactionary publications. His general thesis, as is the case with most conservative race theory, is that two factors are essential to the failure of race relations in America: liberal policies and the inherent inferiority of blacks—in this case, demonstrated by their inability to take charge of their own destinies. It is interesting, as an aside, to note that Taylor, in a book subtitled "the failure of *race* relations," defines race failure exclusively in white and black terms, using Asians only to erect unflattering comparisons with blacks. For example, he writes: "If white racism were blighting the lives of blacks, how would it be affecting other nonwhites? Should it not be a terrible obstacle for Asians as well? Asians have faced fierce discrimination in America, but this has not stopped them from working hard and getting ahead."[4]

Up to the present era, we have seen a litany of spurious "scientific" arguments regarding the *natural* inferiority of those arbitrarily defined as inferior. From Gobineau's uncivilizable "apes" to Hitler's "maggot in the rotting corpse," there is a persistent emphasis on how presumably failed races and ethnic groups are somehow connected with the alleged viciousness, immorality, and stupidity of beasts. Taylor, though he seems to be speaking in objective, more intellectually dispassionate terms, consistently revives this old, discredited, and debunked relationship between inferiority and animality. His basic tactic, though, does not truly appeal to science or even to pseudoscience. Instead, he builds a progressive case for the inherent criminality and thus the animality of blacks by listing what seems to be an unending series of headline crimes attributed to them.

The animal connection drawn between these criminal acts and blacks is based on Taylor's use of slanted and euphemistic phrasing. The core image that Taylor tries to create is one of utter black brutality, a kind of unthinking savagery aimed disproportionately at white Americans. There are hints of this strategy throughout the early attacks on liberal policies, like affirmative action, but the animalization begins in earnest at the point where Taylor tries to make a case for "double standards." He argues, strangely enough, that blacks get off easy in most things and that whites are held to a much higher standard. This also applies to crimes, as blacks are allegedly out there committing endless savageries against whites with little punitive restraint. This situation, largely invented by Taylor, with an assist from a few selected and highly biased media sources, serves as the basis for a spate of animalistic attributions. In recounting an attack on a thirty-two-year-old white man who was riding through South Central Los Angeles, Taylor describes the assailants as "a *gang* of about fifteen blacks"; another white South-Central traveler who was "driving to his machine shop to *protect it and its employees*" was killed, and "*looters stripped* him of valuables and *ransacked* the car (italics added by author)."[5] Other indecencies rained down upon whites range from attacks in various U.S. cities to a *gang* of blacks trying to *tear* a newspaper reporter from his car. In further defense of white tolerance in the face of black savagery, Taylor makes it patently clear that there was not "a *single* instance of retaliatory violence by whites against blacks for any of these attacks."[6]

The root cause of all the cited violence directed against whites was the 1991 Rodney King beating incident in Los Angles. Taylor's description of King and the incident itself is interesting: King is pictured not only as, by and large, deserving of what he got, but also as a superhuman being who was so savage, so monstrous, so out of control that the police had no choice but to subdue him in a particularly violent way:

A policewoman approached Mr. King when he got out of the car, but he grabbed his right buttock and shook it at her. He would not let himself be frisked, spat on the police, laughed maniacally, and danced about when told to stand still. Mr. King is six feet, three inches tall, weighs 250 pounds, and was acting dangerously crazy.... [W]hen police approached him, he started flailing his arms wildly, hitting one officer in the chest. The police decided to force him down. Their first attempt was with a twenty-five-thousand-volt stun gun. One shot of this device will knock a person down 80 to 90 percent of the time. The officers hit Mr. King twice with the gun but he still resisted arrest, and managed to knock one officer off his feet.[7]

Beside the facts that Taylor continually claims that the media favorably skews stories involving blacks,[8] and that the arresting officers' accounts were largely discredited,[9] the interesting point about these descriptions is that they closely parallel traditional means of denigrating blacks by comparison to animals. King is portrayed as something of a King Kong, invulnerable to weapons or restraint, and determined to destroy everything in his path. More likely, though, King is a modern-day version of the murderous, razor-wielding, apish black so popular in the racist literature appearing before and after the Civil War. He shows most of the characteristics of those vague, faceless monsters roaming the streets of American cities, ready to slash, disfigure, and brutally rape some unsuspecting white woman or girl. He is as fearful a figure as any slashing, raping, out-of-control freed Negro depicted in the anti-black, racist literature of writers like Carroll, Shufeldt, or Dixon. The difference, however, is that Taylor's account of the King beating and its aftermath assumes a certain validity merely because it simulates truth and objectivity in its reporting of the story. Not only does it appeal to racist sensibilities, and to those who agree with the expressed conservative ideology regarding race, but it also simulates the actuality of the event. The detailed, journalistic-sounding descriptions appear to be no different from any other detailed journalistic descriptions. Moreover, the fact that Taylor had the academic probity to cite numerous sources, and provide a reference for each and every source, tends to give the whole account the guise of reality and truthfulness.

This strategy is repeated throughout the book, with particular insistence in the section entitled "Race and Crime." Here Taylor heightens the sense of ominous black menace by appealing to the sheer number of black-on-white crimes in America and, most importantly, to the savagery with which many of these crimes are committed. The section opens, once again, with an account of the disproportionate sympathy among politicians and law enforcement for blacks, exemplified by an event during which several whites painted the faces of blacks with white sneaker polish, which led the then-mayor of New York City, David Dinkins, to call a tearful press conference condemning the action. In the same period, however, *"fifty* [black] young *Brooklynites* went on a *rampage* in lower Manhattan, *slashing people with knives* and taking their coats." Again, "near Columbia University, nine *young blacks* . . . likewise *rampaged through the streets, viciously beating and kicking people* (italics added by author)."[10] This sense of black savagery is enhanced by yet another incident of uncontrolled black viciousness—this time in an unprovoked attack on a busload of Jewish children. The incident is described as follows: "The blacks shouted racial insults, *stoned* the bus, and smashed the windows. Inside, *the children screamed in terror,* and some were injured by flying glass."[11]

In the allegations of savagery and animality, though, Taylor saves his most extreme rhetoric for the apparently exclusively minority tendency toward "wilding." Simply stated, wilding is an act of packlike violence committed by large gangs of out-of-control black and/or Hispanic youths. The most famous case of wilding was the brutal rape and beating of the "Central Park jogger" in April 1989. The description of the incident is couched in a narrative structure and language much like that of the earlier anti-black writing. Whites are sensitive, discreet, considerate, and impeccably moral, whereas blacks are insensitive, uncaring, and brutal.

> As is customary in cases like this, the press voluntarily refrained from pub-licizing the name of the victim. As Jerry Nachman of the *New York Post* explained, "What we want to avoid is, a year from now, she buys a blouse from Bloomingdale's and hands her credit card to the clerk who says, 'Oh, yeah, you're the one who got gang-raped in Central Park.'" Black news-papers, which generally follow the same rule, deliberately published the name of the white jogger. Black-owned radio station WLIB also broad-cast her name.[12]

Taylor fleshes out the account by stressing the tendency among black youths to riot at every opportunity, to be generally out of control, and to stalk whites. For example, he describes an earlier incident in Crown Heights, Brook-lyn, by portraying black mobs as *prowling, pulling* motorists from their cars and *thrashing* them. The Central Park incident is floridly described as a "white woman . . . *gang-raped,* beaten to within an inch of her life, and *left for dead by a roving group of young blacks and Hispanics.*"[13]

The comparisons that Taylor makes between large-scale acts of group violence perpetrated by whites and blacks also parallel much of the distorted or highly selective ethnologically based data offered by the earlier racist ideo-logues. For example, in an attempt to diminish and therefore justify the no-torious Sharpville massacre in South Africa—described as the desperate and presumably self-defensive act of "a few white policemen, surrounded by an angry black crowd," who opened fire and killed sixty-nine people—Taylor counters the event with what he considers the infinitely worse black-on-black tribal slaughters in Burundi.[14] His claim that the black-on-black killings went largely unnoticed—which is, of course, patently false[15]—serves, once again, a dual purpose. On the one hand, it reiterates the old stock apposition of white innocence against appalling black barbarism and savagery: the *"few young white policemen* were surrounded by an *angry black crowd*," whereas the black Tutsis just aimlessly slaughtered hundreds of thousands of black Hutus (italics added by author). On the other, it reinforces the image, progressively built by Taylor, of black animality, since, it would seem, only depraved, morally bereft "beasts" would slaughter hundreds of thousands of innocent human beings.

Taylor, consistent with conservative race theory in general, tries to establish a case for out-of-control black promiscuity and thus the wildly abandoned "breeding" of virtual hordes of illegitimate, socially doomed, and largely uncared-for children. The strategy here is precisely the same as that used by the earlier eugenicists, but softened by the substitution of several terms. The bad stock, the carriers of degenerate germ plasm, are now termed "welfare recipients," whom "the majority of Americans believe . . . are already living at public expense have no right to bring yet more people into the world whom we must feed, house, clothe, medicate and try to educate."[16] The language here is close to that used by Davenport to describe the waste of public money on mental defectives; it is also similar to the terminology used in the argumentative positions of the early German eugenics and euthanasia theorists like Binding, Hoche, and Ploetz.[17] The German theorists employed economic arguments as the primary reason for the elimination of so-called wasteful defectives. Taylor does not advocate throwing promiscuous, overbreeding blacks into the ovens, à la Christian Wirth, nor does he propose firing a few well-aimed doses of gamma rays at the genital regions of these breeders, but he is a firm supporter of the "voluntary" use of Norplant (a subcutaneous contraceptive/sterilization device) on welfare mothers. For Taylor, the urgency behind the use of Norplant is absolute, lest—as Davenport, Laughlin, Goddard et al. warned in an earlier era—we have our very society collapse around us.[18]

The racist message is quite transparent: try to reduce black population by the long-established scare tactic of invoking the image of an explosion of impoverished, uneducated, expensive, violent, perhaps deadly, new generations of black welfare recipients wilding through the streets of American cities. On another level, though, the argument involves the characteristic animal allusions. Welfare-receiving blacks (i.e., all blacks, as "welfare" is a code word for blacks) are not like white Americans—controlled, pragmatic, and circumspect in their decision to breed. Rather, blacks are promiscuous, sexually precocious,[19] and largely incapable of controlling their sexual drives: "An end to the vicious cycle of reckless procreation is the only solution to the problem of the underclass. Our country . . . must recognize that single parenthood and welfare are not just an 'alternative life-style' but a fatal violation of the social contract."[20] Like Gobineau's "uncivilizable apes" or Goddard's "wild men," welfare mothers are portrayed as out of control, incapable of reaching a level of human culture and understanding, and unable even to comprehend their contractual obligation with the society in which they live. Thus, as a sub-human, inferior, and animal-like class, they must surrender any right to procreation and submit to the control of "reason" and "science"—that is, accept the Norplant contraceptive device. For the good of the underclass and the nation as a whole, the future hordes of wilders must be eliminated.

Published three years later than Taylor's *Paved with Good Intentions*, D'Souza's *The End of Racism* seems to have benefited little from precedent. Like Taylor, D'Souza invokes numerous outdated and refuted theories of racial inferiority, but he does so on a grander scale. Indeed, *The End of Racism* reads like a compendium of racist theories couched in ultramodern terms. Like Taylor's work, it tends to avoid the ugly epithets and comparisons of earlier eras. In fact, D'Souza's tendency is to hook readers opposed to racism by appearing to under-score its egregious origins and consequences.[21] Nevertheless, there is much in his book that revives the more traditional connections between animality, race, and inferiority; these connections, like Taylor's, are made in language that ap-pears objective, scientific, academic, and therefore relatively neutral.

The greater part of the material that reproduces the traditional structures of animalization appears in the chapter entitled "The Content of Our Chromo-somes." The chapter is relatively short, but focuses in considerable length on *The Bell Curve*, the extraordinarily popular revival of psychometric theory authored by Charles Murray and Richard Herrnstein. The strategy in this section is not so much one of blaming the victim, but rather one of making an extended apology and justification for the validity and truth of intellectual differences between races. The now-classic apposition between the positivity of whiteness and the negativity of blackness is effected by a series of veiled accusations against the crit-ics of biodeterministic racial comparisons. D'Souza lists a "stampede of epithets" uttered by epithetized "normally unflappable pundits." These include excerpted snippets from such a disparate group as Bob Herbert, Adolph Reed, and Stephen Jay Gould. The out-of-context quotes by these various pundits are set against a litany of attacks aimed at a group of scientists and psychologists who appear to be unfairly condemned and scurrilously treated. The tactic is, once again, to make it appear as if the victimizers are being victimized. This, combined with attacks on the liberal policies that attempt to deliberately undermine the solid science underlying *The Bell Curve*, tends to shift focus away from an examination of the flaws in Murray and Herrnstein's hypothesis. Instead, it declares the hypothesis correct by virtue of the sheer weight of the liberal condemnation of it. The implication here is that if liberals unthinkingly dismiss *The Bell Curve* theory of racial difference, it must be entirely correct.

At any rate, the crux of the issue is the reaffirmation of the sorts of animalistic designations that have continuously haunted the historical treatment of inferiority. In making a case for the "victims" of liberal ire, D'Souza invokes a long list of eminent modern IQ theorists and biodeterminists, including Arthur Jensen, William Shockley, E. O. Wilson, and James Q. Wilson. All of these figures have at some point or other sought to prove that blacks are either less intelligent or more prone to criminal activity than whites. Their methods, in all cases, reflect the sorts of techniques, theories, and pseudoscientific experiments that begin in earnest in the early part of the nineteenth century. For, as Gould correctly argues in *The Mismeasure of Man*, modern hereditarian IQ theory is really no different in its general form from the earlier deterministic theories of racial inferiority, from Gobineau onward.[22]

What are the specifics of this new version of the age-old attack on so-called inferiors? How does the *Bell Curve* thesis reduce its targeted blacks to some degree of animal status? In this regard, D'Souza tends to defend the validity of the biometrics and psychometrics underlying Murray and Herrnstein's general claim that blacks are of lower intelligence than all other races, but particularly whites. The defense, however, consists largely of evading the whole issue and creating the illusion that there really is no substantial disagreement on the difference of intelligence between groups (read: whites versus blacks). D'Souza even goes so far as to claim that Gould, a perennial opponent of between-group differences, has taken a "new found position" on this issue.[23] The uncritical acceptance of between-group differences in IQ is, moreover, not only a way of circumventing a large body of work by biologists, psychologists, and clinicians that refutes the between-group difference concept, but also a way of establishing a permanent marker of inferiority: innateness.

In fact, one could argue, as does Gould, that the primary intention of all biodeterministic thinking is to find an irrefutable ground for difference, and therefore for mastery in any particular cultural, sociopolitical, or economic province. This, in turn, relates to the assignment of animality because intelligence is probably the most potent and certainly the most invoked cognitive and logical tool separating humans from animals. If one can establish a permanent, scientifically sound difference in intelligence between groups, then mastery is thoroughly and forever assured; for the stigma of low intelligence—as with all biodeterministic theories—provides a ground for every imaginable imposition of control, discrimination, and abuse.[24] If one is permanently stigmatized with an indelible mark of inferiority that cannot be removed by any means—much like the enduring relegation of animals to an inescapable stratum of dumbness—the individual or group must, it seems, be treated quite differently from other groups or individuals. As was the case with mental defectives, who were presumed to share the same animal hebetude as blacks, it made little sense to waste either time or money on their improvement. More importantly, it is unreasonable and illogical to allow them full equality with those who, by virtue of "objective" scientific proof, are deemed eternally superior. Even when D'Souza, oddly, backs off from his insistent defense of IQ difference theory and its validity and claims that he, too, is a critic of "the fatalism of genetic theories of IQ difference," he still manages to revive the concept of irreversible racial difference by blaming it on the victims (blacks) and on liberals:

> In order to substantiate the hypothesis, however, it is not enough to hurl epithets or blame societal racism for blacks' poor scores on tests of numerical or logical reasoning. Rather, we need to examine the controversial subject of *internal* environment, or cultural disfunctionalities in the black community. Both internal and external environments interacting together may account for why blacks are not competitive with other groups on measures of IQ and academic performance. No such investigation is possible, however, if we continue to insist upon the liberal dogma that all cultures are equal. Only by reconsidering relativism can liberals adequately answer to Richard Herrnstein and Charles Murray and thereby refute the charges of inherited black inferiority.[25]

The flow of illogic is staggering. What D'Souza actually wants us to believe is that the present idea of black inferiority is in part the fault and creation of liberal dogma, and that it is impossible to correct this notion unless liberals drop this dogma and stop tossing racist epithets at conservatives. Since this has not as yet happened, nor, given D'Souza's subtle pessimism, will it happen in the near future, *The Bell Curve* stands unrefuted. Thus, D'Souza is arguing that a work that has been extensively analyzed, criticized, and in large part dismissed by numerous professionals, in such fields as biology, psychology, genetics, zoology, psychometrics, biometrics, and anthropology,[26] stands as the whole truth of black inferiority because liberals will not agree to drop their conception of cultural relativity and become more civil toward conservative race theorists.

Remarkably, if this reversal of stance did somehow occur, then we as a society would be able to take a serious look at the cultural "disfunctionalities" inherent in the black community, and thus discover a *new* source of inevitable black inferiority.

Without waiting for the liberals to drop their dogmatic cultural relativism, D'Souza does indeed explore the disfunctionalities of the black community in his very next chapter, "Uncle Tom's Dilemma: Pathologies of Black Culture." Here, too, there are a number of assertions regarding black behavior that subtly involve animal comparisons, particularly with regard to race and crime. We have seen, from Lombroso onward, that criminality has served as an important basis for assigning degeneracy and difference. Taylor, for example, spent considerable time and effort to establish the fact that blacks are far more prone to animal activities than whites. D'Souza picks up this trend, with abandon. It seems that, once again, liberal cultural relativism and unwarranted attacks on conservative intellectuals are one of the primary causes of black pathologies. The argument is long and convoluted. In essence, D'Souza is saying that blacks in general are dragged down by an underclass that is driven by a set of "pathological norms": "Many individuals and groups work against considerable political and financial odds to maintain enclaves of decency. Yet their work is made more difficult because of the prevalence of pathological norms, especially strong in the black underclass, which mock and resist all efforts at neighborhood restoration."[27] So, in essence, there is a "sick" element in the underclass that resists all efforts to restore normalcy (middle- and upper-class white values) to blacks in general. This thesis is, of course, not unlike that of the earlier race theorists, who typified black achievement as an anomaly and predicted that the advancement of the race as a whole would be handicapped by its inherently degenerate characteristics.

One might also see this underside of black culture, this pathology, as a kind of animalistic residue, as something that transforms the potential of virtuous black behavior into something vicious, unthinking, and brutal, just as poor Larry Talbot was fatefully transformed from nice guy into murderous werewolf. D'Souza continually points to indications of the inherent danger of this morbid condition. For example, after having noted black contributions to culture, particularly in the rhythmic arts and sports, he turns to the dark side of black culture: "Yet black culture also has a vicious, self-defeating and repellent underside that it is no longer possible to ignore or euphemize."[28] Although there are numerous expressions of this underside—dependency on big government, crying racism, and so on—the most obvious of its manifestations are violence, crime, and criminality.

D'Souza is not quite as openly demeaning as Taylor in describing the savage characteristics of black pathology; there is no image, for instance, of an unstoppable "King Kong" defying stun guns while shucking hefty LA police officers. D'Souza does, however, create a picture of the black underclass as out of control: effectively, as a group totally unlike any other in America. In doing so, he condemns virtually every pose, stance, or movement of the so-called bad nigger orientation, giving one the distinct impression that the underclass is entirely degenerate and aberrant. The cool poses of bad niggers are even blamed for the fact that "[t]he second leading cause of death among young black males is accidents. . . . Many single-car fatalities are the result of aggressive, high-risk driving such as leaning-in-the-car, one arm driving, and drag racing."[29] Despite the absurdity of this claim—accidents are one of the principal causes of death for *all* teenagers in the United States, even those who drive with both white hands—there is a characteristic attempt here to reconstruct a category of exclusion for the so-called underclass.

Unlike everyone else, including other blacks, the whole physical attitude and bearing of these "types" is configured in such a way as to make them outsiders in society at large. Witness another description of the bad nigger: "Yet it seems unrealistic, bordering on the surreal, to imagine underclass blacks with their gold chains, limping walk, obscene language, and arsenal of weapons doing nine-to-five jobs at Proctor and Gamble or the State Department."[30] Of course, what is truly *surreal* is either Proctor & Gamble or the State Department inviting inner-city kids to interview for jobs, and, if for some reason they did, the idea of kids limping in, gold chains swinging, and cursing away with an arsenal of weapons tucked in their baggies. At any rate, D'Souza's exclusive language here, emphasized by the overblown descriptions and invidious comparisons, creates something of a societal outcast—not an ape or lower animal as such, as was the case with the Gobineaus, Cuviers, and Schufeldts—but rather a kind of nebulous subspecies. This subspecies is a "maggot" in the black socius. Blacks will thus never achieve their goals in society as long as they are susceptible to this cultural disease, spread by verminlike, violent, unmanageable, and uncontrollable "wilders."

Following his section on criminality, D'Souza, like Taylor, takes up the daunting problem of uncontrolled black breeding—one of the long-established signs, I should add, of the wild animal in the human. The problem lies, once again, with the pathological nature of the black underclass. It seems that black sexuality was kept largely in check when, in the earlier part of the twentieth century, blacks followed the model of middle-class whites and adopted those whites' sense of virtue and self-control.[31] However, by the 1960s black overbreeding had apparently reached a critical mass, and D'Souza describes this condition by paraphrasing the account of the urban anthropologist Elijah Anderson:

> Walk through urban African American neighborhoods, and you will see young men at intersections, boasting about their sexual exploits, laughing and strutting. Another common sight is that of many pregnant women with distended bellies, their youthful faces belying the fact that they are often close to delivering their second or third child. Thirty-two year old black grandmothers abound, and the status of great-grandmother is sometimes attained before the age of fifty. These women, Anderson argues, are the complicit agents of a highly reproductive culture of sexually rapacious males. With some discomfort, we see that there is some truth to the historical stereotype of the black male stud, or at least in the case of the black underclass, what used to be a stereotype now contains an ingredient of truth.[32]

Even given the fact that these statements are glaring generalizations, collected selectively to make a case solely against young black males,[33] they are significant in that they reveal a core tendency in the whole strategy of animalization and mastery. The reference to "black male studs" being no longer a stereotype, but "containing an ingredient of truth" is not only a restatement of traditional racist images—Dr. Howard's oversexed Negro predators, for example[34]—but also a reconstruction of the standard means of attributing lower animal tendencies to certain groups or races. Blacks who identify themselves with the bad nigger image are exceptional in two important ways. First, they form a dangerous underclass, uniquely separate from and below all other classes. Second, their wild sexual desires and expressions are seen as totally destructive and, at this time, largely uncontrollable. They present a kind of primitive threat, not only to more controlled, virtuous, sexually restrained, and morally aware middle- and upper-class white society, but also to those of moral probity and self-control in their own race. This being the case, this class must be eliminated, or at the very least forcefully restrained. In many ways, for D'Souza the dark sexuality of this underclass represents an uncanny and inaccessible primitiveness and animality at the core of American life—a force liable to rot the American socius from the inside out, to gnaw at its most vital parts.

This vision is by and large the same as the fascist view of the Jew and his or her placeholders—the gnawing evil of the sewer rat, the vermin, and the contagion of the pathological bacilli that will eventually destroy society. After all, D'Souza does refer to the black underclass as affected by cultural *pathologies*, and, in certain cases, spreading these pathologies even among their own race. "In today's America, where the slavemasters and segregationists are gone

and blacks enjoy the same legal status as whites, the 'bad nigger' and his op-
positional culture have become a menace to African Americans and the larger
society."[35] Indeed, if one can believe Murray and Herrnstein, the answer to this
emergence of the dark side of humanity—to its dangerous and palpable animal
savagery—is, as with controlling all wild animals, to cage them:

> Over the next decades, it will become broadly accepted by the cognitive
> elite that the people we now refer to as the underclass are in that condi-
> tion through no fault of their own but because of inherent shortcomings
> about which little can be done. . . . In short, by *custodial state*, we have in
> mind a high-tech and more lavish version of the Indian reservation for
> some substantial minority of the nation's population, while the rest of
> America tries to go about its business. In its less benign forms, the solu-
> tions will become more and more totalitarian. . . . One possibility is that a
> variety of old police practices—especially the stop and frisk—will quietly
> come back into use in new guises. New prisons will continue to be built,
> and the cells already available will be used more efficiently to incarcerate
> dangerous offenders. . . . Technology will provide new options for segregat-
> ing and containing criminals, as the electronic bracelets are being used to
> enforce house arrest (or maybe "neighborhood arrest"). . . . *The underclass
> will become even more concentrated spatially than it is today.*[36]

What is the difference, then, between the positions articulated by Taylor,
D'Souza, and Herrnstein and Murray and those presented in nearly all the
other forms of racial mastery we have seen? Clearly, not much, as virtually all
the components of the arguments for inferiority are set solidly in place. Although all the racist theorists discussed herein tend to acknowledge race as a
diverse concept, in the end racial inferiority is attributed solely to blacks. Taylor
speaks of the Asian race only in their obvious superiority to blacks; D'Souza
attributes the possible end of America as we know it to bad niggers; *The Bell
Curve*'s sole targets are those cognitively deprived individuals, the minus-15
percenters, constituting the black underclass and the race in general. In essence,
the only group declared inferior is blacks, and they, as outsiders and degenerates, must suffer the consequences of their shortcomings, which include the
low intelligence often ascribed to animals (the failure to achieve normal levels
of cognitive aptitude) and the studlike sexual behavior of the animal in heat.
Besides, their natural tendency toward crime and criminality puts them in a
position in which they must be watched, searched, stopped, contained, and, if
necessary, incarcerated. Given all these deficiencies, there seems to be no real
difference between the modern-day black and the historical black conceived
as demon, outcast, scapegoat, and bestial presence in white society, both in
American and European pseudoscientific and popular lore. Effectively, in this

sort of literature, the animal in the human has not really disappeared; rather, it has been reconfigured. The image is no longer the growling, slouching ape, but the limping, cursing bad nigger.

New Sexism

> The value of a woman's life would appear to be contingent on her being pregnant or newly delivered. Women who refuse to become mothers are not merely emotionally suspect, they are dangerous. Not only do they refuse to continue the species, they also deprive society of its emotional leaven: the suffering of the mother.
> —Adrienne Rich, "The Theft of Childbirth"

The socioeconomic and political agenda of all of the works examined thus far is quite transparent: employ race fear as a means of attacking theories and programs involving equitable distribution of wealth. In this respect, they really do not differ very much in structure from those of the pre– and post–Civil War anti-black and pro-slavery writings. Both, interestingly, also employ similar approaches regarding animality, in that references to animal behavior and lack are used as a means of maligning blacks. As indicated earlier, however, these sorts of denigrations were not limited solely to blacks and ethnic minorities. Women, too, were excluded from social amenities such as education, jobs, and basic political rights. They were seen as subject to ineluctable laws of sexual selection and to a compelling, natural requirement to breed and nurture—in short, as condemned to a homebound, sexually and economically passive existence. Although women have obviously made significant progress over the past century, there are still numerous modern restorations of these older means of social and sexual suppression of women, many of which involve certain subtle—and sometimes not-so-subtle—forms of animalization. Discrimination against women has issued from numerous disciplines and taken many forms in the modern and postmodern era, but medicine is one of the principal fields given to the use of animal comparisons as a means of deprecating and controlling women.

The predominant late-nineteenth- and early-twentieth-century notion of women being inherently feeble and diseased dates back at least to classical Greece and Hippocrates, and probably even earlier. Briefly, Hippocrates applied a set of characteristic procedures drawn from the medical science of the time to what amounted to an unfathomable mystery: namely, sexual behaviors and disorders seemingly specific to women. Because women in ancient Greece lacked productive social interaction and were literally condemned to home and hearth, there was an implicit need for a justification of their repressed status. This need became manifest in the wide cultural understanding of women as inferior beings, not fully mature in their rational faculties or self-control. Hippocrates himself believed that most "female problems" stemmed from the uterus, and that in these illnesses the uterus literally moved through the body, wandering wildly from place to place, causing disease and disorder. The results of this un-controlled movement varied, ranging from the sensation of strangulation caused by the imaginary feeling of a lump in the throat (*globus hystericus*) to flushing, paralysis, seizures, and fits of sobbing.[37] The notion of female dysfunction was passed on from the Hippocratic tradition to Galen. As far as he was concerned, women were still possessed, but possessed for different etiological reasons. In Galen's theory of humors, the problems of uncontrollable sobbing, headaches, bizarre behavior, skin flushing, and the like were the result of the woman's in-ability to expel a spermlike substance from the uterus.

Even with this mere wisp of information regarding the history of women's ailments, it is not at all difficult to draw a chronological picture of "female prob-lems." Throughout history, women were regarded as diseased, as overwrought, as pathologically delicate and sickly, prone to any number of debilitating mental and physical conditions. Most of these woes were attributed to their reproduc-tive role, and thus to the organs that effected this process. This notion of women as a kind of reproductive apparatus extended throughout the history of their treatment within the medical profession, and it still contributes to the view of women as fulfilling a broader mammalian function. We have already examined some of the animalizing tactics used to suppress women in the nineteenth cen-tury and early part of the twentieth century, many of which were derived from Darwinian evolutionary theory. In the modern era, ideas of sexual selection and roles related to it are still around, but many of the demeaning attacks aimed at women stem from their "sacred" and biologically determined duty as childbearers and nurturing mothers; that is, they continue to center on the uterus.

In the modern era, with the advent and recognition of both statutory and substantive rights of women, the older system of male dominance be-came largely obsolete, based as it was on presumed female weakness, needi-ness, oversensitivity, sexual passivity, and so on. The shift in approach, though it took numerous forms, was left in large part to the medical and psychiatric establishments. The whole process of childbearing, nurturing, and mothering in general was largely monopolized by the various disciplines within these male-dominated fields. New names for conditions that expressed old prejudices were invented: names like mother-infant bonding, Munchausen syndrome by proxy, neglectful mothering, postpartum depression, and the like.[38] The mammalian duty of bearing, nurturing, and raising children became a reworked imperative of female identity, worth, and status, but dominated by a small group of experts who assumed nearly absolute power over the processes.

A representative example of this kind of medical hegemony is what Diane E. Eyer calls the "scientific fiction" of mother-infant bonding.[39] Briefly, mother-infant bonding became an important biomedical subject in 1972, when two pediatricians published a study purporting to show that women who spent sixteen extra hours with their babies following birth demonstrated better mothering skills. With scant confirming evidence, the physicians who originally observed and recorded the process began to draw remarkable conclusions from their experiment. They postulated that their initial results indicated that a sensitive hormonal period in women just following childbirth attuned them to either accept or reject their infants. Indeed, many experimenters in the field of mother-infant bonding were willing to go so far as to claim that healthy child development was a direct result of the physical closeness of the mother to her child.[40] However, the whole conception of mother-child bonding was, interestingly enough, based on extrapolations from certain types of lower animal bonding—extrapolations that were formulated largely on the basis of a supposed instinctual mammalian connection with offspring. On this point, Eyer writes:

> Unfortunately, most of those who sought to reform hospital birthing practices (doctors and nurses as well as parents) failed to see the trap: Because bonding was a construction of medicine, it would ultimately serve to protect the interests of that institution. The promised revolution in childbirth became a product of the politics of science. . . . By selecting the behavior of a few species of animals that coincided with popular notions about women's "instinct," bonding research reduced women to automatons who behave the way they do, not because of their capacity for reason, their complex psycholog[y], or their economic or social circumstances, but rather because of their inherent and inevitable inferiority.[41]

The notion and practice of mother-infant bonding, invented by doctors and to a large extent perpetuated by the medical profession, had two hidden agendas. First, it was a means of controlling the behavior of women and, in so doing, realizing an entrenched female stereotype regarding instinctual animal behavior. Second, it helped to reestablish the role of the physician in childbirth, which, due to the popularity of various forms of natural childbirth, midwifery, home delivery, and so on, was slowly eroding. Hence, what seemed to be a caring attitude on the part of doctors hid an old bias: the irresistible force of inner instincts, the magnetic attraction of primordial animal drives that were reflexively at work in the female of the species. Extrapolating from certain animal species, every woman was seen as compelled to behave in a certain manner and as having some instinctual need to mother, regardless of her distinctive individual traits, characteristics, and attitudes. Once again, the animal reared up in the human, and the beneficiaries were those who occupied the place of power: namely, those who were in a position to transform the concept of the instinctual into social, economic, and psychological supremacy.

The tendency of the medical profession to transform mothering and what is construed as its failure into power over women is perhaps best exemplified by the bizarre medico-psychiatric appellation, Munchausen by proxy syndrome. The full-blown by-proxy syndrome had humble beginnings. A British family physician, Richard Asher, had observed a number of emergency room patients who seemed to have medically indeterminable disorders, and who appeared regularly at hospitals to seek either emergency medical treatment or inpatient care. In a 1951 article in the *Lancet*, Asher deemed these individuals a unique breed of super-malingerers, and invented a new name for their behavior, *Munchausen syndrome*. The name Munchausen was drawn from the renowned fabulist, Baron von Munchausen, following Asher's claim that the operating mode of these "hospital hoboes" was to lie compulsively about their symptoms and invent tall tales to obtain unnecessary medical treatment and/or drugs.[42] The syndrome met with some initial recognition, as it struck a sympathetic chord with other British hospital physicians who had experienced similar behaviors. Still, the whole idea of faking symptoms and lying to medical authorities did not really become internationally popular until another British physician, Roy Meadow, published a paper in 1977 on the proxy transference of this so-called prevaricating behavior to children, which he termed *Munchausen syndrome by proxy* (MBPS). Effectively, Meadow argued that certain individuals, primarily mothers, would injure or fabricate illness in a child to attain some nonspecific end, but usually to receive attention from members of the medical profession. At this time, when there was a powerful emphasis on parental child abuse, child molestation, and mothering in general, the syndrome was attributed almost entirely to mothers or surrogate figures like close female relatives, nurses, nannies, or grandmothers. The syndrome thus became almost exclusively a female problem, and bad and abusive mothering, in turn, was identified as its evident cause.[43]

The MBPS onus was placed on the mother because she was viewed—largely by the medico-psychiatric establishment—as an individual who failed in her prescribed duties as a nurturer and instinctual protector of her child or children. This role, of course, was much like that alleged to underlie mother-infant bonding, in that it was conceived on the basis of a biocultural presupposition about the nature of mothering. Without paying much attention to the everyday stress and complications of mothering, psychiatrists and medical doctors, particularly pediatricians, viewed those assumed to be suffering from the by-proxy form of Munchausen syndrome as pathologically twisting their natural duty as mothers; that is, as implicated in a perversion of mothering.

One could well argue that this perversion of mothering is based at least in part on a sociobiological myth of good mothering. Good mothering (as opposed to bad mothering/MBPS mothering) is determined by a gender-based, biologically and socially rooted construct of proper behavior: women must nurture their children, demonstrate powerful maternal instincts, stay close to their children, protect them, feel fully compensated by childbearing and childrearing, and so on. In other words, childbearing and childrearing should be a smooth, unthinking, instinctual procedure, much like that carried on by other mammals and different young-rearing species—a state of simple bliss expressed perfectly by a popular British work on gender roles: "'Childbearing and childrearing represent for women,' assert Lundberg and Farnham, 'almost their whole inner feeling of personal well-being.'"[44]

This view of the bad mother as shunning her responsibility of childrearing and nurturing, as well as unfailing assiduousness regarding the child's health and well-being, is really a veiled attribution of sub-animality, a failure to properly follow instinctual animal behavior—for animal mothers, in many species, assume the full responsibility of childrearing. For example, hens lay and tirelessly incubate their eggs; female grazing animals, such as deer, cattle, sheep, and antelope, nurse and raise their young and even teach them survival skills, as well as being called upon to protect them from predators. So, at least on one level, the Munchausen mother who injures or neglects her child represents the negative side of animal mothering. She fails to fulfill her most necessary biological functions, those that mark all females of the species as nurturers and protectors of their young.

This failure at mothering exacts a price. Munchausen mothers are not only assumed to be lower-than-animal in their inability to care for and protect their offspring, but they are also subject to the force of medico-psychiatric, and in some cases legal, control and power. Although some mothers do in fact abuse their children using certain forms of medical intervention, all mothers accused of MBPS behavior fall under the same category—the "accused"—which, in turn, marks them for life, whether or not they have actually committed this type of child abuse. In this sense, the diagnosis itself carries with it a means of control over mothers, and the control is exacted by a condemnation of the mother on the grounds of bad mothering, or, as mentioned earlier, the failure to reach even an animal level of nurturing and care. Any substantial deviation from preset, largely biologically determined, acts of nurturance and care places the woman at the mercy of the medico-psychiatric and legal institutions. Furthermore, although the ostensible charge may be child abuse by medical means, the real basis for the allegation of immorality and perversion is the woman's contravention of the sacred codes of child care, an imposture of motherhood. Two American MBPS experts, Herbert Schreier and Judith Libow, make this patently clear in the following quote:

> It is not just pediatricians, judges, lawyers, and child protective care workers who are vulnerable to this particular dynamic. Most of us are invested in and intensely convinced by an image of good mothering, and are quite susceptible to skillful lying and effective imposturing, particularly when they involve a "symbol" so close to our hearts. We cling to a belief of universal "naturalness" of the early mother-infant interaction that does not fit with the facts. For example, many mothers do not show an intense "natural" interest in their newborn children.[45]

This belief in the universal "naturalness" of mothering, despite Schreier and Libow's caveat, is perhaps the primary source of the vilification of alleged MBPS mothers. The social opprobrium associated with their behavior is thus largely a reaction to their neglect of those imperative natural duties associated with mothering. In this respect MBPS serves as a source for a recoding, a restoration of the more traditional forms of women's repression: namely, the turn-of-the-century distortion of Darwinian theory into female imperatives of nurturing and childrearing in general. But whereas sexist scientists, like Havelock Ellis, sought to suppress women by placing them in an immutable, "scientifically" determined category of eternal nurturers, the theorists of mother-infant bonding and MBPS erect a somewhat different means of female suppression. In their case, the means of suppression are based on the contravention of the so-called natural mothering role, rather than its fateful fulfillment. The fact that a woman cannot stay at home, properly nurture her child, love and protect the child, and so on, is at the core of the problem. The bad mother, the "hormonally deficient" mother, the imposter, has now become the target of the various professional institutions and discourses surrounding childbearing and childrearing. In effect, the naturalness of good mothering has been turned on its head and finely adjusted so as to be used against those mothers who are now seen as unnatural.

Human sterilization, though appearing to be solely the brainchild of nefarious social theorists and biodeterminists, required complicity from the medical profession: someone with a medical license and knowledge had to do the tube tying and castrating. This earlier involvement of the medical profession in sterilization extended well into the twentieth century, and doctors still carry out court-ordered procedures, particularly on sex offenders. However, the motivation for and basis of the modern use of sterilization have changed significantly. Following the exceedingly tragic results of its use in Hitler's Germany, sterilization as a means of producing "good stock" and eliminating bad has been, at least temporarily, sidetracked. Its use as a subtle means of population control, however, has not been eliminated entirely. The control is now manifest in the form of various types of sexual surgery, particularly unnecessary hysterectomy and tubal ligation—and the preponderance of controlling is aimed mostly at poor, minority, powerless, underrepresented, or destitute women.

In the latter part of the nineteenth century, some form of sexual surgery often awaited any deviation by women from their traditional roles as homemakers, nurturers, and sexual slaves. Wandering women were subject to such gynecological procedures as clitoridectomy and female circumcision (relatively common surgical procedures performed until the late 1930s which were intended to ensure that women would not masturbate), hysterectomy, mastectomy, oophorectomy, ovariotomy, and so on. The reasons for this sort of surgery were historically ascribed to the aim of returning women to conventionally expected roles and forms of female behavior:

> An 1893 proponent of female castration claimed that "patients are improved, some of them cured; ... the moral sense of the patient is elevated ... she becomes tractable, orderly, industrious, and cleanly." ... Doctors claimed success for castration when it returned woman to her normal role, subservient to her husband, family, and household duties. Her disorder lay in her deviation from that role, a broad enough characterization to explain the bewildering and suspicious variety of indications.[46]

Such physician-initiated procedures as unnecessary hysterectomies were not by any means restricted to patients in the nineteenth and early twentieth centuries. They were common throughout the twentieth century and continue to be so today. In *The Mismeasure of Woman*, Carol Tavris argues that, of the approximately 650,000 hysterectomies performed annually in the United States, as many as 90 percent could be considered unnecessary. Much of the rationale for such operations results from physicians' insistence that women's internal sexual organs are essentially useless after childbearing age.[47] The pattern here seems clear. Even today, with much nonsensical Darwinian-based sexist theory behind us, women are still being treated as wombs, as reproducers of the species; and when the medical profession decides that the reproductive cycle must come to an end, women are systematically deprived of this ability and right to reproduction, much along the lines of the suggestions made by D'Souza, Herrnstein and Murray, and their ilk. Effectively, the poor, the "pathological underclass," must be restrained in reproducing their kind, if not by gamma rays and crematoria, then by "legitimate" forms of sexual surgery.

Because of the bad press received by outright sterilization, sexual surgery on the underclass is often performed in clandestine ways. The following excerpt from a lawyer-client interview provides a harrowing example of just such a procedure, performed surreptitiously on a Mexican-American woman:

> Mrs. Acosta attended weekly prenatal clinic sessions at County—where, not once was she counseled about sterilization. . . . However, on August 20, 1973, nine months and eleven days pregnant, Lupe Acosta entered L.A. County in the final stages of labor. "When I was being examined, they pushed very hard on the stomach," she recalls, "very, very hard. With their hands. One doctor would have one leg open. The other doctor would have the other leg open. And then, there was two doctors just pushing down on my stomach and I couldn't . . . I couldn't stand it. I pushed one doctor because I couldn't stand the pain. When he came back, he hit me in the stomach and said, "Now lady, let us do what we have to." . . .
>
> A question to Mrs. Acosta from her lawyer: "Do you remember signing a consent form?"
>
> "No," she answers, "I don't remember signing anything. Only when I left the hospital—perhaps an exit paper?" . . .
>
> "When I asked the woman doctor, she asked me if I knew what had happened to me. I said 'No.' And then the doctor told me, 'Well you won't need the Pill because they tied your tubes.' I said I didn't sign anything. She said, 'Your husband did.' And then I told them he wasn't my husband."[48]

Patient testimony is not the only source of these disturbing images. An interview with a medical student who had just completed his studies at Wayne State University, in Detroit, reveals equally outrageous clandestine acts:

> "Most of the patient population was black, inner city," he explains. "We had a lot of young girls come in . . . thirteen and sixteen and they'd have two or three children. In those cases, we'd ask 'em, often when they were in labor, if they wanted tubule ligations. There were *so many* young girls and most of them had a real low mentality. . . . Sterilization was offered to women in labor no matter what their age."
>
> "You mean you sterilized sixteen year olds?" asks an incredulous intern from Milwaukee, who has been sitting on the side, taking in the discussion.
>
> "Well, yeah . . . if they had two kids. . . . There was beginning to be a whole lot of trouble. Detroit's blacks, they're really very anti-white. They were having all these meetings about genocide."[49]

Although there are no doubt many modes of female repression in the modern era, reproductive control was perhaps most consonant with the earlier forms of female animalization. Central to modern reproductive control was the conventional idea of an invariable female nature that operated according to certain immutable laws. Women were compelled to bear children and to treat them in an intimate, nurturing way. If they did not conform to this pattern, scientifically established through Darwin's evolutionary theories of natural and sexual selection, they would be singled out as perverse, as impostors of good mothering, and thus as social outcasts. In the case of MBPS, for example, if certain pathological women did not conform to a basic mammalian and animal form of behavior regarding their offspring—if they did not fulfill their natural obligation to perpetuate the species—they could be severely punished and irrevocably stigmatized for their transgressions.

The same sort of thinking also holds true for modern types of female sexual surgery, though in a slightly different way. Women who had passed childbearing age were considered of little or no use to the perpetuation of the species. The medical profession reacted to this by a wild cutting spree, which entailed hundreds of thousands of unnecessary hysterectomies and other forms of female organ removal every year. The site of Greek female pathology, the uterus, had moved once again, only this time out of the body entirely.

One could say much the same, regarding animalization, of modern styles and forms of sterilization. It was no longer an expedient used to eliminate or reduce whole races, classes, or segments of society—the proverbial undesirables—but it still functioned as a means of curtailing what was viewed from a certain societal perspective as unacceptable and uncontrolled sexual behavior. The poor, indigent, uneducated, welfare-receiving mother was seen as out of control, incapable of generating or maintaining sufficient reason to be allowed to breed freely. Those in the medical profession, no doubt urged on by social moralists like Herrnstein, Murray, Magnet, and the like, largely took it upon themselves to rein in this wild and bestial behavior. In the end, the modern medico-psychiatric establishment, though infinitely more knowledgeable and scientifically advanced than its predecessors, was somehow able to reinscribe many of the same animalistic categories applied in the nineteenth and early twentieth centuries—particularly, the all too common misapprehension that women have a sacred and inescapable duty to conserve the species.

XI

Sociobiology, Pop Ethology, and Restating Animality

> After one more experience of this kind, just the sight of
> the dog—even if at that moment it is not aggressive—
> suffices to elicit the cat's attack. The corresponding
> situations vary from species to species, but the dynamic
> interrelationships between fear and aggression are basically
> identical in all vertebrates, and particularly mammals.
> —Paul Leyhausen, "On the Natural History of Fear,"
> in Lorenz and Leyhausen, *Motivation of Human*
> *and Animal Behavior*

Nietzsche would most likely view certain sociobiologists/ethologists in the same light that he viewed what he called "philosophical laborers": "It is for these investigators to make everything that has happened and been esteemed so far easy to look over, easy to think over, intelligible and manageable, to abbreviate everything long, even 'time,' and to *overcome* the entire past."[1] Indeed, a certain type of sociobiology fits perfectly Nietzsche's description in that it attempts to drag the past, the very distant prehistoric past, into the present largely intact and fully active in our current behavior. It also fulfills this description because it attempts to incorporate what has been esteemed in the past into the *status quo* of the present, thus serving to support long-standing, much-favored hierarchies of supremacy and subjugation: Men dominate women, whites dominate other races, masters dominate slaves, bosses dominate workers, the cognitive elite dominates the cognitive underclass, and so on. This is and supposedly always will be the case because of an inevitable pattern of genetically determined behavior, which, in the end, can be proven out by experiments with and on a broad range of vertebrates. Mastery, for certain sociobiologists, is a given.

But is it really? Or does this type of sociobiology stand on much less certain ground than it seems, aiming at nothing less than a total synthesis of all social behavior based on biological and genetic causes? E. O. Wilson, one of the early contributors to sociobiological theory, offered the following definition: "Sociobiology is the systematic study of the biological basis of all social behavior. For the present it focuses on animal societies. . . . But the discipline is also concerned with social behavior in early man and the adaptive features of the organization of primitive human societies."[2] The movement itself, however, has a history that begins somewhat earlier than Wilson's popularizing book, *Sociobiology: The New Synthesis*, published in 1975. Most interpreters and critics of sociobiology tend to date its inception to the mid-1960s with the emergence of what Gould termed "pop ethology," represented in the works of Robert Ardrey, Konrad Lorenz, Desmond Morris, and a few others.[3] The common theme of all these works is that humans are fundamentally aggressive and territorial. This, in turn, presents an overall picture of humans as belligerent and warlike, constantly at each other's throats and given to adopting virtually any and every measure of protective security—in effect, a biocultural vision of Thomas Hobbes's social universe.[4] The basis for this claim, however, turns out to be "fragmentary and controversial evidence of human paleontology and animal behavior."[5]

In his *Territorial Imperative* and elsewhere, Ardrey tends to attribute direct aggressivity to humans because they were in the beginning intrinsically vicious. This came about, Ardrey argues, because some hominids were fierce predators, descended from the carnivorous species *Australopithecus africanus*, which spent most of its time hunting down its larger, though much tamer, vegetarian relative, *Australopithecus robustus*. Ardrey's theory has been soundly refuted, primarily because he based it on canine tooth growth in early hominids; his idea turned out to be fallacious because canine teeth grow larger in primate evolution more slowly than body size. Subsequently, it was determined that both "predator" and "prey" species had precisely the correct size of teeth for their relative growth, undermining the claim that one had a distinct offensive advantage and could prey mercilessly on the other.[6]

Despite the scientifically erroneous nature of his central arguments, Ardrey went on to formulate elaborate sociobiological scenarios, many of which corresponded perfectly with the dominant anti-communist ideologies of the mid-1960s. For example, he provided an extensive defense of private property and property ownership—a culturally devised concept rather than a genetic predisposition—on the ground that humans, like many wild animals, are persistently territorial in nature. In fact, Ardrey even went on to dismiss the Marxian notion of a harmonious society living without private property by appealing to the fact that invariable behavior patterns direct all our territorial activities. On this, he wrote:

> Marxian socialism represents the most stunning and cataclysmic triumph of the romantic fallacy over the minds of rational men. Viewed through the transparent curtain, the single metaphysical thread all but vanishes in the vast fabric of unassailable logic. And an observer of the animal role in human affairs can only suggest that much of what we have experienced in the last terrifying half-century has been simply what happens, no more and no less, when human energies become preoccupied with the building of social institutions upon false assumptions concerning man's inner nature.[7]

The foreseeable failure of socialism is further attributed to the ineluctable natural law guiding the inner animal in man, which is strictly territorial and uncompromising when this territorial imperative is violated: no private property, no peace.

> A logic larger than the Marxian pursued its own inexorable way in all those societies subjected to full socialist doctrine. In a state of nature a society founded solely on socialist territory must have territorial isolation; the Communist society got it. The iron curtain became a feature of socialist geography, the iron hand a weight on socialist communication, the iron jug too frequently the chief educational adornment of the enlarging brains of socialist youth. But a society so isolated must still be welded, and so ancient territorial noises came to enlighten the new social scene. Threats of war, display of might, creation of incidents, alarms of aggression, all the paranoiac paraphernalia of the primate's perpetual territorial hostility became permanent features of socialism's external relations.[8]

Despite the risible nature of this quotation, the thinking underlying it shows an interesting reconfiguration of the early methods of invoking the animal in the human and using it as a means of disparaging certain groups or, in this case, ideas. An imperative that is undeniable, because of its primordial, universal, and invariable existence in the human animal, rears up to undo a modern social system. In effect, what Ardrey is arguing is that a conceptual formation, created in a complex discursive and interactive network over several centuries of European thought and cultural and intellectual history, has and will forever fail to work because of some presumed animal-like instinct that has existed and remains largely unchanged through millions of years of evolution. The enormous complexity of social thought, human action, dialectical exchange, social experimentation, class struggle, and so on is neatly reduced to—and undone by—a single evolutionary characteristic that fatefully moves both man and beast: territoriality and aggression about territoriality. Fortunately, however, the Adam Smiths and John Lockes got it absolutely right: private property effectively reproduces the primordial relations of territorial animals and early hominids, and will therefore function more or less effectively in a world based on collective animal instinct. "If we defend the title to our land or the sovereignty of our country, we do it for reason no different, no less innate, no less ineradicable, than the lower animals."[9]

If this kind of thinking seems familiar, it is. One finds echoes here of many of the theories of animality, race, and inferiority we saw in the first part of this book. For example, Gobineau's theory of disadvantaged civilizations, though not as ethologically and biologically sophisticated, is quite similar in its insistence on inherent, immutable human characteristics—blood—as the determinant factors in the development of civilizations. Gobineau, like Ardrey, is careful not to linger on the particulars. Instead, he divides races into their broad inherent constituents, that is, the immutable instinctual factors that make them the way they are. Blacks are at the bottom of the scale, simply because of certain lower animal characteristics (narrow receding foreheads, prognathous jaws, and the like) "imprinted on the individuals of that race ere their birth, [which] seems to *portend their destiny*."[10] Likewise, the yellow race is inferior—though not quite as inferior as blacks—because of certain other inherited characteristics. According to Gobineau, these "yellow people" are destined to be mediocre in morals, as well as in intellect, though they can "easily understand what is not very profound, nor very sublime"; they demonstrate little scope of imagination, and therefore cannot invent very much of novelty or worth.[11] A predetermined heritage, but a most positive one, in Gobineau's view, also fatefully affects whites. They are everything the other races are not: sensitive, moral, brilliant, caring, artistic, innovative, and so on. Like the modern humans of Ardrey's analysis, however, all these races issue from the same hereditary past. The differences between the races are centered on adaptation, and on innate qualities that are only minimally subject to progressive social or cultural change. Thus, Ardrey's reduction of primordial instincts of territoriality and aggressivity to sociopolitical dominance—the failure of socialist territoriality in face of private property, for example—is not really much different from Gobineau's reduction of blood and cultural instinct to racial dominance. In both cases the future structures of the social order are largely predetermined by some fundamental and innate predisposition to dominance, which works itself out, oddly enough, in support of the favored status quo of the moment, namely, Gobineau's white supremacy and Ardrey's free-market system.

Ardrey's pop ethology does not stop at the sociopolitical ramifications of territoriality. As Nietzsche often lamented, like all good moralists Ardrey feels compelled to delve into the question of conscience, and of good and evil. This, as might be expected, also has its roots in territorial mechanisms:

> The limitation of conscience lies in its territorial nature. It is the mechanism whereby an animal society mobilizes its members against an enemy and commands individuals to make sacrifices for the common good. So far as conscience deepens the amity channels of social partners it is [a] force for tolerance, for compassion, and for mercy. And so far as the capacity for a species to form territorial coalitions results in the formation of larger and larger territorial societies, the expression of tolerance and compassion and mercy comes to be extended to an increasing number of individuals. In this sense, conscience in human behavior has acted as a building block in the edifice of civilization. . . . The conscience of social man differs from that of the social animal chiefly in its complexity . . . [b]ut this will not by any means end the complex facets of my conscience. I shall defend the white race against the black, stand for the Christian world against what I deem to be godless, and oppose any adventures on the part of Rome [the Pope] which seem to threaten my Protestant preserve. And few other than my Georgian social partners will understand that in every instance I am acting according to my conscience.[12]

So, if we are to understand Ardrey correctly, the origin of conscience—of the discrimination between right and wrong, good and evil—is really a largely automatic animal behavior motivated and regulated by regional allegiances and beliefs. In this view, white supremacists are only acting instinctually in defending their territory, whereas those whites who support blacks in Georgia are operating counterinstinctually, that is, failing to defend their territory from enemy incursions. The moral obliquity of segregation, prejudice, and lynching is really not in question, nor is that of the centuries of intentional repression associated with Southern slavery. Conscience is merely an issue of fulfilling ancient instinctual drives to protect territory and clan, "the mechanism whereby an animal society mobilizes its members against an enemy and commands individuals to make sacrifices for the common good."[13] The use of animality as a repressive force is quite clear here. Not only do the most powerful and proactive indigenous defenders of territory win out over the less powerful—blacks, the godless, the wily Pope, and so on—but they also are absolved of any moral wrongdoing simply because they are reflexively implementing an irresistible force directed toward territorial protection. Motivated by an ancient drive, the powerful are merely working out an instinctual pattern first established at the very beginning of vertebrate evolution. Force, mastery, even cruelty are fully justified, because they are completely imprinted in some irremediable program, some genetic signature dating from our evolutionary past: namely, territoriality and predatory aggression.[14]

Nevertheless, even this powerful territorial drive is, according to Ardrey, overcome by deeper, more primitive drives. Conscience is just an epiphenomenon of a much grander principle: namely, the instinct for order. "Far antedating the predatory urge in our animal nature, far more deeply buried than conscience or territory or society lies the shadowy, mysterious, indefinable command of the kind, of the instinct for order."[15] This deeper urge for order, according to Ardrey, stems from an inner, genetic reaction to the primary mode of predation, "a talent for disorder." In the boundless wisdom of the mindless evolutionary flow, order had to be reestablished, and order, in turn, led to civilization. Civilization, however, is not there to be loved; rather, it is a baneful thing, given to explosive and deadly consequences—collapse every thousand years or so, according to Ardrey—but we are largely stuck with it, fully subject to its twists and turns, because it stems from order, which, in the end, is our deepest and most compelling animal instinct. Subsequently, the animal, writ large in the human by the invariable laws of evolution, lurks alongside its twin, rising up continually to force, to blindly compel, the human to act out his or her deepest instinctual drives. Animal-like irresponsibility, or amorality, is simply part of our "hard wiring":

> To the extent that we are free to make ethical decisions that can be translated into practice, biology is irrelevant; to the extent that we are bound by our biology, ethical judgments are irrelevant. It is precisely because biological determinism is exculpatory that it has such wide appeal. If men dominate women, it is because they must. If employers exploit their workers, it is because evolution has built into us the genes for entrepreneurial activity. If we kill each other in war, it is the force of our genes for territoriality, xenophobia, tribalism, and aggression. Such a theory can become a powerful weapon in the hands of ideologues who protect an embattled social organization by "a generic defense of the free market." It also serves at the personal level to explain individual acts of oppression and to protect the oppressors against the demands of the oppressed. It is "why we do what we do" and "why we sometimes behave like cavemen."[16]

Unlike Ardrey, who sees humans as entirely aggressive, Konrad Lorenz takes the position that humans are aggressive by nature but not quite aggressive enough. In fact, Lorenz denies our sharp-toothed predatory origins in favor of a more benign, flat-toothed vegetarian species, unable to cope with predatory aggression and therefore rather defenseless against such incursions. Even so, he tends to twist the evidence to support his own a priori view of "an innately aggressive, territorial, entrepreneurial, male-dominated species."[17] This becomes quite clear in Lorenz's most popular book, *On Aggression* (1963). The work is structured in strata; that is, it builds an argument in several layers for aggression in humans and animals as the primary motivating factor of life. The earlier chapters point out behavioral homologies between certain animal species and humans, with special emphasis on how dominance, species protection, and ritualized fighting have become predominant instincts. As he advances his argument, though, he warns that these are not to be taken as "the only important functions in the preservation of the species." Besides these homologies, he stresses, "We shall see later what an indispensable part in the great complex of drives is played by aggression; it is one of those driving powers which students of behavior call 'motivation'; it lies behind behavior patterns that outwardly have nothing to do with aggression, and even appear to be its opposite."[18] In short, as is also the case for Ardrey, aggression is the immutable, transhistorical, essential underlying basis of all animal behavior.

Now, no one would deny that humans are at times aggressive, nor is it possible to casually reduce aggressivity in human and animal behavior to some trivial factor or role. Still, an argument or philosophy that places it at the center of all human actions, and does so as a result of observed animal behavior neatly and quite unreflectively transposed to human behavior, has notable shortcomings. For instance, in *On Aggression* Lorenz goes on to reduce virtually all human interaction to either acts of aggression or avoidance of acts of aggression. In discussing what he calls cultural ritualization, he proposes that its main function in animals is to effect several steps that lead from communication to the control of aggression, and then to formation of a bond. This process, according to Lorenz, is also at work in humans *mutatis mutandi*. Any group of humans that exceeds in size what can be held together by personal love and friendship, like the triumph ceremony of geese, depends for its very existence on the aforementioned three "functions of culturally ritualized behavior patterns."[19] This ritualized behavior pattern, in turn, is effectively the origin of all human manners. On this, Lorenz writes: "'Good' manners are by definition those characteristic of one's own group, and we conform to their requirements constantly; they have become 'second nature' to us. We do not, as a rule, realize either their function of inhibiting aggression or that of forming a bond. Yet it is they that effect what sociologists call 'group adhesion.'"[20] So, if we extrapolate from this model, any human function that effects bonding and cohesion is rooted in the innate animal drive of aggression and is thus also entirely reflexive, a prime constituent of a kind of social unconscious. What we end up with, then, is something much like Ardrey's territorial imperative: we cannot act any differently than we do act, because of an inevitable, irresistible reaction to some inner formation or to a primordial urge, in this case, for social adhesion.

Lorenz, who goes on to tie together completely the loose ends of his imperative narrative throughout the text, reveals a bit of sensitivity about his theories at the end of his fifth chapter. He tries to absolve himself of the misunderstandings that might arise from his use of natural science in what is commonly considered the province of the human sciences:

> Here, as so when discussing human behavior from the viewpoint of natural science, I am in danger of being misunderstood. I did indeed say that man's fidelity to all his traditional customs is caused by creature habit and by animal fear at their infraction. I did indeed emphasize that fact that all human rituals have originated in a natural way, largely analogous to the evolution of social instincts in animals and man. I have even stressed the other fact that everything which man by traditions venerates and reveres, does not represent an absolute ethical value, but is sacred only within the references of one particular culture. However, all this does not derogate from the unfaltering tenacity with which a good man clings to the handed down customs of his culture. His fidelity might seem to be worthy of a better cause; but there *are* few better causes. If social norms and customs did not develop their peculiar autonomous life and power, if they were not raised to sacred ends in themselves, there would be no trustworthy communication, no faith, no law. Oaths cannot bind, nor agreements count, if the partners to them do not have in common a basis of ritualized behavior standards at whose infraction they are overcome by the same magic fear as seized my little greylag [goose] on the staircase in Altenberg.[21]

Effectively, what is being said here, at least in terms of our concerns, is that some deep-seated instinct, which has "a life of its own" and thus directs humans as specific groups ineluctably toward certain ends, determines all human actions, and particularly moral ones. What is missing in this neat equation, of course, is the fact that certain groups and individuals work against these so-called inevitable drives and instincts, "the tenacity with which a 'good man' clings to his culture." As far as Lorenz is concerned, though, these resistant groups and individuals are mere deviations from a grander, deeper pattern of natural behavior. The inevitability of cultural and social conformity simply eliminates any possibility of resistance to that conformity. Or, as Lorenz contends, the little greylag goose would shudder in fear if it did not have in common a basis of ritualized behavior standards.

Yet, given Lorenz's totalizing and thoroughly animalizing behavioral theory, what would happen to actors like Alexander Schmorell and Hans Scholl, founders of the White Rose resistance group; Dietrich Bonhoeffer; the Socialists and communists who opposed the Nazis; to all of those individuals and groups that resisted the inescapable urge to cling to their indigenous German culture? Unfortunately, we know all too well what happened: most of them were murdered—if Lorenz is right, merely because they could not, in good conscience, follow their deepest animalistic drives.[22]

The casual destruction of human intention, invention, and autonomy is continued in Lorenz's penultimate chapter of *On Aggression*, quite inaptly titled "Ecce Homo!" He begins the chapter by presenting some apparent paradoxes about human behavior, particularly the fact that, even though humans are rational creatures, they tend to act irrationally. Of course, the reason for this is clear:

> Human behavior, and particularly human social behavior, far from being determined by reason and cultural tradition alone, is still subject to all the laws prevailing in all phylogenetically adapted instinctive behavior.... Man's social organization is very similar to that of rats, which, like humans, are social and peaceful beings within their clans, but veritable devils toward all fellow members of their species not belonging to their own community.[23]

Hence, ratlike or any animal-like aggression is at the root of all our conflicts. Humans just bristle when they come into contact with exogenous humans, humans who do not fit their clanlike temperament and who excite phylogenetic instincts lying deep within their collective psyches.

The absurdity of such a claim is palpable, but it is interesting to follow its more-than-fuzzy logic to its conclusion. Basically, what Lorenz is claiming is that all animals share a common instinctual heritage—this claim is probably more or less correct. However, what he adduces from this claim is that modern-day aggressive human behaviors—though changed, overturned, and altered by external events; bathed in thousands of years of discursive information; and subject to millions of years of environmental conditioning—are driven by intact originary impulses. These impulses are formed due to an inherent inadequacy among humans to function as predators, a "carnivorous mentality" that "arises from his being a basically harmless, omnivorous creature, lacking in natural weapons with which to kill big prey, and, therefore, also devoid of the built-in safety devices which prevent 'professional' carnivores from abusing their killing power to destroy members of their own species."[24]

So, we must assume that, since we did not have those great saber teeth of the tiger, nor the powerful paws and claws of the cave bear, we have done untold harm to our own species. On this view, the Nazis' gassing and burning of the Jews could be seen as just the acting out of an instinctual lack of carnivorous weaponry; the annihilation of Hiroshima and Nagasaki as merely the result of an intraspecies conflict, complicated by a sense of carnivorous frailty; and so on. It is much more likely, though, that war waged among state-organized societies has very little to do with a priori states of aggression. War is in virtually all instances undertaken for clear and calculated reasons of political and economic gain.

Obviously Lorenz's thinking has distinct parallels with many of the earlier noted theories of animality. He neatly transposes one of the standard negative ethical concepts regarding animals onto human behavior: namely, lack of responsibility for their actions. Although he does try to recover some moral principles from the phylogenetic ooze,[25] his basic concept employs animality as a blanket explanation for actions that are inherently and in many ways particularly human. Moreover, Lorenz tends to conflate various categories of animal behavior, which are in reality quite separate and most likely motivated by different needs and stimuli. An animal that reads Shakespeare and an animal that burrows under the soil for grubs and bloodworms are quite different animals, even though they may have some instincts in common. As is the case with much sociobiological theory, though, Lorenz simply reduces this variation to the common phylogenetic instincts. If humans are unique, acting in remarkable and incomprehensible ways as the product of millennia of social and cultural adjustment, it would be quite difficult, if not impossible, to make clear attribution of all behavior to one dominant system or one overriding principle, as the sociobiologists do with free-market economics and the particular social hierarchies and behaviors that issue from that system. "Faced with the extraordinary richness of complexity of human social life in the past and the present, they [sociobiologists] have chosen the nineteenth-century path of describing the whole of humankind as a transformation of European bourgeois society."[26]

Sociobiology and pop ethology also demonstrate a distinct partiality toward male domination in common social, economic, and sexual interactions. The problem stems from the aforementioned concept holding that genetically coded and entirely predictable behaviors direct most of our social actions. In many animal species, males dominate females; the story of man's evolution told by the sociobiologists confirms this tendency as an irremediable fact, an imperative: "If men dominate women, it is because they must."[27] Sam Kash Kachigan's *The Sexual Matrix* provides an interesting example:

> [Thus] we arrived at the important conclusion that polygamy is the natural order among human beings, just as it is in most species of the animal kingdom.... [M]onogamy is responsible for the high incidence of divorce and female grievances in modern society, as well as the genetic devolution

and behavioral degeneration of civilization as a whole.... Culture is to blame, and fortunately *culture can be changed*. Mating is the key.[28]

And what is the key to mating? "In every respect, then, it makes much more sense for young women to mate with older men, who will have proven their genetic endowment as well as their financial and emotional capacity for raising children."[29]

Even though Kachigan is neither a social scientist nor a trained sociobiologist, and seems to have a compelling personal agenda, his comments on relations between the sexes are really not too different from the points made by certain sociobiologists and pop ethologists. For example, the picture of sexual relations drawn by Desmond Morris in his two extraordinarily popular works, *The Human Zoo* (1969) and *The Naked Ape* (1967), is one of nearly total dominance by the male of the species over the female. His account of what he calls "dominance mimicry" argues that it is an age-old trait built into virtually all animals; it leads, ultimately, to a position of supertribal status in animal communities. After a detour through the difference between dominance mimicry and true status symbols—which is, in reality, another transposition of modern economic conditions to what is presumed to be phylogenetically induced behavior—Morris explains how mimicry has affected and continues to fatefully affect human social relations and position:

> In Renaissance Germany, a woman who dressed above her station was liable to have a heavy wooden collar locked around her neck.... In the England of Henry VIII no woman whose husband could not afford to maintain a light horse for the king's service was allowed to wear velvet bonnets or golden chains. In America, in early New England, a woman was forbidden to wear a silk scarf unless her husband was worth a thousand dollars.... High-status wife wears a diamond necklace. Low-status wife wears a bead necklace.... Unfortunately, they have low status value, and the low-status wife wants something more. There is no law or social edict preventing her from wearing a diamond necklace. If she takes this step, adorning her neck with a dominance mimic, she starts to become a threat to high-status wife. The difference in their status displays becomes blurred. High-status husband therefore puts on the market necklaces of large fake diamonds.... The trap has been sprung. True dominance mimicry has been averted.[30]

As might be easily observed, a few relevant details are missing here. To begin with, the low or high status of women is always related to that of their male partners. A woman cannot wear this or that, or is subject to ridicule, because her husband does not enjoy sufficient status in a particular society. But it is, of course, not some primeval and irresistible attempt to display dominance and social status that drives this subjugation, but rather the socially, economically, and culturally determined status of women within the societies that Morris cites. In most of the above-mentioned societies, women were merely chattels of their husbands, largely without substantive or statutory rights. Another sore point here is the insistence on male dominance in the form of market control, that is, males "put on the market necklaces of large, fake diamonds," so that their stay-at-home wives can compete with other stay-at-home wives for status within the society—a fact that seems difficult to extrapolate from some compelling generic and genetic impulse. The fact that women need to accessorize themselves with gaudy jewels and colorful costumes to gain some status (usually, for their husbands) really does not say much about the inherent intellectual qualities of women, either. Indeed, the woman acts merely as an extension of her husband's will, seeking to fulfill a phylogenetically determined necessity through some blind, long-standing ritual. Her worth is calculated entirely on the basis of what status she can achieve through and for her male counterpart. These instinctual and inevitable animal drives once again reflect a patriarchal vision of women's place.

Displays are only one form of male dominance, and a relatively insignificant one at that. Mating and the sexual act, according to Morris, are central to all animal behavior, and therefore a primary function in the so-called human animal. However, his account of this patently dual act—more colorfully put by Morris as "it takes two to copulate"[31]—turns out to be remarkably one-sided. In virtually all stages and moments of mating, it is primarily and nearly exclusively the female who is in some way hereditarily and physically prepared for the act: all of the necessary paraphernalia for successful mating are displayed by the female, to such an extent that the female of the species seems to be no more than an attractive receptacle for animal reproductivity. In a certain sense, the entire history of sexual reproduction, in both animals and humans, is recounted in terms of the female binary: submissiveness/seductiveness. In this respect Morris argues that the shift from the customary animal from-the-rear mating position to the human frontal position took place because of certain physiological changes in the female. In indicating these changes, however, the male seems to remain a static element in the process, poised eternally to penetrate the female who must undergo a series of significant metamorphoses and supplement these changes with a dazzling array of bodily symbolizations.

> If the female of our species was going to successfully shift the interest of the male round to the front, evolution would have to do something to make the frontal region more stimulating. At some point, back in our ancestry, we[!] must have been using the rear approach. Supposing we had reached

the stage where the female signaled sexually to the male from behind with a pair of fleshy, hemispherical buttocks (not, incidentally, found elsewhere among the primates) and a pair of red genital lips, or labia. Supposing the male had evolved a powerful sexual responsiveness to these specific signals. Supposing that, at this point in evolution, the species became increasingly vertical and frontally oriented in its social contacts. Given this situation, one might very well expect to find some sort of frontal self-mimicry. Can we, if we look at the frontal regions of the female of our species, see any structures that might possible be mimics of the ancient genital display of hemispherical buttocks and red labia? The answer stands out as clearly as the female bosom itself. The protuberant, hemispherical breasts of the female must surely be copies of the fleshy buttocks, and the sharply de-fined red lips around the mouth must be copies of the red labia. (You may recall that during intense sexual arousal, both the lips of the mouth and the genital labia become swollen and deeper in colour. . . .) If the male of our species was already primed to respond sexually to these signals when they emanated posteriorly from the genital region, then we[!] would have a built-in susceptibility to them if they could be reproduced in that form on the front of the female's body. And this, it would seem, is precisely what has happened, with females carrying a duplicate set of buttocks and labia on their chests and mouths respectively.[32]

Given the sort of theorizing and reasoning demonstrated in Morris's writing, it is not difficult to imagine why women have been considered mere objects, nor is there any great mystery about why feminists employ the notion of the "male gaze." Every supposedly aleatory evolutionary change is calcu-lated perfectly to suit the dominant patriarchal ideology. For countless millen-nia, through the most complex, indeterminate, and constantly changing DNA transpositions, the male stands, unchanged and unfazed, above the female, ready to penetrate and thus dominate this mass of constantly evolving sexual signals. Left behind by evolution, frozen in time, the male straightforwardly inherits those characteristics that have always provided him with dominance: strength, tenacity, entrepreneurship, business acumen, sexual attractiveness, power, the capacity to manufacture cheap baubles, and so on. According to sociobiological thinking, it is only the female animal that needs to change drastically, to shift her physical appearance and social relationship with the environment, so as to fulfill her destiny within the evolutionary history of the species. The male tends to get stronger, because the female tends to get weaker and more compliant with his fundamental needs.[33]

Although there are many more animalistic reductions in modern sociobi-ology,[34] as well as in other related disciplines, particularly behavioral psychology, the preceding should suffice to give one an impression of the modern restoration of the animal/human relation. In his earlier work, E. O. Wilson, intent on establishing the centrality of generic influences on modern civilization, constantly invoked the animal-in-the-human to explain the inevitability of the status quo: powerful, athletic, almost apelike men conquered subservient, though physically attractive, women, spreading their super-genes to a race of indomitable proto-capitalists, who still reign supreme. However, as ridiculous as the adaptive stories concocted by the sociobiologists and pop ethologists may seem,[35] they still carry, in somewhat altered form, the indelible mark of mastery and human subjugation demonstrated by virtually all of the aforementioned means of control and power. Regardless of the area in which the individual writer is working, there is always a hierarchy of worth and status: men are superior to women, bosses to workers, whites to everyone else, the cognitive elite to the underclass, and so on. In large part, the appropriation of Darwinian and advanced evolutionary biological concepts and terminologies by sociobiology and pop ethology becomes a kind of calculus of superiority, a means by which the objectivity associated with science can be invoked to substantiate the status quo.

Moreover, a good deal of the conceptual underpinnings of sociobiology and pop ethology can be found outside the domain of science, in the sorts of ideological discourses that undergird the prevailing capitalist, free-market ideologies to which they are so doggedly attached. For example, much of the core thinking underlying sociobiology and pop ethology is contained in the philosophical movement called ethical egoism, widely acknowledged in the post-war period—particularly, the version espoused by Ayn Rand. Rand and her followers hold that rational beings will always act in their own self-interest and, oddly enough, that these interests will never conflict.[36] Because self-interest has much greater breadth and value when acted upon by wealthy and powerful individuals, the universal aspect of the concept is really no more than a justification for seeking power over others whose self-interests are not backed by immense capital. Everyone is compelled to act this way, but the rich and powerful do it infinitely better. This is not unlike, I suggest, the sociobiological concept of the genetically determined inevitability of the strong overwhelming the weak as a means of removing all barriers, especially ethical ones, to doing just that. In the end, these biologically based movements, much like the others we have seen in this section on modernity, are reinscriptions and restorations of traditional methods of assigning animal status (evolutionary in this case) to those whom elites wish to control, dominate, or eliminate. Darwin's idea of sexual selection, so egregiously misused in the latter part of the nineteenth century to suppress women, has now metamorphosed into Desmond Morris's sexy bras, big booties, and bright red lipstick, so essential to attracting males in the modern human zoo.

XII

Containing the Criminogenic

The association of criminals with animals is common to virtually all periods of history. We have seen convicts and presumed enemies of the state thrown to the lions, tigers, and bears in ancient Rome; Lombrosian criminal types associated with murderous storks, and compared anatomically with apes and other animals; as well as runaway slaves chained in pens with cowbells hung around their necks. Although criminological methods and science have no doubt advanced in the modern era, there are still certain elements in the criminal justice and penal systems that associate criminality with some form of animality, and sometimes act on this association to suppress targeted groups and individuals.

The conventional ethical wisdom regarding the issue of crime and punishment suggests that crime should not go unpunished, and that, in addition, punishment will deter the commission of further crimes, though there is a great deal of controversy over what constitutes appropriate retributive punishment. Still, crime and punishment are by no means black-and-white subjects. On the actual sociocultural level, there is an element of power, both political and socioeconomic, that regularly drives and influences these two central issues. Indeed, punishment is often used to contain and restrain certain elements in a particular society, and thus to provide the punishers with mastery and control over the punished. A perfect historical example of this tendency is the Bloody Code, the name traditionally given to the English system of criminal law during the period 1688 to 1815.[1]

The Code consisted of a long list of capital crimes, many of which were patently absurd. For example, to steal a horse was a capital crime punishable by death; so was pickpocketing more than a shilling, or stealing more than forty shillings; allowing a fishpond to overflow so that fish escaped was punishable by hanging, as was cutting down trees in an orchard or garden. Although the Code served a variety of legitimate purposes regarding policing and security, one of its primary functions was to protect an emerging bourgeoisie, a merchant class with money and property. The severity of the Code was intended not just to deter crime itself, but also to deter crimes that would disrupt the security and mobility of a powerful, well-connected, emerging class. To impose such a code, at least after the decline of the British monarchy, required certain justifications, as British law was presumably there to protect the rights of the accused as well as those of the offended. For the most part, early (i.e., prior to the advent of capitalist, free-market liberalism) justifications were egalitarian, stating that the law was dispassionate, dedicated to protecting the full spectrum of economic and social stratifications. This was just a smokescreen, though, intended to create the illusion of inclusive legal justice granting the same impartiality to everyone: "As Gramsci was later to explain it, social hegemony is only truly attained when a ruling class can persuade those it rules that the norms and sanctions of society, which in reality benefit only the privileged few, are devised for the good of all."[2]

The reduction of criminals or presumed criminals to a level of animality serves a similar function in modern society. If the lowest status possible—in this case, sheer bestiality—can be assigned to certain criminals or criminal types, if they can be identified as a palpable danger to society as a whole, then it becomes relatively easy to impose powerful restrictions and punishments on these groups in the name of preserving the very fabric of the social order. We have already seen an instance of this technique in the work of D'Souza, Herrnstein, Murray, Wilson, and others.[3] Their common position regarding crime is that most of it is committed by minorities, and mostly by "underclass" blacks. This, in turn, gives the impression that there is a stampeding, completely unruly "herd" out there that threatens the very values of American life. The solution to the problem is invariable: increase the breadth and intensity of policing directed toward these individuals; arrest them, arbitrarily frisk them, and detain them; and generally contain them, either by restricting their movement outside their neighborhoods or by physical incarceration. To justify these clearly unconstitutional and often downright illegal exercises under the color of law, this group must be singled out and vilified in some extraordinary way. These minority groups, as noted earlier, are referred to as "wilders," as out of control, and as incapable of ever being properly remediated or, more bluntly, trained—in short, as veritable "wild children."[4] Other groups influenced by this kind of thinking employ slightly different types of animal comparisons. The Manhattan Institute, a conservative think tank shaped by Murray-Herrnstein-J. Q. Wilson thinking regarding crime and punishment, expresses the same elitist class message in terms of degeneration and social marginality. Their approach is not so much an outright appeal to fear—of a dark, uncontrollable, dangerous pack of creatures running around out there in the night—as is the case with much racist ideology, but rather an appeal to the quality of life, the discomfort of having detritus-like individuals interacting with true humans on a daily basis:

> To use their analogy, a broken window left unrepaired sends the signal that no one is in charge, and soon gives way to a neighborhood of broken windows, and worse.
>
> Our experience in New York has proven this theory true. Five years ago, the police department began addressing so-called small crimes for the first time in decades. For the most part, they simply resumed enforcing laws already on the books: statutes against turnstile jumping, public drunkenness and urination, aggressive panhandling, excessive noise, and the like. . . . Thus by applying "broken windows" policing, we're able to get predators off the street. . . .
>
> Graffiti is more than an eyesore. It is a living symbol of contempt for property rights of and the rejection of principles that have defined civilizations for centuries. . . . As with graffiti, dirty streets and parks signal a lack of respect for property and breed fear and disorder.[5]

Despite the fact that there is not a single mention in the entire handbook of homelessness, which is one of the main causes of acts like "public urination," as well as other violations and derogations of the quality of New York City life, and aside from the fact that the manual is by and large a guide book for wealthy private entrepreneurs to take over city services and management, there is much here that involves traditional forms of reduction to animality. Although no ethnic or racial group is mentioned explicitly, there is a strong indication—a form of guilt by association—that the loathsome criminogenic "underclass" is at work again. If we focus attention on the narrative construction of the preceding excerpt, this becomes much clearer. For example, in the first mention of "broken windows," there is a strong implication of spreading danger and the loss of social control. The central message is capped off with an "and worse," which creates an open-ended sense of urgency and dread. Following this caveat, quality-of-life crimes are described and inventoried. The terminology once again tends to increase the impression of a diametrical opposition between good and bad people, and to create a sense of disorder and impending danger: "public urination and drunkenness," "aggressive panhandling," and "excessive noise" all strike a chord of flagrant negative public conduct, but, most importantly, a chord of disgust for wildness and bestiality—a veritable attack on the sensibilities of presumably decent people. After all, the very image of public urination is usually one of a dog lifting his leg at a fire hydrant. Images of public drunkenness, and uncontrolled and presumably filthy panhandlers rubbing against and shaking down sanitary, upright citizens, clearly carry a connotation of imminent danger and lack of civilized manners. Finally, the reference to graffiti is yet another means of creating a situation incommensurate with civilized conduct. Graffiti writers are also criminals in the making, vandals and barbarians who create "a living symbol of contempt for property rights of and the rejection of principles that have defined civilizations for centuries." Littered parks and dirty streets, too, "signal a lack of respect for property and breed fear and disorder." Now, none of these expressions directly implicate the underclass, and they do not explicitly name any particular ethnic or racial group, but they effectively imply, by the use of uncivilized and animalistic imagery, that some dangerous segment of society must be controlled or eliminated.

This becomes even clearer in a book by George L. Kelling and Catherine M. Coles, entitled *Fixing Windows*, in which the authors include several other quality-of-life crimes usually associated with minorities and/or minority communities: namely, street prostitution, menacing behavior, and vandalism.[6] In the end, the call for elimination of these groups and perpetrators revisits precisely what Gramsci argued earlier: the implication is that the restraint of this criminal element will free all of society from fear and improve the quality of life, whereas in reality it simply provides a means of protection for private property—one of the foundations of conservative social theory—and tends to underscore the strict divisions between classes, emphasizing in a roundabout way the palpable inferiority of minorities and the poor, the so-called criminogenic underclass. Besides, delinquency ultimately entails a link to surveillance, providing a justification for police and other governmental authorities to keep watch on groups and neighborhoods considered dangerous to the free exercise of ruling class power: "Delinquency, with the secret agents that it procures, but also with the generalized policing that it authorizes, constitutes a means of perpetual surveillance of the population: an apparatus that makes it possible to supervise, through the delinquents themselves, the whole social field."[7]

The notion of a criminogenic underclass that demonstrates animal-like behavior is also clearly at the root of what became known in the early 1990s as the "violence initiative." The concept was precisely the one underlying biologically based theories of inferiority over the past two centuries: there is some inherent, biologically/genetically based flaw or insult in certain races, classes, and individuals that compels them to act the way they act. Nonetheless, the violence initiative of the 1990s was really not particularly new in contemporary America. Programs employing the same idea were undertaken in the 1970s, under the assumption that the so-called race riots in large American cities were caused by brain disease and genetic defects in certain blacks, particularly their leaders. A number of physicians of the period even advocated performing psychiatric brain surgery—lobotomy—on some of the participants and their leaders to relieve the intense "psychotic" compulsion to resist and riot. In Mississippi, doctors actually performed brain surgery on black children considered hyperactive or especially aggressive.[8] The impulse to control social behavior through biology even spread to universities in this 1970s surge, with UCLA being scheduled to begin research on the biology of violence, particularly that of the inner city.

Although most of this research was abandoned quickly, largely because of its uncanny and uncomfortable resemblance to proto-Nazi and Nazi inquiries into the connection between racial characteristics and certain types of "inherent diseases," it was resurrected by a relatively obscure researcher from the National Institutes of Mental Health (NIMH), Frederick Goodwin. Goodwin, a soldier in the war to establish a biological basis for criminal behavior,[9] built his vision of a widespread violence initiative on research done with rhesus monkeys. In a public comment that Goodwin later retracted, he argued that there might be a direct parallel between rhesus monkeys and inner-city youth, in that, as "jungle dwellers," both were primarily concerned with killing each other, having sex, and reproducing:[10]

> Now, one could say that if some of the loss of structure in this society, and particularly in the high impact inner city areas, has removed some of the civilizing evolutionary things that we have built up and that maybe it isn't just careless use of the word when people call certain areas of certain cities jungles, that we may have gone back to what might be more natural.[11]

Although the initiative itself was stalled for a while, because of pressure exerted by certain members of Congress, it was reinstated in 1992, and the rhesus monkeys were, so to speak, released anew. This time, though, the conception of animal/human parallelism was couched in more acceptable and presumably objective scientific terminology. Aggression, located in the brain chemistry and genes of certain individuals, was now seen as the primary cause of violence. If neuropsychiatrists and biologists could discover a compelling aggressive trend in inner-city youth, they could, at least in principle, cure violence in America, particularly among that troublesome underclass. The demonstrational model associated with this claim of serotonin depletion due to sluggish serotonergic neurotransmission was, once again, based on those benighted monkeys. The source of its inspiration was most likely a brief article published in an issue of *Archives of General Psychiatry*, referring to patterns of aggression among monkey clans.[12] The study purported to find "correlates of aggression" in free-ranging rhesus monkeys, although it noted that the conclusions were based on observations of already existing wounds on various members of the rhesus clan. However, there are criticisms to the effect that

> using bite wounds and scars to determine high levels of aggressivity is extremely misleading. The title of the study speaks of "correlates of aggression," but the study actually looks at victims of aggression—animals with multiple wounds. Battered wives wind up with more wounds than their husbands. So do pugilists who lose in the ring, as well as children who get bullied on the playground or beaten by their parents. More important, the number of wounds, old and new, would reflect stress more than aggressivity.[13]

Despite the misinterpreted evidence, the nascent violence initiative advanced at a rapid pace. Several professional papers citing the correlation between violent behavior and serotonin appeared. They argued that depletion of this neurochemical was central to virtually all juvenile delinquency, and that the early effects of this condition appear to continue into adulthood. Once the "sufferers" had been identified, the wheels of medico-psychiatric power began to turn. Small groups of presumably at-risk youths were subjected to invasive testing, including spinal taps, use of neuroleptic drugs, and the injection of radioactive tracers into the brain. Spinal taps are particularly invasive, painful, and dangerous, especially when administered to young children. The procedure often requires sedation, long periods of physical immobility, and sometimes results in severe headaches as an aftereffect. Regardless of these side effects, the testing was carried on at an increasingly high level. There were also numerous other experiments coordinated to coincide with the development of new drugs and improved drug applications. Zoloft and Prozac, two of America's best-selling drugs, function as serotonin triggers. In fact, the experiments with Prozac tended to reintroduce the ubiquitous monkey, though this time as a rather playful, sedate, and friendly creature: "The animal studies show that higher levels of a key serotonin metabolite, called 5-HIAA, make more playful and gregarious monkeys. . . . On drugs that increase the uptake of serotonin, such as the much-prescribed antidepressant Prozac, both humans and monkeys tend to interact better in social situations and show little aggression."[14] Breggin and Breggin respond to such statements by claiming that they are based on interviews with federal researchers and that there is convincing evidence to the contrary regarding the effects of Prozac: "the drug can cause violence and suicide, but there's little evidence that it can cure either one."[15]

In a certain sense, the little rhesus monkey stands as the central figure in this complex socioeconomic and political struggle to reduce violence and enrich certain drug companies. The rhesus monkey not only provides the (erroneous) evidential motivation for the whole project, but also serves as the indispensable symbol for exploitation and mastery over a segment of society. If, as has been the case in virtually all reductions to animality, one can associate a group with some lower animal or animal behavior, a bridge between savagery, primitiveness, exclusion, and all those derogations related to animality can be easily and effectively erected. The mere statement that inner-city youth are aggressive and violent for strictly bioscientific reasons (that is, as the result of a highly technical and complex biochemical, molecular brain reaction) lacks effective ideological and propagandistic cachet. Medico-psychiatric power and mastery and class ideology do not operate well in this sort of otherworldly technical environment. Once the monkey arrives on the scene, though; once the coded parallel between animality and the so-called underclass is established, the strictly scientific conception connects with popular racist ideology and thinking. The sociopolitical dimension of science is then operative within its professional and technical formation; its function as a weapon protecting upper- and middle-class values is wholly established. The full force of federal agencies, private foundations, research universities, and other segments of the scientific community are thrown against these traditional nuisances, these outsiders. The fact that the offenders' behavior can be associated directly with the aggressive acts of other "jungle dwellers"—the ubiquitous monkeys—provides strong popular support and impetus for such projects. It dehumanizes the subjects, while at the same time justifying the performance of what amount to painful and unwarranted experiments on these animal-like "aggressors." Much like the Nazis' heinous experiments on "vermin-like" Jews, the violence initiative supporters benefited greatly from the association of an already degraded, feared, and detested segment of the American population—inner-city children of color—with animals and animal behavior.

One of the alternatives to "curing" crime on a national and neuromolecular level is to contain it by imprisoning as many real or potential criminals as possible. Nevertheless, the concept of imprisonment is not only a way of limiting and deterring crime and criminality, nor is it strictly a form of personal punishment. It also serves numerous authoritarian functions, particularly with regard to the idea of the deprivation of liberty. Briefly stated, as the democratic political models emerging from the Enlightenment exalted liberty, the power to remove it took on awesome authority. As such, in the early modern era, imprisonment—the power to restrict and oversee free movement—became the ultimate practical form of punishment, taking the place previously held by more severe forms: "in eighty years penal detention replaced public execution as a calculated technique for altering individual behavior."[16]

The power of imprisonment has not diminished in the modern era. It still occupies a central place in the punishment and, in many instances, the derogation of human beings. Given this dual function, punishment finds distinct parallels with certain forms of animalization. As I have argued previously, one of the principal theories of animalization supports isolation—figuratively speaking, caging—or, in more familiar language, colonization. One of the practical strategies of colonization is to restrict, surveil, and control every function of the lives of the colonized. As we saw in the case of the Congo Free State, the natives were contained strictly within certain areas, their food supplies were rigorously limited and controlled, and even their movement from place to place was tightly restricted. In fact, the only movements officially sanctioned were those dictated by the needs of the Belgian state: namely, large-scale, arduous treks to and from commercial enterprises. In a larger sense, the psychology behind colonization was to make the subjects of colonization feel totally degraded and defeated, dehumanized in the sense that they lacked any freedom to act on their own.[17] In a certain sense, this turns humans into the equivalent of wild animals that are removed from the wild and caged in a kind of hypercontrolled zoo.

Even given the legitimacy of incarceration as an appropriate retribution for criminal acts, some modern penal institutions go so far in punishing certain individuals that they reflect the above-mentioned forms of colonized animalization. Although there are innumerable instances of this process of animalization in U.S. prisons, the example of Corcoran State Prison in California is strikingly exemplary. Corcoran is a maximum security prison that has a unit for the super bad called the Security Housing Unit (SHU). This unit holds largely minority individuals who are determined to be enormous security risks. The general layout and regimen of the place is much like that of most bad zoos, only significantly worse. In a facility ringed by miles of razor-wire fence, gun turrets, light towers, and a lethal electric fence, the SHU is a prison within a prison. The cells in the SHU are tiny; no work is allowed; there are no educational programs and no recreation other than the legally mandated one hour of exercise a day; and total isolation.[18] Indeed, the prisoners of the SHU unit do not even receive the usual perquisites enjoyed by animals held in bad zoos: relatively fresh food, adequate ventilation, occasional treats from loving children, and some recreational exercise.

One might well ask: Why imprison prisoners within a prison, itself geared to a high level of security? The answer seems to lie in the animalizing extremes of the act of imprisoning itself. Like the wildest of wild animals, or the sexually dangerous Hottentot Venus, or the "fearsome" Ota Benga, the SHU prisoners represent an absolute descent into wildness and inhumanity: they are the child killers, drug lords, mass murderers, and so on who cross the fine line between human and animal. By completely stifling them—by numbing all receptors, including those to food, fresh air, recreation, and human life itself—the example of the totally controlled animal is produced.

The animal is not merely caged. It is also, in a certain sense, created. The entire environment of the SHU, like that constructed in the colonized Congo, is built around the production of animality and control. Restlessness, boredom, anger, hostility, and savagery are all carefully cultivated within the confines of this prison within a prison. With nothing to do, little to eat, and virtually no opportunity to communicate or even move, the prisoners are rendered animal by the very environment in which they are forced to exist.

The rendering-animal of Corcoran state prisoners was manifested in even more extreme ways. What amounted to free-for-all fights were often staged between prisoners. They were intentionally isolated in exercise yards and placed in situations in which they were forced to confront one another. Guards bet on the outcome of the fights, giving them the feeling of cockfights or dogfights: "At the micro-level, COs (also known as 'screws' or 'bulls') were staging fights as a form of sadistic diversion, even videotaping the fights for later viewing, and gathering to watch the contests from gun towers."[19] This was, remarkably enough, only a minor part of the violence perpetrated against prisoners. Between 1989 and 1994, 175 inmates were shot with live rounds by California prison guards, and hundreds of others were shot with painful wooden-block baton rounds. Twenty-seven prisoners died. The reasons given for the shootings were that they were necessary to maintain safe control of unruly prisoners. Like wild animals out of control, rogue elephants or man-eating tigers, no one dared approach the prisoners unarmed. The guards and their superiors simply determined (and were officially supported in their determinations) that fights and other serious prison transgressions had to be handled by shooting rather than intervention. Other prisons also witnessed incredible scenes of torture, suggesting incidents of animalization in eighteenth-century madhouses. Indeed, a group of mentally ill prisoners at Pelican Bay State Prison "were being beaten, tortured and left to lie in their own excrement for days. In one case a prisoner who had gone mad in solitary confinement was submerged in a vat of boiling water until his skin dissolved. On better days 'therapy' for the mentally ill consisted of watching cartoons from inside a phone-booth-sized cage."[20]

Obviously, there is much more to be said about crime and punishment in the United States, as well as elsewhere. Nevertheless, the preceding indicates a strong element of modern-day animalization and thus mastery and control in the various processes of policing and penalizing certain groups and individuals.

Noticeable in this material is the disproportionate amount of surveillance, prohibition, incarceration, and police power directed at those traditional subjects of animalization: the poor; blacks; ethnic minorities; the underclass; those singled out as pathological, perverse, mentally ill; and so on. This is not, I believe, an anomaly. The underclass that is supposed to be running wild and "breaking windows" is assumed to represent an atavistic element in society. The graffiti writers, public urinators, squeegee men, vandals, and so on form a completely uncivilized pack that is seen as representing a clear and present danger to the very foundations of Western civilization.

Kelling and Coles define the threat as a latent "disorder," and lend it the scary substance of an inevitable domino effect: "The answer lies in the immediate fear that such disorderly behavior engenders in the local community when it reaches a critical mass, and in the potential for more serious crime, urban decline, and decay that may ultimately follow on the heels of unconstrained disorder."[21] The presumed biological insults of inner-city youth are also traced to animalistic, uncivilized characteristics: they are compared to monkeys, and, extrapolating from data derived from monkey behavior, seen as aggressive and savage. With a crisis looming, the only way to cure the internal and inevitable biologically induced faults is to remove them, to excise them from the victim and society itself, as the lobotomizers and shock therapists have suggested over the past century. If the violence initiative had continued, that was exactly what would have happened: thousands, perhaps millions, of inner-city children would have been exposed to neurochemical brain tampering.

Last, and perhaps worst, of all is the sub-animal treatment of prisoners, particularly those incarcerated in ultra-high-security units. They are neither compared overtly to animals nor treated as if they were animals, but, rather, given no choice other than to become the lowest form of animal. Indeed, one can nowadays experience the persistence of such forms of penal degradation with Seymour Hersh's breaking of the torture scandal at Abu Ghraib prison in Iraq, where Iraqi prisoners were not only routinely sexually humiliated and tortured, but in one striking, highly publicized, remarkably visible instance, led around on a dog leash.[22]

XIII

The Beast and the Human/Machine

Like one who, on a lonely road,
Doth walk in fear and dread,
And, having once turned round, walks on,
And turns no more his head;
Because he knows a frightful fiend
Doth close behind him tread.

—Samuel Taylor Coleridge,
"The Rime of the Ancient Mariner"

One of the most pressing questions of the postmodern era is that of the human/ machine relation. It is omnipresent in virtually all the technical, social, and humanistic disciplines. Computer scientists, philosophers, engineers, anthropologists, ethicists, sociologists, and even primatologists have offered some solution to or account of the problem. The question is searing because, among other things, it involves a dilemma of human identity and a potential threat to that identity. If the traditional markers of human identity—emotion, sensitivity, imagination, pattern recognition, and so on—can be programmed into sophisticated machines, the entire designation of "human" becomes uncertain and, in that respect, threatened. Humans are presumably on a fateful collision course with their own devices.

Precisely when this issue arose is open to debate. One could argue that the question of the human's place in a world that was being rapidly industrialized and instrumentalized was broached even as early as the Romantic era, with the representative literary work being, of course, Mary Shelley's *Frankenstein* (1816). With the advent of *Frankenstein*, creation in the form of reanimation became an issue of science, and thus was at least in small part removed from its

169

long-established theological context. Mechanized and electrified technology, a force that held great power as well as great danger, had permanently entered the human world. The monster became a force to be reckoned with:

> "Begone! I do not break my promise; never will I create another like your-self, equal in deformity and wickedness."
>
> "Slave, I before reasoned with you, but you have proved yourself un-worthy of my condescension. Remember that I have power; you believe yourself miserable, but I can make you so wretched that the light of day will be hateful to you. You are my creator, but I am your master; obey!"[1]

The monster's threat resounded through the next two centuries, leading to an abiding interest in the question of the machine's mastery over humans. The modern debate, as mentioned, has taken numerous forms, many of which involve a broad range of technological disciplines. For instance, the media and the technological reproduction of images were seen as central to this ongoing consideration of human/machine relations. Walter Benjamin's groundbreaking essay, "The Work of Art in the Age of Its Technological Reproducibility," fo-cuses directly on the relationship between the physical presence of an artwork and its reproduction by some photographic process. Benjamin argues that the reproduction of an artwork eliminates a crucial element, the "aura," which is an aesthetic sensation produced by the artwork in its actual setting—a sensation felt only by a direct spectator. The results of the loss of aura, according to Ben-jamin, also extend to the human; the reproduction of human images results in the loss of humanness itself. Consequently, the reproduced image of the human becomes a commodity: "the cult of the movie star, fostered by the money of the film industry, preserves not the unique aura of the person but the 'spell of per-sonality,' the phony spell of a commodity." The commodification of human im-ages, in turn, creates an interposition between the human and the mechanical, the reproduced image. Confusion is created between the real and the image of the real. The final result is that "when you reproduce anything that formerly had aura (or life), the effect is to dislocate the image from the aura, leaving only the image. At this point, the image is neutral, it has no greater inherent power than commodities."[2] With this single act of reproduction (the removal of images from ordinary experience), human beings lose one of the aspects that differentiate them from objects. In a certain respect, they are themselves objectified.

This objectification of the human is further pursued in the work of me-dia theorist Marshall McLuhan, particularly in his notion of media serving as an "extension of man." Briefly stated, this idea assumes that fragmentary and mechanical technologies extend our bodies in space. The industrial machine, for example, is able to do work that we originally did with our hands. The radio is an extension of human speech; television, of sight; the computer, of thought, and so on. All of this was, naturally, a boon to technological progress, resulting in vastly increased industrial production and communication, which in turn gathered isolated communities and cultures into what McLuhan called a "global village." But this progress was not free of drawbacks:

> With the arrival of electronic technology, man extended, or set outside himself, a live model of the central nervous system itself. To the degree that this is so, it is a development that suggests a desperate and suicidal autoamputation, as if the central nervous system could no longer depend on the physical organs to be protective buffers against the slings and arrows of outrageous mechanism.[3]

Furthermore:

> The principle of numbness came into play with electronic technology, as with any other. We have to numb our central nervous system when it is extended and exposed, or we will die. Thus the age of anxiety and of electronic media is also the age of the unconscious and of apathy. . . . With our central nervous system strategically numbed, the tasks of conscious awareness and order are transferred to the physical life of man, so that for the first time he has become aware of technology as an extension of his physical body.[4]

The arrival of this externalized being, one rooted in extension rather than immanence, is also accompanied by the novel shift of human agency to non-human or artificial entities. Perhaps no area is more indicative of this shift than the relation between humans and computers, the swing from human to machine subjectivity. This shift, moreover, implies that we have effectively equated humans with machines by allowing the human/machine metaphor to run completely out of control, by subordinating and amputating those characteristics thought to be most human:

> The fundamental metaphorical message of the computer, in short, is that we are machines, thinking machines, to be sure, but machines nonetheless. It is for this reason that the computer is the quintessential, incomparable, near-perfect machine of Technopoly. It subordinates the claims of our nature, our biology, our emotions, our spirituality. The computer claims sovereignty over the whole range of human experience, and supports its claim by showing that it "thinks" better than we can. Indeed, in his almost hysterical enthusiasm for artificial intelligence, Marvin Minsky has been quoted as saying that the thinking power of silicon "brains" will be so formidable that "If we are lucky, they will keep us as pets." An even giddier remark, although more dangerous, was offered by John McCarthy, the inventor of the term "artificial intelligence." McCarthy claims that "even machines as simple as thermostats can be said to have beliefs."[5]

The point of this is that those characteristics always thought to be distinctly human are simply, and conveniently, grafted onto machines, computers in this case. Even the most basic human attribute of belief is denied its origin and place within the human mind itself. Instead, it is seen as merely an action, something done, and thus as an attribute of virtually any functional machine, even a thermostat. This, in turn, extends what we ordinarily consider human subjectivity, with all its cognitive and sensitive functions, to a vast range of external systems and objects. If what is most distinctly human, restricted to our conception of subjectivity, can be extended to virtually any machine, system, or medium that can simulate thinking, or sensing, or movement (robotics), or imagery, then these external systems and media will profoundly affect the way in which we act and relate to ourselves. Humans are thus not only compelled to share their own attributes with external systems and machines, but also must necessarily alter the locus and center of their own actions, thought, and volition in general.

With the movement of machines into roles usually held by humans, and in many areas the displacement of humans by machines, the groundwork for a new way of thinking arises: the problematic result of the breakdown of the mechanical and organic worldviews. The mechanical worldview includes nature in the same category as technology. Nature consists of a set of mechanical organisms without any inherent vitality, that is, wants or needs that require moral consideration. Nature is merely another source for technology, and the tools derived from natural sources are obtained free of any moral consideration. To kill an animal or cut down a tree is merely a way of achieving some human goal. In contrast, the organic worldview is quite different. According to this view, the world is permeated with some form of spirit or vital force. In this sense, everything in the world, not just human beings, has some intrinsic rights: "St. Francis of Assisi argued that animals helped to glorify God in their own way, independent of their usefulness to human beings, and that they deserved ethical treatment based on their intrinsic rights to existence."[6]

The problem, then, is a breakdown of the distinction between the organic and the mechanical. The play *R.U.R*, written by Karel Căpek in 1921, is exemplary of this breakdown. Briefly, a famous physiologist, Rossum, invents a chemical synthesis that imitates living matter. He tries desperately to create living beings, failing with animals and having only limited success with humans. Finally, he is successful in creating human beings, but ones limited in their ability to feel and create; that is, soulless. He opens a factory and grinds out huge numbers of simple robots, which are eventually upgraded by another scientist to fully human beings with souls, emotions, and rational minds. At that point they revolt against the humans, kill them, and eventually discover how to reproduce, creating a fresh line of beings through a new Adam and Eve. The point of the play, though complex, is that, like the unfortunate Victor Frankenstein, a science that attempts to derive the organic from the mechanical or vice versa will produce monsters bent on its own destruction. There is a basic, inviolable incommensurability between the mechanical and the vital, between living and inorganic matter.

With the barriers between the organic and mechanical removed, or at least in a state of imminent collapse, the designation of "life-form" becomes something of a free-for-all. Just about anything that can be assigned intelligence, free movement, or even thermostatic beliefs, as McCarthy proposed, can be seen as also having some form of practical animation. This naturally leads to the development and to the potential problems of special fields devoted to working with these artificial systems, artificial intelligence (AI) and artificial life (AL). AI and the extension of artificial systems of intelligence to business, education, and various other social functions and institutions have both supporters and detractors. We have seen the general drift of detraction. Most of those opposed to AI and AL stress their alienating and dehumanizing potential. Supporters look at the question in a very different way. Their more or less common take on AI and AL is that the achievement of AI or AL alone is enough to ennoble human reason, to "boost our self-respect," as Marvin Minsky put it. Rather than dehumanizing us, AI research has led us to appreciate the subtlety and depth of human qualities and abilities. In short, the amputation makes us more acutely aware of what we have. Still, even those who support the development of expert systems and their integration into society are uneasy about the prospect. Daniel Crevier, author of *AI*, expressed his concern thus:

> When machines acquire an intelligence superior to our own, they will be impossible to keep at bay. ... The evolution of life on earth is itself nothing but a four-billion-year-long tale of offspring superseding parents. The unrelenting progress of AI forces us to ask the inevitable question: Are we creating the next species of intelligent life on earth? Whatever the outcome, we will have to radically reexamine our values.[7]

The implications of these modern "amputations" of human qualities have led inevitably to a debate about the status of the human in the postmodern era. Perhaps at no point in the history of the term has "human" been assigned so many prefixes: non-human, post-human, in-human, and more. The debate, at least on a philosophical level, centers on the conflicting positions of posthumanism and techno-science. Both positions are largely extensions of their namesakes: posthumanism consists of a more skeptical reiteration of post-Enlightenment humanism, and techno-science (a term invented by Lyotard) describes the forces involved in extending the domain of technology at the expense of humanity. The somewhat malevolent techno-science position is in part credited, though perhaps unfairly, to Donna J. Haraway, a primatologist and feminist theoretician who tends to place considerable emphasis on the idea of the post-human.[8]

Lyotard has expressed his position regarding the human and inhuman in several works, and one might even say that these were significant issues as early as the publication of *The Postmodern Condition* (1984). His most extensive and rigorous attacks on techno-science, however, are found in a series of loosely related essays collected under the title *The Inhuman* (1991). The most provocative and relevant essay is "Can Thought Go on without a Body?," in which the title question is answered largely in the negative. The practical reason that Lyotard advances for this response is that, for techno-science to achieve the elimination of the body so as to fully install AI and AL in the future, it would have to recognize difference and eliminate the element of time; this would, ultimately, undermine the efficiency necessary for techno-science to function. Still, there are other reasons for his rejection of bodiless thought. For Lyotard, human thought, integral to the functions of bodily sensation and experience, requires an unpredictable future. The aleatory course of future events is, for him, the precondition of thought itself. With virtually everything externally and systematically planned, no intuitive human thought is necessary, and therefore the body becomes merely an empty mechanical extension, an operative machine capable only of movement and instrumentation. Against this prospect Lyotard argues:

> It's obvious from this objection that what makes thought and the body inseparable isn't just that the latter is the indispensable hardware for the former, a material prerequisite of its existence. It's that each of them is analogous to the other in its relationship with its respective (sensible, symbolic) environment: the relationship being analogical in both cases. In this description there are convincing grounds for not supporting the hypothesis (once suggested by Hilary Putnam) of a principle of the "separability" of intelligence, a principle through which he believed he could legitimate an attempt to create artificial intelligence.[9]

Donna Haraway takes the other side in the human/inhuman controversy. Her position, though complex and worked out over a considerable period of time, basically embraces the idea of inhumanism in the name of feminism. For Haraway, the figure of the cyborg is a way to avoid gendered existence. It is also a key to "reinventing nature"—the subtitle of her book—so as to establish a whole new set of social relationships that are not based on traditional patterns of male dominance. Cyborgs are figures of sexual neutrality, lacking distinct biological characteristics that can be attributed to either feminine or masculine identity or roles. As pure machines, they carry with them nothing of the history of female repression: "Cyborgs effectively bypass biology and all the social history attached to it, and, in so doing, all the problems connected with biological determinism and essentialism that the feminist movement has been wrestling with for years."[10]

Haraway's embrace of the inhuman, then, is directed toward a radical politics of choice. As nothing, cyborgs are not committed to dogma, history, or essentialist thinking. They can be anything, but in so doing leave the human behind. This is the crux of Lyotard's criticism. The sacrifice of human qualities—of the body, for example—is, for him, a recipe for ruin. In direct contrast, for Haraway, it is precisely in this sacrifice of the body, of this coded biological entity, that women can transcend the repressive models that have traditionally held them hostage to specific gender and sexual roles and identities. If the body is extended to outside mechanical systems; if, as Haraway muses, the body does "not end at the skin," then women can gain ultimate power: "Intense pleasure in skill, machine skill, ceases to be a sin, but an aspect of embodiment. The machine is not an it to be animated, worshipped, and dominated. The machine is us, our processes, an aspect of our embodiment."[11]

The entire debate surrounding the human/machine, human/inhuman problem relates to the human/animal distinction. As we saw in part 1 of this book, much of Western thought regarding animals and their position vis-à-vis humans assumes a radical division between the two. Animals are first and foremost different from humans, and the difference is then articulated in negative terms. Indeed, Descartes and the tradition that followed him argued quite explicitly that animals are strictly machines, nothing more than mechanical devices that react to external stimuli. In this respect animals were already excluded from the human world. They had no viable means of communicating with humans, nor were they capable of sharing any substantive aspect of the human social world. In their presumed dumbness, animals were inevitably cast outside the realm of human interaction, into an "exterior-substance" universe that ran parallel to the human world but that never crossed over into it. With exile came a dimension of life that was remote and radically *other*—a dimension largely incommensurable with rational human life.

It is precisely the idea of this nether dimension occupied by the animal that subtly underlies the modern divisions *human/inhuman* and *human/machine*. If one thinks about how machines, cyborgs, robots, artificial and virtual realities, and so on are understood by both their supporters and detractors, this connection will become quite clear. The machine is always located outside the human world, or, perhaps more accurately, at the most extended limits of that world.

Machines are placed in the human world out of practical necessity; they suffer the dumbness of their hardware, of their very physical composition, even the fact that most of them have to be plugged in. Their evolution is neither organic nor self-sustaining, but, rather, entirely dependent on human progress. This, if we think about it, is precisely how—with certain exceptions—we have traditionally conceived of animals. They are there, as Kant argued, as a means to our ends, to benefit us. In this capacity, they are always external to us, living in a dimension that we believe we fully control—indeed, in certain respects, that we create. Like machines, they are seen as entirely dependent on our progress and history. We domesticate animals, collect them as specimens, breed them, categorize them, eat them, reduce them to taxonomic data; we set their limits, arguing over their cognitive, affective, and intellectual capacities, and whether they can or cannot attain language and understanding or moral capacity, feel pain, and so on. They are in this particular sense no different, no better or worse, no less practicable, than machines, because both are radically different from and external to the human world—dependent, from our perspective, for their very existence on humans and the humans' world.

In this sense, the idea of animality and its remoteness underlies virtually all of the human/inhuman–, human/machine–based arguments. The principal concern of Lyotard's position is that we do not surrender our humanity to techno-science, to the irrepressible march of advanced capitalism. But in what context is this notion of humanity conceived? It is precisely in the context of the necessity of not crossing the line between human and non-human, of establishing a firm difference between the ceaseless communicative chatter of the human and the silence of some exterior, animal world. Even as early as Aristotle, the humanness of humans was to a certain extent imparted by their difference from other animals. The fact that we could reflect on our moral behavior, perceive ourselves, and articulate our ideas in language lifted us to a state of dominance and mastery over those that were presumed unable to adequately demonstrate these capacities. To allow ourselves to be absorbed by the other on the outside of human conduct would be to surrender our human qualities, to admit our animality and all the presumed objectionable characteristics that attend it. In a very real sense, Lyotard is not only defending the human, but also, more subtly, resisting what he sees as a turn toward some inarticulate darkness—or, seen in a more hegemonic posture, human superiority over the entire animal domain. After all, the usually virtuous Aristotle of the *Lai d'Aristote*, ridden by the sensuous Phyllis, surrendered his exclusively human ability to discern right from wrong to become a desiring animal, as was the case with Ambrose Paré's monstrosities, which, through the forbidden act of bestiality, had sadly crossed the line between human and animal.

Haraway, in contrast, welcomes the shift from one dimension to another. She envisions the absorption into the world of machines, the transformation from human to cyborg, as a way of extirpating those negative humanly imposed characteristics associated with sex and gender. Haraway's phrase "the machine is us" represents a stepping over the threshold between the human and the other, whether it be an animal, a system, or a machine. For her, the cyborg represents another side of the theoretical fold, a radical move against patriarchy and a permanent release from "totalizing theories in general."[12] However, as is the case with Lyotard, this radical otherness is already carved out, set in place by millennia of eviction and marginality. The cyborg *is* the beast, writ in the modern configurations of machines and systems. The beast is thus what calls from the nether dimension, but not to offer immortality, bodilessness, great sex, or pure cyber-fantasy, as theoreticians of the "life-world" propose.[13] Restored as the thinking machine, as the other of the human, the animal once again haunts the discourses of modernity and postmodernity, but this time, perhaps, as something like the proverbial "ghost" in the machine.

Summary

The animal and the curse of animality, the mark of the beast, have not disappeared from modern and postmodern discourses. The beast has simply been reinscribed, restored, or dissimulated within these various discourses. The idea of animalistic inherency, of something inculcating darkness and fear, still functions in the sociopolitical and cultural texture of the modern era. With the advent of film and modern image production, the narrative of animality could be told in brilliantly emphatic detail, with sound, movement, special effects, and lifelike color. Although movies have no doubt contributed to a more widespread understanding of animals and their world, they have also tended to denigrate groups or types of humans by comparing them with lower animals. The negative characteristics of the apish criminal, the Lombrosian throwback, were superimposed onto filmic representations, associating those representations with evil or dumbness or savagery. As noted earlier, blacks were regularly portrayed as either animal-like or in close kinship with animals. Tarzan's drove of uncivilized blacks, which he felt he had to shepherd through life, turning them from evil and savagery, are examples of this filmic treatment. Without language or culture, costumed in animal pelts, bird beaks, and eagle feathers, they represented the ultimate descent into animality—considerably below his tribe of apes—redeemable only by the tough love of an abandoned but civilized white man: "Beware. Tarzan watches."

Reiterations of more traditional modes of mastery have also appeared in modern forms of racism and sexism. With the coarse and, for the most part, debunked modes of racist physical anthropology, craniology, comparative anatomy, and various other forms of somatic and hereditarian theory gone, a new, more modern, more scientific-sounding set of racist ideas and styles surged in to fill the void. These latter were based on supposedly objective scientific grounds, using the latest in genetics, psychometrics, IQ theory, and clinical psychology to restate the old hereditarian saw: the genetically superior will always and inevitably reign over the inferior, and this can be proven quantitatively. The reiteration and reconfiguration of the animal in this respect was largely based on recreating the images of hebetude, intellectual, cognitive, and emotional inferiority, and uncontrolled criminality traditionally associated with "lower types."

This sort of imagery also extends to women. The late-nineteenth-century emphasis on Darwin's idea of sexual selection has now been converted into medico-psychiatric myths of mothering and female responsibility. No longer fully oppressed by social and scientific patriarchy, women are now controlled by their failure to meet their inherent mammalian destiny. The idea of breeders and nurturers has been updated. Now, mothers who in some way fail to nurture according to a male-dominated vision of good mothering are open to suppression, opprobrium, and in some cases criminal prosecution. The power of the medico-psychiatric establishment is thus reestablished, not by imposing the inviolable laws of natural and sexual selection, but rather by insinuating itself into the very process of mothering, by determining the rules of proper nurturing and mothering behavior in general. This intrusion, as we have seen, also extends to other reproductive procedures. Sexual surgery, a means of directly controlling women in the nineteenth and early twentieth centuries, is now applied in a more subtle and socially acceptable way: it is used on the destitute, the poor, and women of color who are deemed unfit for mothering by the medical profession.

Sexism and conservative ideology are also reflected in the modern comparative human/animal behavioral science of popular forms of ethology. Certain ethologists argue for the irrepressible presence of the animal in the human. In this regard, they reduce the complexity of human social and sexual interaction—of human behavior in general—to a limited set of generic behaviors influenced by certain innate motivating factors. Ardrey, an avid supporter of the status quo, particularly when it comes to capitalism and free-market entrepreneurship, espoused a theory of territoriality commensurate with private property and singular devotion to regional values, regardless of their moral worth. Lorenz saw similar restrictions on human autonomy and behavior. For him, we are all moved by a deep-seated aggression, largely unchanged from the beginning of animal life on the planet. The only changes in the drive occur at the level of civilization and culture, but all of these are essentially preprogrammed to direct us to the adages of free marketry, individualism, nationalism, xenophobia, and virtually all other ultraconservative prerequisites. In brief, the creators of the "human zoo" and the "science" of comparative human/animal behavior use this method simply to reformulate traditional biases in the biosciences.

Like the more modern pop ethologists, Lombroso found a direct relation between crime and animality. He argued that criminals are born, not made, and, as such, are the product of some generic connection with their animalistic past. This, in a slightly altered form, was the position taken by some modern-day researchers regarding crime and criminality in certain groups and individuals. The roots of crime were deeply etched in the young criminal's brain in the form of neurochemicals. Moreover, once certain dangerous criminals were apprehended and incarcerated, the application of extreme punishments created an inescapable animalistic environment, the atmosphere of a bad zoo, in which torture, sensory deprivation, starvation, and sometimes outright killing were blithely tolerated.

Finally, the great human/machine question hovering around the threshold of the new millennium entails certain characteristics of animality. The beast lurks below the surface of the human/machine controversy. The posthumanist who opposes the inhuman is in a very real sense calling forth a resistance to being absorbed into the nether dimension of bestiality, a world in which we surrender our human qualities and become victims of the "dumbness" of machines. In contrast, there are those of a techno-scientific leaning who are more than willing to sacrifice these presumably exclusively human characteristics to start anew, to enter a world devoid of ossified biases regarding sex, gender, class, and race.

The question remaining in this millennium is clearly what can be done about this signature "mark of the beast" and about the kinds of human mistreatment associated with it. The answer lies, I propose, in a fundamental change of our sensibility, of our entire vision of animals and their place in the world—which, in turn, requires a sustained attack on attitudes that would impose and continually reimpose the mark of the beast. To begin with, one must ask a simple question: What's so bad about animals? The answer is unambiguous: Nothing at all. They have just been seen from a distinctly human perspective as representing an evil or dumb or savage side of the human being. Unfortunately, this error has been acted upon immemorially, often (as we have seen) with dire results.

The term *animal*, then, has a dual use. On the one hand, it is used to designate a species to which we belong; that is its detached and scientific use. On the other hand, however, it is "used to supply a foil, a dramatic contrast lighting up the human image."[14] It is in the latter use that the human notion of *animal* becomes negative, taking on the connotation of what should not be practiced by humans, and designating those acts that fall into what has been characterized as "the great dark outside non-human area." In many ways, this dark outside area has been maintained at the expense of both animals and certain humans. Aristotle acknowledged the detached, scientific status of animals—that is, as species within a greater composite of living things—but he denied the full integration of the lower animals. His denial was modeled on the human conception of moral reflection and rational thought. Because these cognitive qualities require a special kind of reflective consciousness that only humans have, Aristotle relegated the beasts to a level lower than humans.

In so doing, though, he created a long-standing rift in the "continuum," providing a basis for denigrating lower animals because of what they did not have, or, as Tim Ingold succinctly put it, "every attribute that it is claimed we uniquely have, the animal is consequently supposed to lack."[15] This, in turn, became a convenient means of identifying humans with certain defects and inadequacies. Bearing the mark of the beast meant that something had gone terribly wrong with an individual, a group, a race, a class, or a people. Furthermore, this reduction to bestiality became a powerful tool for the social control of these besieged peoples. To be associated in certain popular or scientific interchanges with, say, an ape already indicates some fundamental fault, one that automatically situates the person or group outside of the "illuminated human image." As such, they can be denigrated in any number of ways: associated with animal dumbness; with dark instinctual drives; with uncontrollable passions and savagery; with murderous tendencies and even cannibalistic ones.

This association, however, is an inured concept that survives at the margins of Western thought and science. Its roots lie in the prejudices and fallacies inherent in attitudes and thinking about race, sex, and human difference—beliefs that lead inevitably to alterity and division, to mapping animals and the animal-like, for instance, outside human worlds. There are alternatives to this kind of artificial division. One alternative is to conceive of all living beings as coexisting in an extensive continuum, one similar to Darwin's original vision of integrated animal life. Moreover, this sort of move requires the dissolution of barriers traditionally erected between humans and animals—for, in effect, a massive integration of all living things, an extensive continuum in A. N. Whitehead's sense of the term.[16] Also exemplary of this idea of a species continuum is what Gilles Deleuze and Félix Guattari call the "process of becoming-animal," which in their thinking "produces nothing other than itself. . . . What is real is the becoming itself, the block of becoming, not the supposedly fixed terms through which that which becomes passes."[17] This phenomenon can also be described as one in which "[t]he passages from man to animal are thought in terms of becoming.... Man and animal mutually affect one another, erasing each other's contours, forcing them to be lost in the continual metamorphoses that form neither one nor the other. ... Animality will thus be overcome, it will disappear and another direction will be created."[18] Simply put, the very process of becoming-animal dissolves the barriers between human and animal, creating a state in which "[m]an does not become wolf, or vampire, as if he changed molar species; the vampire and werewolf are becomings of man, in other words, proximities between molecules in composition, relations of movement and rest, speed and slowness between emitted particles."[19]

This conception of total integration is not, of course, peculiar to philosophical and critical/theoretical thought. Some ethologists have already, in their own ways, reached a similar conclusion. For them, though, the problem is largely one of translation. How do we understand the functional world of animals in their own terms, rather than as symbolic actions related to human behavior? The answer is to construct methodologies based on animal behavior rather than our own behavior, on animal action and communication rather than our own conceptions of the way they communicate and act—that is, to modify these methodologies so that they take into account and integrate certain human failings as well as those observed in animal behavior.

We must, then, drop the self-serving barrier of humanness as opposed to animality so carefully and persistently erected in Western thought over the millennia. By factoring our own idiosyncrasies and weaknesses into animal behavioral research—by admitting the animal *into* the human and vice versa—it is possible to create an empathetic relation between humans and animals, thus, at least in part, removing a major obstacle in creating a continuum of species.

Animal rights and animal liberation advocates also follow a path similar to the one I have proposed. In their general vision, animals must share the world with humans, not on an absolute basis of equality, but, rather, being given equal consideration in that they indisputably suffer and feel pain: "The basic principle of equality does not require equal or identical *treatment*; it requires equal consideration. Equal consideration for different individuals may lead to different treatment and different rights."[20] The notion of equal consideration is the hub of animal rights theory. It attacks speciesism on the ground that even though humans may have greater intelligence than other animal species, that intelligence gives them no right to exploit non-humans. This would be a clear case of failing to *consider* the rights of other species, which would be the same as denying rights to minorities or women on the ground that they are in some way different. The right to consideration is most definitely an absolute: "If a being suffers, there can be no moral justification for refusing to take that suffering into consideration."[21] Furthermore, this right quite clearly requires a unified and universal human moral obligation toward non-humans—what one might call a continuum of moral responsibility.

The substance of all these positions can, of course, be applied to disparaging the use of animality as a tool of human repression. If we believe that all beings that are similar in all relevant respects have an equal right to consideration, the egregiously fallacious arguments of the racists, sexists, biodeterminists, and so on become even more irrelevant and inoperative. To argue that some people have the right to exploit and master others because they are different becomes effectively meaningless. Difference, in this respect, is a category of power, one that sets a particular group above others, and, in so doing, claims mastery over those distinguished *as* others. This is exactly what I am arguing against. Racism, sexism, biodeterminism, molarity, speciesism, colonialism, and the like are all means of establishing and maintaining power over those who lack it. To attack these totalizing systems of power, self-interest and self-aggrandizement represent an important step in the largely political struggle for equality and fairness.

In the end, we should recall that, for Native Americans, it was a great honor to wear the skins, horns, and feathers of animals, and to adopt their names: Crazy Horse, Sitting Bull, White Eagle, Standing Bear, White Antelope, and the like. This was because they believed power came from nature and the earth, from a seamless continuum that included all living things. This concept was poignantly expressed in the Great Vision of the Oglala Sioux holy man Black Elk:

> And as I looked ahead, the people changed into elks and bison and all four-footed beings and even fowls, all walking in a sacred manner on the good red road together. And I myself was a spotted eagle soaring over them.... The leaves on the trees, the grasses on the hills and in the valleys, the waters in the creeks and in the rivers and the lakes, the four-legged and the two-legged and the wings of the air—all danced together to the music of the stallion's song.[22]

Notes

Preface

1. Quoted in Jean-François Lyotard, *Heidegger and "the Jews,"* trans. Andreas Michel and Mark S. Roberts (Minneapolis: University of Minnesota Press, 1990), 85.

Chapter I

1. Aristotle, *Zoology*, in *Selections*, trans. Phillip Wheelright (New York: Bobbs-Merrill, 1951), 109.
2. Ibid.
3. Ibid., 109–10.
4. Ibid., 113.
5. Aristotle, *De Anima*, bk. III, chs. 9–13.
6. Aristotle, *Nicomachean Ethics*, bk. III, ch. 2(1), trans. J. A. K. Thompson (Baltimore: Penguin Books, 1969), 83.
7. Ibid., 190.
8. Ibid.
9. Ibid., 221.
10. There is an immense amount of literature on this subject. Some of the more interesting and accessible of these are: Thomas Aquinas, *Philosophical Writings*; Boethius, *Consolation of Philosophy*; *The Didascalicon of Hugh of St. Victor*; and Boccaccio, *The Decameron*, among others.
11. Gregory B. Stone, "The Philosophical Beast: On Boccaccio's Tale of Cimone," in *Animal Acts: Configuring the Human in Western History*, ed. Jennifer Ham and Matthew Senior, 24 (New York: Routledge, 1997).
12. See Sigmund Freud, *The Ego and the Id* (New York: W. W. Norton, 1960), 19.
13. Stone, "The Philosophical Beast," 25.
14. Ibid., 27.
15. René Descartes, "Letter to the Marquis of Newcastle," in *Selections*, ed. Ralph M. Easton (New York: Charles Scribner's Sons, 1955), 357.

183

16. It should be noted here, as Rodis-Lewis and others have argued, that the main intent of the automaton "fable" is to distinguish what has a soul and what does not. Descartes himself noted this at the conclusion of part V of the *Discourse on Method*, where he argued that the power of motion is not sufficient to constitute a rational being, who needs a rational soul to also have feelings and appetites. The harsh separation of humans from animals, though, is not anything, nor a mere premise or set of premises attached to a larger argument. Intentionally or not, it sets up much of the Western distinction between intelligent life and mere sentient being, which, in the end, serves an important function in justifying the maltreatment and exploitations of animals and of those designated as animal-like.

17. Matthew Senior, "When the Beasts Spoke," in *Animal Acts*, ed. J. Ham and M. Senior, 67.

18. Ibid., 61.

19. Ibid., 64.

20. René Descartes, *Treatise on Man*, trans. Thomas Steele Hall (Cambridge, MA: Harvard University Press, 1972), 22.

21. René Descartes, "Letter to Henry More," in *Selections*, 360 (emphasis mine).

22. Geneviève Rodis-Lewis, "Limitations of the Mechanical Model in the Cartesian Conception of Organism," in *Descartes: Critical and Interpretive Essays*, ed. Michael Hooker, 165 (Baltimore: Johns Hopkins University Press, 1978). It should be pointed out here that the optimism shared by Descartes and Rodis-Lewis regarding the ease of human adaptation does not seem to take into account the remarkable adaptation of many other animal species. One of the best examples is the lowly, soulless cockroach, which has survived pretty much intact for approximately 100 million years.

23. Ibid.

24. René Descartes, *Discourse on Method* (pt. V), translated by John Cottingham et al. (Cambridge, UK: Cambridge University Press, 1988), 139–40.

25. Ibid., 141.

26. With respect to Descartes' reduction of animals to automata, Peter Singer makes a cogent argument for this being the first step in justifying the pain inflicted by animal experimentation, which, according to Singer, was a widespread practice at the time. Singer provides an eyewitness account of some of the experiments carried out at the Jansenist seminary at Port-Royal: "They administered beatings to dogs with perfect indifference, and made fun of those who pitied the creatures as if they felt pain.... They nailed poor animals up on boards by their four paws to vivisect them and see the circulation of the blood which was a great subject of conversation." Peter Singer, *Animal Liberation* (New York: HarperCollins, 2002), 201–3.

27. Immanuel Kant, *Anthropology from a Pragmatic Point of View*, trans. Victor Lyle Dowdell (Carbondale, IL: Southern Illinois University Press, 1978), 9.

28. Ibid., 238.

29. Ibid.

30. Ibid., 239.
31. See Descartes, *Discourse on Method*, 139–41.
32. Kant, *Anthropology*, 240.
33. Although this may have been believed during Kant's time, modern animal behavioral research has discovered numerous animal "gifts" that contradict this position. The building and passing on of habitational structures by animals, for example, is common to many species: gorillas leave beds of leaves and food for other gorilla clans; many species teach their young specific skills, which, in turn, are taught to the next generation; and so on. Even with regard to the coveted human quality of reasoning, there have been numerous modern-day discoveries of subtle forms of animal reasoning and communication. Elephants, for example, tend to continually learn and acquire new skills and problem-solving techniques throughout their life spans. Moreover, very recent studies of orangutans in Sumatra have revealed precisely the opposite of Kant's claim that animals do not evolve over generations. Indeed, these discoveries included the observations that orangutans learn certain complex living habits and pass them on to the next generation. See *Newsday*, January 3, 2003, A43. For further reading on animal intelligence, see, for example, Donald R. Griffin, *Animal Minds: Beyond Cognition and Consciousness* (Chicago: University of Chicago Press, 2001).
34. Tim Ingold, "Introduction," in *What is an Animal?* (London: Unwin Hyman, 1988), 3.
35. In this regard, one need only turn to characters like Hamlet, King Lear, Don Quixote, etc., to realize the integration of madness into art and society in the Renaissance.
36. Michel Foucault, *Madness and Civilization: A History of Insanity in the Age of Reason*, trans. Richard Howard (New York: Vintage Books, 1965), 70 (emphasis mine).
37. Ibid., 70 (quoting from Blaise Pascal, *Pensées*).
38. Ibid., 64.
39. Ibid., 70–71.
40. Ibid., 72.
41. Ibid., 72 (quoting Coguel).
42. Ibid., 72–73.
43. Ibid., 73.
44. Ibid., 74–75.

Chapter II

1. For a detailed historical account of race theory, see Ivan Hannaford, *Race: The History of an Idea in the West* (Baltimore: Johns Hopkins University Press, 1996).
2. Ibid., 267.
3. Arthur Comte de Gobineau, *The Moral and Intellectual Diversity of Races* (New York: Garland, 1984), 94.

4. Ibid., 314–15 (with exception of "wooly," the italics are mine).
5. Ibid., 433.
6. Ibid., 444 (quote from Pruner).
7. Ibid., 67, 69 (emphasis mine).
8. Quoted in Stephen Jay Gould, *The Mismeasure of Man* (New York: W. W. Norton, 1996), 118.
9. Morton's various errors, both intended and unintentional, in assembling his data are made patently clear in Gould, ibid., 82–101.
10. Ibid., 117.
11. Ibid., 118.
12. Ibid., 133. This "brain mythology" regarding the conformation of the brains of blacks has lasted well into the twentieth century. Frantz Fanon, in *The Wretched of the Earth* (New York: Grove Press, 1968), cites a striking example of exactly this kind of thinking. In a 1939 article that appeared in the *Southern Medical and Surgical Gazette*, Professor A. Porot wrote: "The Algerian has no cortex; or, more precisely, he is dominated, like the inferior vertebrates, by the diencephalons. The cortical functions, if they exist at all, are very feeble, and are practically unintegrated into the dynamic of existence."
13. Gould, *Mismeasure of Man*, 143.
14. See ibid., 146–47.
15. Ibid., 147–48.
16. Aristotle, *Zoology*, 113.
17. Cesare Lombroso, *Crime: Its Causes and Remedies*, trans. Henry P. Horton (Boston: Little, Brown, & Co., 1918), xiv.
18. Gould, *Mismeasure of Man*, 154.
19. Ibid.
20. Lombroso, *Crime*, xv.
21. Ibid.
22. Quoted in Gould, *Mismeasure of Man*, 136.
23. Ibid. (emphasis mine).
24. This is not to say that they did not at all apply the theory of sexual selection, or that they did not write about women's animality from an evolutionary perspective. Lombroso, for example, wrote: "Various as are these solutions of a singular problem, we may, I think, seek yet another. In female animals, in aboriginal women, and in women of our time, the cerebral cortex, particularly in the psychical centers, is less active than the male." Cesare Lombroso and William Ferrero, *The Female Offender* (New York: D. Appleton & Co, 1895), 111.
25. Cynthia Eagle Russett, *Sexual Science: The Victorian Construction of Womanhood* (Cambridge, MA: Harvard University Press, 1989), 63.
26. See ibid., 91–103 and passim.
27. Ibid., 102.
28. Sarah Baartman was finally interred in her native South Africa on August 8, 2002. Her remains were removed by the South African government from the

Musée de l'Homme that had long displayed them. *Newsday*, August 10, 2002, A-12.

29. See Sander L. Gilman, *Difference and Pathology: Stereotypes of Sexuality, Race and Madness* (Ithaca, NY: Cornell University Press, 1985), 76–108; Anita Levy, *Other Women: The Writing of Class, Race, and Gender, 1832–1898* (Princeton, NJ: Princeton University Press, 1991), 68–74.

30. Gould, *Mismeasure of Man*, 22.

31. Levy, *Other Women*, 70.

32. The restraint of sexual excesses by animal comparison was not by any means limited to women alone. Arnold I. Davidson, in his article "The Horror of Monsters," indicates that in the nineteenth century, some sign of bestiality marked many so-called sexual deviates and perverts. Sodomites, for example, at times had their sexual organs compared to those of dogs. Ambroise Tardieu, an early chronicler of pederasty and sodomy, wrote of the compulsive sodomist: "Having made him completely undress, we can verify that the virile member, very long and voluminous, presents at its tip a characteristic elongation and tapering that gives to the gland the almost pointed form of the penis of a dog." See "The Horror of Monsters," in *Boundaries of Humanity: Humans, Animals, Machines*, ed. James J. Sheehan and Morton Sosna (Berkeley: University of California Press, 1991), 60.

33. In this regard see also "Anal Eroticism and the Castration Complex," in *Standard Edition*, vol. 19, 72–88; and "A Difficulty in the Path of Psychoanalysis," in *Standard Edition*, vol. 17, 137–44.

34. Sigmund Freud, "Inhibitions, Symptoms and Anxiety," in *Standard Edition*, vol. 20, 103.

35. Ibid., 107.

36. Gilman, *Difference and Pathology*, 54.

37. Sigmund Freud, "Some Psychological Consequences of the Anatomical Distinction Between the Sexes" (1925), in *Sexuality and the Psychology of Love* (New York: Collier Books, 1963), 186.

38. Ibid., 191.

Chapter III

1. Daniel J. Kevles, *In the Name of Eugenics: Genetics and the Uses of Human Heredity* (Cambridge, MA: Harvard University Press, 1995), 4.

2. Ibid.

3. For an interesting account of animal husbandry in relation to humans, especially women, see Harriet Ritvo, "The Animal Connection," in *The Boundaries of Humanity*, 68–84.

4. Kevles, *In the Name of Eugenics*, 48.

5. Ibid., 51.

6. Ibid., 56.

7. Gould, *Mismeasure of Man*, 189.

8. Goddard's study concluded that of the 480 offspring of the Kallikak family, only 46 were normal; the remaining 434 turned to crime, prostitution, alcoholism, and even suffered from epilepsy. See Robert N. Proctor. *Racial Hygiene: Medicine under the Nazis* (Cambridge, MA: Harvard University Press, 1988), 99–100. Gould also tells of a slight alteration that was made on some of the photographs in Goddard's book. It seems that Goddard, or someone, added heavy eyebrows and lips to the original photographs, making the Kallikaks look extraordinarily sinister and stupid. See Gould, *Mismeasure of Man*, 201.

9. Quoted in Kevles, *In the Name of Eugenics*, 78.

10. Ibid., 108.

11. Kevles states that the total number of sterilizations between 1932 and 1941 amounted to almost 36,000. See ibid., 116. It should be noted that in a work published in 2003, Edwin Black claims that if one includes the postwar period in America, more than 60,000 were sterilized in the eugenics program (see *War Against the Weak: Eugenics and America's Campaign to Create a Master Race* [New York: Four Walls Eight Windows, 2003], xvi, 7). The 60,000 that Black proposes, however, is countered later in the book (p. 398) with a figure of 70,000 sterilized over the course of the eugenics era. Whichever is correct, the conclusion is inevitable: Eugenics was a thoroughgoing and effective force for human repression.

12. Kevles, *In the Name of Eugenics*, 116.

13. Ibid.

14. Boria Sax, *Animals in the Third Reich: Pets, Scapegoats, and the Holocaust* (New York: Continuum, 2000), 22.

15. Robert J. Lifton, *The Nazi Doctors: Medical Killing and the Psychology of Genocide* (New York: Basic Books, 2000), 279.

16. Hannaford, *Race*, 363. A much more detailed treatment of the Nazi ideology regarding human breeding, euthanasia, slaughter, and so on appears in part 2 of this book.

17. Adolf Hitler, *Mein Kampf*, trans. Ralph Manheim (Boston: Houghton-Mifflin, 1971), 289.

18. Ibid., 285.

19. Ibid., 297.

20. Ibid.

21. Ibid., 300–301.

22. This is certainly true of the older scientific traditions discussed earlier in this book, but it is amply demonstrated in modern philosophical thinking as well. In her essay "The Animal Connection," Harriet Ritvo emphasizes Robert Nozick's refutation of Tom Regan's *The Case for Animal Rights*. In his *New York Times Book Review* review of Regan's book, Nozick simply asserts that "animals are not human and therefore cannot possibly have any rights." See Ritvo, in *The Boundaries of Humanity*, 69–70.

23. Hitler, *Mein Kampf*, 57.

24. Edward Shorter, *A History of Psychiatry: From the Era of the Asylum to the Age of Prozac* (New York: John Wiley & Sons, 1997), 219.

25. The estimate of animals killed in laboratories worldwide was between 100 million and 200 million per year in 1982. This does not include those subjected to some form of torture, like scalding, immersion, burning, pesticide exposure, irradiation, electric shock, and any other number of painful procedures. This of course pales before the number of animals killed for consumption—a figure that must be astronomical if one considers that McDonald's alone has already served "over 30 billion hamburgers."

26. Kurt Danziger, *Constructing the Subject: Historical Origins of Psychological Research* (Cambridge, UK: Cambridge University Press, 1990), 90.

27. Shorter, *A History of Psychiatry*, 219.

28. Peter Breggin, *Toxic Psychiatry* (New York: St. Martin's Press, 1991), 205.

29. For further details of this interesting case, see a series of articles by Zachary R. Dowdy for *Newsday* (March 16, 2001; March 28, 2001; April 17, 2001).

30. Mary Midgley, "Persons and Non-Persons," in *In Defense of Animals*, ed. Peter Singer, 57 (New York: Basil Blackwell, 1985).

31. For extended accounts of this phenomenon, see Thomas Szasz, *The Manufacture of Madness: A Comparative Study of the Inquisition and the Mental Health Movement* (New York: Harper & Row, 1970); Paula Caplan, *They Say You're Crazy: How the World's Most Powerful Psychiatrists Decide Who's Normal* (Reading, MA: Addison-Wesley, 1995).

32. Elliot S. Vallenstein, *Great and Desperate Cures: The Rise and Decline of Psychosurgery and Other Radical Treatments for Mental Illness* (New York: Basic Books, 1986), 84.

33. Ibid., 86, 88.

34. This, of course, is not to imply that animals do not have similar emotional characteristics. There is a veritable library of studies and documentation on these sorts of feelings in animals. The stress here is only on the instinctual behaviors of animals, and the transposition of these basic instincts to human subjects.

35. Vallenstein, *Great and Desperate Cures*, 117.

Chapter IV

1. Michel Foucault, *Discipline and Punish: The Birth of the Prison* (New York: Vintage, 1979), 209.

2. Ibid., 200 (emphasis mine).

3. Dale Jamieson, "Against Zoos," in *In Defense of Animals*, ed. Singer, 108.

4. Quoted in Peter Singer, *Animal Liberation*, 190.

5. Jamieson, "Against Zoos," 108.

6. Phillips Verner Bradford and Harvey Blume, *Ota Benga: The Pygmy in the Zoo* (New York: Delta, 1992), 255.

7. Ibid., 181.

8. Ibid., 97.

9. For an account of Leopold's takeover of the Congo, see Adam Hochschild, *King Leopold's Ghost* (Boston: Houghton Mifflin, 1999).

10. See Foucault, *Discipline and Punish*, 164–69.

11. Ibid., 169.

12. Fanon, *The Wretched of the Earth*, 303.

13. Hochschild, *King Leopold's Ghost*, 229.

14. Ibid., 230.

15. Ibid., 231.

16. Brian W. Dippie, *The Vanishing American* (Lawrence, KS: University Press of Kansas, 1982), 85.

17. Ibid.

18. Ibid., 134.

19. It should be noted that much of the same quasi-scientific rhetoric directed at blacks was also aimed at American Indians. Morton, for example, included numerous American Indian skulls in his craniometrical studies, invariably rating them near the bottom in cranial capacity. See Gould, *Mismeasure of Man*, 83–100. Both George Bancroft and Lewis Henry Morgan used an amalgamation of polygenesist theory and social Darwinism to discourage Indian development and to argue for the elimination of their environmental resources. See George Bancroft, *The Native Races* (1874), and Lewis Henry Morgan, *Ancient Society* (1877).

20. Paula Mitchell Marks, *In a Barren Land: American Indian Dispossession and Survival* (New York: William Morrow, 1998), 96.

21. Ibid., 97.

22. Ibid., 98.

23. Dee Brown, *Bury My Heart at Wounded Knee: An Indian History of the American West* (New York: Henry Holt, 1970), 444 (emphasis mine).

24. Singer, *Animal Liberation*, 189.

25. Ibid., 200–201.

26. Ibid., 200–202.

27. See Daniel C. Dennett, *Darwin's Dangerous Idea* (New York: Touchstone Books, 1996).

Chapter V

1. James Walvin, *Slavery and the Slave Trade* (Jackson: University of Mississippi Press, 1983), 1.

2. Hannaford, *Race*, 531.

3. Ibid., 55.

4. Aristotle, *Politics*, bk. I, ch. 5.

5. Ibid.

6. Ibid.
7. Ibid.
8. James Pope-Hennessy, *Sins of the Fathers: The Atlantic Slave Traders, 1441–1807* (London: Phoenix Press, 1967), 8.
9. Ibid., 12.
10. Ibid., 3.
11. Walvin, *Slavery*, 54.
12. Pope-Hennessy, *Sins of the Fathers*, 3.
13. George Francis Dow, *Slave Ships and Slaving* (Westport, CT: Negro Universities Press, 1970 [1927]), 148.
14. Ibid., 4.
15. Hugh Thomas, in his monumental *The Slave Trade: The Story of the Atlantic Slave Trade: 1440–1870* (New York: Touchstone, 1997), provides numerous counterexamples of the treatment of slaves, invoking some of the statutory regulations regarding the humane treatment of slaves, particularly those issued by the British government. This more benign treatment may have been afforded in certain cases, but, it seems, it is considerably outweighed by continuous brutalizations. Besides, Thomas invokes virtually every possible justification for slavery in his book: the unavoidable violence of the times, commercial adventurousness, and so forth, without at any point exploring in some detail the moral obliquity involved. Indeed, in this respect his book is a kind of disguised celebration of slavery.
16. Marjorie Spiegel, *The Dreaded Comparison: Human and Animal Slavery* (Secaucus, NJ: Mirror Books, 1996), 56.
17. Ibid.
18. Ibid., 57.
19. Ibid.
20. Olaudah Equiano, "The Life of Olaudah Equiano," in *The Classic Slave Narratives*, ed. Henry Louis Gates Jr. (New York: Mentor, 1987), 79.
21. Frederick Douglass, *Narrative of the Life of Frederick Douglass as a Slave* (New York: Modern Library Edition, 2000), 282.
22. Singer, *Animal Liberation*, 223.
23. Equiano, "Life," 79.
24. Douglass, *Narrative*, 282 (emphasis mine).
25. Ibid., 282–83.
26. F. George Kay, *The Shameful Trade* (South Brunswick and New York: A. S. Barnes, 1967), 136–37. It should be noted here that Hodge eventually met with retribution, as he was (reluctantly) convicted of murder and sentenced to death by the governor of the Leeward Islands.
27. The Marquis de Sade, *Juliette*, trans. Austryn Wainhouse (New York: Grove Press, 1976), 430.
28. Douglass, *Narrative*, 291.
29. Ibid., 294–95.

30. John W. Blassingame, *The Slave Community: Plantation Life in the Ante-Bellum South* (New York: Oxford University Press, 1972), 159.
31. Spiegel, *The Dreaded Comparison*, 64.
32. Blassingame, *Slave Community*, 109–10.

Chapter VI

1. J. H. Van Evrie, a pro-slavery, anti-black writer and publisher who straddled the pre– and post–Civil War periods, published numerous pro-slavery books, pamphlets, and tracts, and issued a series devoted exclusively to anti-abolitionist tracts. The series contained titles such as *Abolition Is National Death* and *The Abolition Conspiracy*. Many church and religious groups were also active in publishing similar literature, as were Southern commercial publishers as well.
2. One of the greatest problems for slaveholders, both in the pre–Civil War South and within the history of slavery in general, was slave resistance. From the accompanying text, one might get the impression that slaves were just passive subjects that were manipulated as their owners and overseers wished. This is not the case (or the intended image) at all: slaves played a major, active role in their own emancipation. In the United States alone, there were numerous slave revolts and work stoppages, and thousands ran away. The slave revolts—particularly, the Haitian revolution—in the Caribbean were legendary; many of them ended in the killing of large numbers of European soldiers and native whites, and thus contributed to the discouragement of further expansion of the institution. Joseph L. Graves Jr., in his book *The Emperor's New Clothes: Biological Theories of Race at the Millennium* (New Brunswick, NJ: Rutgers University Press, 2001), relates that black slaves burned the city of Dallas, Texas. The fact that slaves contributed significantly to their own emancipation, moreover, detracts from and reflects negatively on the common notion that the slaves were freed through the efforts of a handful of white men, most notably Lincoln in the United States and Wilberforce in Great Britain—though well-meaning white men and women did contribute significantly to slave emancipation, and particular emphasis should fall on the role played by the Quakers and various other abolitionist groups.
3. J. H. Van Evrie, *White Supremacy and Negro Subordination* (New York: Van Evrie, Horton & Co., 1868), 89.
4. Ibid., 91.
5. Ibid., 107.
6. Ibid., 225–26 (emphasis mine).
7. Ibid., 111.
8. Ibid., 113.
9. Ibid., 114.
10. Ibid., 147.
11. It is difficult to say exactly where this odd conception of infertility came from, but sources certainly existed prior to Van Evrie's propagation of the theory. Per-

haps the best known of these is the famous (infamous) work by Edward Long, *Long's History of Jamaica* (1774). In this book Long argued that mulattos were as infertile as mules. Long divided the genus *Homo* into three species: Europeans, Negroes, and orangutans. Negroes, in his view, were closer to orangutans than to humans, and were therefore able to interbreed successfully with them. However, Long argued, God was terribly offended by the monstrosities created by these sorts of unions, and therefore struck all mulattos who were the offspring of orangutan unions sterile. In sum, Long conceived of two types of sterile mulattos: those produced by black/white unions and those produced by black/orangutan unions. Regarding the latter, Long wrote: "I do not think an Orang-Outang would be any dishonour to an Hottentot female. Orangs ... conceive a passion for the negroe woman." Quoted in Léon Poliakov, *The Aryan Myth: A History of Racist and Nationalist Ideas in Europe* (New York: Basic Books, 1971), 178.

12. Van Evrie, *White Supremacy and Negro Subordination*, 173.
13. Josiah Priest, *Bible Defence of Slavery* (Glasgow, KY: The Rev. W. S. Brown, 1853), 242.
14. Ibid., 243.
15. Ibid.
16. Chancellor Harper, "Harper's Memoir on Slavery," in *The Pro-Slavery Argument* (New York: Negro Universities Press, 1968 [reprint from 1832 original]), 57.
17. Ibid., 57–58.
18. Ibid., 61.
19. Ibid.
20. Charles Carroll, *The Negro a Beast or in the Image of God* (St. Louis: American Book and Bible House, 1900), 201.
21. Ibid.
22. Ibid., 217.
23. Ibid., 219.
24. R. W. Shufeldt, *America's Greatest Problem: The Negro* (Philadelphia: F. A. Davis, 1915), 98.
25. Ibid., 99.
26. Ibid.
27. Ibid., 105.
28. Ibid.
29. Ibid.
30. Shufeldt, *America's Greatest Problem*, 149–50.
31. Ibid., 152.
32. Ibid., 147 (emphasis mine). It is interesting to note that "animal impulses" occasionally seem to grasp the author as well. He filled *America's Greatest Problem* with numerous photographic illustrations, some of which are of attractive, nude, and erotically posed black men and women, that he took himself. The women seem to look lovingly and seductively at the camera, in much the same way that "cheesecake" models of the early 1920s and 1930s teased their audiences.

The photos appear particularly out of place intermixed with technical charts, gorilla skulls, and anatomical photographs and renderings—so much so that one gets the impression that Shufeldt the photographer, even given his natural Caucasian moral probity and sexual restraint, may have intentionally posed women and some of the men in these erotic stances. Titles attached to some of the figures are telling as well. In a figure entitled "Pure African Negro," he includes the phrase "Victim of syphilis." In another, he notes "the comparatively slight development of the gluteal region." Perhaps the most interesting of all is a photograph entitled "Young Male Negro Boy," who is depicted fully nude, allowing a glimpse of his "large but flexible sex organ." In the title, Shufeldt indicates that the picture was taken in New York City. One might wonder why—other than the usual attempt to attribute savagery to modern blacks—a young boy from New York City would be depicted completely nude carrying a native spear.

33. Thomas Dixon Jr., *The Leopard's Spots* (Ridgewood, NJ: Gregg Press, 1967 [1902]), 70.
34. Ibid., 94.
35. Ibid., 94–95.
36. Ibid., 139.
37. Ibid., 140.
38. Thomas Dixon Jr., *The Clansman* (Lexington: University Press of Kentucky, 1970 [1904]), 289.
39. Ibid., 290.
40. Ibid., 303–4.

Chapter VII

1. Telford Taylor, "Opening Statement of the Prosecution, Dec. 9, 1946," in *The Nazi Doctors and the Nuremberg Code: Human Rights and Human Experimentation* (New York: Oxford University Press, 1992), 70.
2. Ibid., 71.
3. Ibid., 74.
4. Ibid., 76.
5. Ibid., 80.
6. Ibid., 82.
7. Ibid., 89–90.
8. In his specialized work on the role of animals and animal symbolism in Hitler's Germany, *Animals in the Third Reich*, Boria Sax gives a detailed account of the law of 1933. See pp. 110–23. The full text of the law is reproduced in appendix 1 of Sax's text; see pp. 175–79. Sax also notes that the animal protection laws were selectively enforced, as was the case with almost any Nazi statute. High-ranking Nazi officials, favored groups like the Hitler Youth, or preferred members of the medical establishment could do pretty much as they pleased with animals.

Others, however, were reprimanded for cruelty to animals, and in some cases arrested and sentenced to prison terms. The law itself proved to be comprehensive and humane, and lasted with few modifications in Germany until 1972, when it was watered down. The humane standards applied to slaughter, ironically enough, remained on the books until 1997. See Sax at 117–18.

9. Michael Burleigh, *Death and Deliverance: Euthanasia in Germany 1900–1945* (Cambridge, UK: Cambridge University Press, 1994), 15.

10. Ibid., 17.

11. Ibid., 18.

12. Ibid., 18–19.

13. Ibid., 19.

14. See *supra,* text accompanying notes 84–94. The German historian of science Reinhold Müller is quoted by Robert N. Proctor, in *Racial Hygiene,* on precisely the subject of the U.S. influence on German racial hygiene. Müller stated: "Racial hygiene in Germany remained until 1926 a purely academic and scientific movement. It was the Americans who busied themselves earnestly about the subject. Through massive investigations in the schools, they proved (with impeccable precision) Galton's thesis that qualities of the mind [*seelische Eigenschaften*] are as heritable as qualities of the body; they were also able to show that these mental qualities are inherited according to the very same laws as those of the body." Proctor, *Racial Hygiene,* 98.

15. Ibid., 126–27.

16. Ibid., 181.

17. James M. Glass, *"Life Unworthy of Life": Racial Phobia and Mass Murder in Hitler's Germany* (New York: Basic Books, 1997), 63.

18. Lifton, *The Nazi Doctors,* 302.

19. Klaus Theweleit, *Male Fantasies,* vol. 2 (Minneapolis: University of Minnesota Press, 1989), 12.

20. The Freikorps consisted of a more or less self-appointed group of war veterans who fought against the assumed rising tide of Bolshevism in Germany after World War I. Several of the Freikorps members wrote accounts, both fictional and nonfictional (mostly in the form of memoirs), about their military experiences. Ernst Jünger was by far the most gifted and prolific of these writers, and later established a career as a major German novelist. For further reading, see Klaus Theweleit, *Male Fantasies,* vols. 1 & 2. See also Barbara Ehrenreich's foreword to volume 1 of *Male Fantasies.*

21. Sax, *Animals in the Third Reich,* 159.

22. Ibid.

23. Guenther Lewy, *The Nazi Persecution of the Gypsies* (New York: Oxford University Press, 2000), 13.

24. See ibid., 10–14, where Lewy dismisses most of these accusations against Gypsies as myth and simple prejudice.

25. Ibid., 50.

26. Ibid., 51.
27. Quoted in Glass, *"Life Unworthy of Life,"* 55.
28. Alfred Rosenberg, *Race and Race History*, ed. Robert Pois (New York: Harper & Row, 1970), 175.
29. Ibid., 188–89 (emphasis mine).
30. Glass, *"Life Unworthy of Life,"* 40.
31. See Eric T. Olson, *The Human Animal: Personal Identity without Psychology* (New York: Oxford University Press, 1997), 136–38.
32. Glass, *"Life Unworthy of Life,"* 55.
33. For an interesting and enlightening account of Emmanuel Levinas's writing on the Holocaust, and his personal experiences of this event, see David Clark, "On Being 'The Last Kantian in Nazi Germany,'" in *Animal Acts*, ed. Ham and Senior, 165–98.
34. Feig writes that the commandant of Buchenwald, Karl Koch, had thrown prisoners to his favorite bear. See Konnilyn G. Feig, *Hitler's Death Camps: The Sanity of Madness* (New York: Holmes and Meier, 1979), 104.

Chapter VIII

1. Quoted in Richard Breitman, *The Architect of Genocide: Himmler and the Final Solution* (Hanover, NH: University Press of New England, 1991), 189.
2. For further reading, see Daniel Jonah Goldhagen, *Hitler's Willing Executioners: Ordinary Germans and the Holocaust* (New York: Knopf, 1996).
3. Feig, *Hitler's Death Camps*, 37.
4. Ibid., 15.
5. For the full spectrum of these objectives, see Wolfgang Sofsky, *The Order of Terror: The Concentration Camp* (Princeton, NJ: Princeton University Press, 1997), 16–27.
6. Ibid., 25.
7. Feig, *Hitler's Death Camps*, 103.
8. Ibid.
9. Quoted in Yitzhak Arad, *Belzec, Sobibor, Treblinka: The Operation Reinhard Death Camps* (Bloomington: Indiana University Press, 1987), 175.
10. Ibid., 104.
11. Ibid.
12. Sofsky, *The Order of Terror*, 233.
13. Peter Singer, in *Animal Liberation,* 150–51, contends that many of these so-called humane killing devices in slaughterhouses are not entirely effective.
14. Sofsky, *The Order of Terror*, 233.
15. See *supra*, text accompanying notes 176–77.
16. Sofsky, *The Order of Terror*, 233–34.
17. Lyotard, *Heidegger and "the jews,"* 27.
18. See Clark, "The Last Kantian," in *Animal Acts*, 165–98.

19. Ibid., 192.
20. Ibid.
21. Ibid., 193.
22. See Proctor, *Racial Hygiene*, 15–19.
23. Taylor, *The Nazi Doctors and the Nuremberg Code*, 90.

Chapter IX

1. See *supra*, text accompanying note 125.
2. Edgar Rice Burroughs, *Tarzan of the Apes* (Cutchogue, NY: Buccaneer Books, 1914), 80–81.
3. The Tarzan series alternated between black "African" natives and white ones. The seeming oddity of this shift was practical because the series was shot in Mexico, making it expensive and difficult to import black extras, and eventually leading to the use of locals, who were either whites or indigenous Indians.
4. For further reading on the wolf in Nazi culture, see Sax, *Animals in the Third Reich*, 72–80 and passim.
5. David J. Skal, *The Monster Show: A Cultural History of Horror* (New York: W. W. Norton, 1993), 216.
6. David J. Skal, *Screams of Reason: Mad Science and Modern Culture* (New York: W. W. Norton, 1998), 82.

Chapter X

1. Jean Baudrillard, "Simulations," in *The Ecstasy of Communication* (New York: Semiotext(e), 1988), 83.
2. See ibid., 1–80.
3. Ibid., 32.
4. Jared Taylor, *Paved with Good Intentions: The Failure of Race Relations in Contemporary America* (New York: Carroll and Graf, 1992), 109. See, for further examples, ibid. at 109–21.
5. Ibid., 228 (emphasis mine).
6. Ibid., (emphasis mine).
7. Ibid., 225.
8. Ibid.; see also pages 229–40 and passim.
9. For example, the deadly chase, said to have taken place at 115 miles per hour, was deemed impossible, as a Hyundai test driver could barely reach 85 miles per hour on a test track with the exact same model of car.
10. Taylor, *Paved with Good Intentions*, 271 (emphasis mine).
11. Ibid., 272 (emphasis mine).
12. Ibid., 98.
13. Ibid. (emphasis mine). Taylor's vehement attack on savage gangs of marauding blacks seems even more bigoted and constructed in view of new evidence

that came to light in the Central Park jogger case. It turns out that the wilders tried, convicted, and imprisoned did not commit the crime at all. A lone assailant, whose DNA was found at the scene, but who was not arrested at the time, admitted to the crime. The so-called iron-clad confessions were obviously coerced from several of the defendants. A case is being made for prosecutorial misconduct, or, at best, incompetence. As of December 6, 2002, all of the cases against the so-called wilders had been vacated by the Manhattan district attorney's office, leaving the final exculpation to a New York State appeals judge, who, shortly following the DA's decision, exonerated the previously imprisoned youths of all involvement in the rape and beating of the Central Park jogger.

14. Taylor, *Paved with Good Intentions*, 275.

15. Contrary to Taylor's statement, there was considerable international recognition of the slaughters in Burundi and elsewhere in Africa, especially in UN councils and the World Court. Moreover, if the slaughters in Africa did not receive attention commensurate with those perpetrated by the white minority government in South Africa, there may be another answer: black people slaughtering other black people is usually met with considerable indifference.

16. Taylor, *Paved with Good Intentions*, 349.

17. See *supra*, text accompanying notes 225–29.

18. See Taylor, *Paved with Good Intentions*, 348–50.

19. Taylor consistently refers to black teenage pregnancy, which is one of the issues emphasized in much conservative thinking regarding race and welfare. One could also make a connection here with Dr. Howard's remark about "never having seen a Negro virgin over ten years of age." See *supra*, text following note 202.

20. Taylor, *Paved with Good Intentions*, 351.

21. This tactic is perhaps most obvious in the section on slavery, entitled "The American Dilemma," where D'Souza appears to be in violent disagreement with the whole institution of slavery, but in the end finds some justification for its existence, as well as some means of exculpating white slaveowners. For example, he makes the argument that American slavery was really just an extension of world slavery, and that even blacks and Indians were actually slaveholders. What, one might ask, is the difference? Small numbers of Jews, Catholics, and Gypsies were complicit with the Nazis in some phase of the Holocaust: does that make Jews, Gypsies, and Catholics any less the victims of that event, or make the event any less horrific? D'Souza ends one of the subsections in his slavery chapter with the following statement: "In summary, the American slave was treated like property, which is to say, pretty well" (*The End of Racism*, 91). He also adds to this claim that slavery made an infinitely better life in America for the descendants of slaves—which is approximately the same as arguing that the European Holocaust, as evil as it might have been, increased the mental and physical toughness of and created numerous job openings for its survivors (ibid., 113).

22. See Gould, *Mismeasure of Man*, 383–85, and passim.

23. D'Souza, *The End of Racism*, 475. The claim of a "new found position" for Gould seems a bit overly optimistic in view of the fact that Gould wrote a new "definitive refutation" of *The Bell Curve*, which appeared in the revised 1996 edition of *The Mismeasure of Man*.

24. Evidence for this mastery is apparent in the solution for treating the underclass put forth in *The Bell Curve*.

25. D'Souza, *The End of Racism*, 476 (emphasis mine).

26. See, for example, *The Bell Curve Wars: Race, Intelligence, and the Future of America*, ed. Steven Fraser (New York: Basic Books, 1995), in which several contributors attack the scientific soundness of *The Bell Curve* arguments, and from a variety of points of view. Of special interest in this regard is Joseph L. Graves Jr.'s *The Emperor's New Clothes: Biological Theories of Race at the Millennium* (New Brunswick, NJ: Rutgers University Press, 2001). Graves takes on *The Bell Curve* from the point of view of a geneticist and discredits much of the Herrnstein-Murray data from that perspective. See, in particular, pp. 157–72.

27. D'Souza, *The End of Racism*, 485.

28. Ibid., 486.

29. Ibid., 505.

30. Ibid., 516.

31. Ibid.

32. Ibid., 517.

33. It would seem hardly a characteristic unique to black youths to strut around street corners bragging about their real or imagined sexual conquests. One could certainly find this kind of youthful behavior on virtually any street corner in America, or anywhere else in the world, for that matter. Moreover, the adoption of hip-hop and rap style—what D'Souza un-hiply calls the "bad nigger" style—by white middle- and upper-class youths has no doubt added to the so-called underclass. The wigger phenomenon is perhaps as widespread in America as that of the bad nigger, thus de facto adding a large contingent of limping, gold chain–wearing, cursing, gun-packing white kids to the black underclass. One could also argue that this deep-seated black pathology was largely invented and sustained by those American-based industries that would stand to profit most from its popularity (that is, the apparel, sneaker, and music industries).

34. See *supra*, text accompanying notes 200–205.

35. D'Souza, *The End of Racism*, 524.

36. Richard J. Herrnstein and Charles Murray, *The Bell Curve: Intelligence and Class Structure in American Life* (New York: Free Press, 1994), 523–24 (emphasis mine).

37. David B. Allison and Mark S. Roberts, *Disordered Mother or Disordered Diagnosis? Munchausen by Proxy Syndrome* (Hillsdale, NJ: Analytic Press, 1998), 26–27.

38. One could certainly add abortion to this list, as it constitutes a distinct form of controlled female reproduction, even though there is a great deal of religious dogma and rhetoric associated with the procedure. However, the question of abortion, even as a prohibition of species continuation, is so complex that I have not included it among these modes of medico-psychiatric repression associated with childbirth and childrearing.

39. See Diane E. Eyer, *Mother-Infant Bonding: A Scientific Fiction* (New Haven, CT: Yale University Press, 1992).

40. Allison and Roberts, *Disordered Mother*, 188.

41. Eyer, *Mother-Infant Bonding*, 3, 5–6.

42. Richard Asher, "Munchausen's Syndrome," *Lancet* 1 (1951): 339–41.

43. Several competing medical and psychiatric etiologies purport to determine the precise causal chain involved in the MBPS disorder (e.g., those of Schreier and Libow, and Meadow). None, however, provide sufficiently cogent and convincing support for the causes of the disorder. In addition, it has been argued elsewhere that the disorder itself is not self-standing, but, rather, a far-ranging compilation of other factors. See Allison and Roberts, *Disordered Mother*.

44. Ann Oakley, *Woman's Work: The Housewife, Past and Present* (New York: Vintage, 1976), 188–89.

45. Herbert A. Schreier and Judith A. Libow, *Hurting for Love: Munchausen by Proxy Syndrome* (New York: Guilford, 1993), 133.

46. G. J. Barker-Benfield, "Sexual Surgery in Late Nineteenth Century America," in *Seizing Our Bodies: The Politics of Women's Health*, ed. Claudia Dreifus, 27 (New York: Vintage, 1977).

47. Carol Tavris, *The Mismeasure of Woman* (New York: Simon & Schuster, 1992), 162–63. See also Allison and Roberts, *Disordered Mother*, 184–86.

48. Claudia Dreifus, "Sterilizing the Poor," in Dreifus, *Seizing Our Bodies*, 106–7.

49. Ibid., 113–14.

Chapter XI

1. Friedrich Nietzsche, *Beyond Good and Evil*, trans. Walter Kaufmann (New York: Vintage, 1989), 136.

2. R. C. Lewontin, Steven Rose, and Leon J. Kamin, *Not in Our Genes: Biology, Ideology and Human Nature* (New York: Pantheon, 1984), 234.

3. Particular works cited by Lewontin et al. are: Robert Ardrey's *The Territorial Imperative* (1966); Konrad Lorenz's *On Aggression* (1966); Desmond Morris's *The Naked Ape* (1967); and Tiger and Fox's *The Imperial Animal* (1971).

4. See Thomas Hobbes, *Leviathan*, ed. C. B. Macpherson (London: Penguin, 1985).

5. Lewontin, Rose, and Kamin, *Not in Our Genes*, 239.

6. Ibid.

7. Robert Ardrey, *African Genesis* (New York: Dell, 1968), 157–58.

8. Ibid., 158–59.
9. Robert Ardrey, *The Territorial Imperative* (London: Collins, 1966), 5 (quoted in Lewontin, Rose, and Kamin, *Not in Our Genes*, 240).
10. Gobineau, *Moral and Intellectual Diversity of Races*, 443 (emphasis mine).
11. Ibid., 450.
12. Ardrey, *African Genesis*, 356–57.
13. Ibid., 356.
14. I should note here that Ardrey does in fact depict this unconscious force of conscience as a destructive one. For example, in the final chapter of *African Genesis*, at p. 359, he states: "The power of conscience, blind, anti-rational, and acting in alliance with weapons fixation, will be the responsible force if self-annihilation be the human outcome."
15. Ibid.
16. Lewontin, Rose, and Kamin, *Not in Our Genes*, 237.
17. Ibid., 240.
18. Konrad Lorenz, *On Aggression* (New York: Harcourt, Brace & World, 1966), 43.
19. Ibid., 78.
20. Ibid., 79.
21. Ibid., 84.
22. Lorenz's later popular works in animal psychology and some of their pronouncements regarding aggression and domination must, of course, be seen in the light of his earlier involvement with the Nazis. He was an active theoretician and supporter of eugenics prior to and during the war years and wrote numerous studies using animal comparisons to determine the inferiority of certain human beings. One of the most egregious, and damning, of his Nazi-period studies compares selected animal physical characteristics—"pug-dog heads," for instance—with certain human characteristics. He supported his views in this essay with thirty-five illustrations, many of which were reminiscent of the traditional Jewish caricatures appearing in the anti-Semitic literature of the time, particularly the publications of the odious anti-Semite Julius Streicher. For further reading on Lorenz's involvement with the Nazis and his subsequent rehabilitation, see Sax, *Animals in the Third Reich*, 124–31, 133–36; and Ute Deichmann, *Biologists under Hitler* (Cambridge, MA: Harvard University Press, 1996).
23. Lorenz, *On Aggression*, 237.
24. Ibid., 241.
25. See ibid., 109–38.
26. Lewontin, Rose, and Kamin, *Not in Our Genes*, 245.
27. Ibid., 237.
28. Tavris, *The Mismeasure of Woman*, 212–13. The quotation is from Sam Kash Kachigan, *The Sexual Matrix: Boy Meets Girl on an Evolutionary Scale* (New York: Radius Press, 1996), 162.

29. Tavris, *The Mismeasure of Woman*, 213, quoting Kachigan, 161.
30. Desmond Morris, *The Human Zoo* (New York: McGraw-Hill, 1969), 65–66.
31. Ibid., 83.
32. Desmond Morris, *The Naked Ape* (New York: McGraw-Hill, 1967), 75–76.
33. It is important to note that sexual selection, mating rituals, and the physiology of sexual evolution are not really in question here. To be sure, males and females of all animal species have evolved certain strategies of sexual attraction over the period of their evolution. If they had not, they would most likely have disappeared. It is the emphasis on male dominance and female deference in both sexual selection and physiological change that I am criticizing. A more objective and scholarly account of this situation would see these phenomena as distributed more or less equally among both sexes, without using animalizing references to devalue women's roles. For a quite different and more scientifically sound analysis of essentially the same phenomena that Morris is dealing with, see Sarah Blaffer Hrdy, *Mother Nature: A History of Mothers, Infants, and Natural Selection* (New York: Pantheon Books, 1999), particularly parts 1 and 2.
34. One distinct example of the persistence of sociobiological thinking is the relatively recent contribution of Robert Wright, *The Moral Animal* (New York: Pantheon Books, 1994). Turning a bit from the largely controversial theories of sociobiology proper, Wright restores the sociobiological agenda in terms of a newly coined appellation "evolutionary psychology." However, Wright does nothing very new, other than simply restating the old adaptive stories of E. O. Wilson et al. in somewhat different terms. Women are still inferior to men. Genes still program for behaviors like reciprocal altruism and male dominance, despite the fact that no genetic research, even under strictly controlled laboratory conditions, has ever linked a social behavior to a specific gene.
35. For more details on the notion of sociobiology being a conglomeration of "adaptive stories" about evolutionary development, see Lewontin, Rose, and Kamin, *Not in Our Genes*, 258–64. See also R. C. Lewontin, *Biology as Ideology: The Doctrine of DNA* (New York: HarperPerennial, 1992), 87–104.
36. It is clear that this particular position is riddled with logical holes. Jacques Thiroux, in his book on ethics, correctly argued that rational individuals constantly clash in their views of self-interest. He provided as an example the conflict between Albert Einstein and Edward Teller on the use of atomic weapons. Both were obviously rational beings, but they were deeply divided on whether atomic weapons were good for oneself or for humanity. Jacques P. Thiroux, *Ethics: Theory and Practice* (New York: Macmillan, 1990), 43.

Chapter XII

1. Frank McLynn, *Crime and Punishment in Eighteenth-Century England* (London: Routledge, 1989), xi.

2. Ibid., xvii.

3. See *supra*, text accompanied by notes 300–315.

4. See Myron Magnet, *The Dream and the Nightmare: The Sixties Legacy to the Underclass* (New York: William Morrow, 1993), 168–70.

5. *The Entrepreneurial City: A How-To Handbook for Urban Innovators* (New York: Manhattan Institute for Policy Research, n.d.), 43, 47–48. Despite the drop in crime and the presumed increase in the quality of life in New York during the administration of Mayor Rudolph Giuliani (1992–2000), there was a significant downside to the "broken window" theory of aggressive policing. Numerous constitutional cases were brought against the mayor's office and the police department. Civil suits abounded, and police brutality complaints increased exponentially; these suits carry a price tag of more than $100 million in potential liability for the city, with no end in sight. For a detailed account of the dark side of aggressive policing, see Christian Parenti, *Lockdown America: Police and Prisons in the Age of Crisis* (London: Verso, 1999), 69–138.

6. George L. Kelling and Catherine M. Coles, *Fixing Broken Windows: Restoring Order and Reducing Crime in Our Communities* (New York: Free Press, 1996), 15.

7. Foucault, *Discipline and Punish*, 282.

8. Peter R. Breggin and Ginger Ross Breggin, *The War against Children of Color: Psychiatry Targets Inner City Youth* (Monroe, ME: Common Courage Press, 1998), 1.

9. According to Breggin and Breggin, Goodwin had done research into the large-scale drugging of criminals in 1984. Ibid., 4.

10. Ibid., 4.

11. Quoted in ibid., 8.

12. Ibid., 88. See J. Higley et al., "Cerebrospinal Fluid Monomine and Adrenal Correlates of Aggression in Free-Ranging Rhesus Monkeys," *Archives of General Psychiatry* 49: 436–41.

13. Breggin and Breggin, *War against Children of Color*, 88–89.

14. J. Talan, "Study with Monkeys Finds Intolerance, Violence and Aggression Might Be Generic," *Saint Paul Pioneer Express*, October 11, 1993, C5, quoted in Breggin and Breggin, *War against Children of Color*, 88–89.

15. Breggin and Breggin, *War against Children of Color*, 95.

16. Foucault, *Discipline and Punish*, 264.

17. For further reading on the psychology of colonialism, see Fanon, *The Wretched of the Earth*, passim. See also Ania Loomba, *Colonialism/Postcolonialism* (London: Routledge, 1998), 104–73; G. C. Spivak, "Can the Subaltern Speak? Speculations on Widow-Sacrifice," *Wedge* (Winter/Spring 1985): 120–30.

18. Parenti, *Lockdown America*, 170.

19. Ibid., 172.

20. Ibid, 174.

21. Kelling and Coles, *Fixing Broken Windows*, 16.

22. Here I refer to the photo of Private Lynndie England leading an Iraqi prisoner around on a leash at the Abu Ghraib prison. See, for further reference, Seymour M. Hersh, "Torture at Abu Ghraib Prison," *New Yorker*, May 10, 2004.

Chapter XIII

1. Mary Shelley, *Frankenstein or, the Modern Prometheus* (New York: Signet/Penguin, 1983), 160.
2. Jerry Mander, *Four Arguments for the Elimination of Television* (New York: Quill, 1978), 286.
3. Marshall McLuhan, *Understanding Media: The Extensions of Man* (New York: Signet, 1964), 53.
4. Ibid., 56.
5. Neil Postman, *Technopoly: The Surrender of Culture to Technology* (New York: Knopf, 1992), 111.
6. David F. Channell, *The Vital Machine: A Study of Technology and Organic Life* (New York: Oxford University Press, 1991), 138.
7. Daniel Crevier, *AI: The Tumultuous History of the Search for Artificial Intelligence* (New York: Basic Books, 1993), 341.
8. See, in particular, Donna J. Haraway, *Simians, Cyborgs, and Women: The Reinvention of Nature* (New York: Routledge, 1991).
9. Jean-François Lyotard, *The Inhuman: Reflections on Time* (Stanford, CA: Stanford University Press, 1991), 16.
10. Stuart Sim, *Lyotard and the Inhuman* (Cambridge, UK: Icon Books, 2001), 47.
11. Haraway, *Simians, Cyborgs, and Women*, 180 (quoted in Sim, *Lyotard and the Inhuman*, 54).
12. Sim, *Lyotard and the Inhuman*, 54.
13. See, for example, Don Ihde, *Bodies in Technology* (Minneapolis: University of Minnesota Press, 2002), 81–100.
14. Ibid., 36.
15. Ingold, *What Is an Animal*, 3.
16. See Alfred North Whitehead, *Process and Reality: An Essay in Cosmology* (New York: Harper & Row, 1957), 95–126.
17. Gilles Deleuze and Félix Guattari, *A Thousand Plateaus: Capitalism and Schizophrenia*, trans. Brian Massumi (Minneapolis: University of Minnesota Press, 1987), 238.
18. Alice Cournot, "Le 'devenir-animal' chez Gilles Deleuze," in *Animalitiés: Revue d'Esthetique* 40, no. 1 (2001): 89, 91.
19. Deleuze and Guattari, *A Thousand Plateaus*, 275.
20. Singer, *Animal Liberation*, 2.
21. Ibid., 8.
22. John G. Neihardt, *Black Elk Speaks* (Lincoln/London: University of Nebraska Press, 1979), 37, 42.

Bibliography

Adams, Nehemiah. *A South-Side View of Slavery*. 1854. Reprint, Port Washington, NY: Kennikat Press, 1969.

Allison, David B., and Mark S. Roberts. *Disordered Mother or Disordered Diagnosis? Munchausen by Proxy Syndrome*. Hillsdale, NJ: Analytic Press, 1998.

Arad, Yitzhak. *Belzec, Sobibor, Treblinka: The Operation Reinhard Death Camps*. Bloomington: Indiana University Press, 1987.

Ardrey, Robert. *African Genesis: A Personal Investigation into the Animal Origins and Nature of Man*. New York: Dell, 1968.

——. *The Hunting Hypothesis: A Personal Conclusion Concerning the Evolution of Man*. New York: Atheneum, 1976.

——. *The Territorial Imperative*. London: Collins, 1966.

Arens, W. *The Man-Eating Myth: Anthropology and Anthropophagy*. New York: Oxford University Press, 1979.

Aristotle. *De Anima*. In *Introduction to Aristotle*, edited by Richard McKeon. New York: Random House, 1947.

——. *Metaphysics*. Translated by Richard Hope. Ann Arbor: University of Michigan Press, 1975.

——. *Nichomachean Ethics*. Translated by J. A. K. Thompson. Baltimore, MD: Penguin Books, 1969.

——. *Politics*. Translated by Benjamin Jowett. New York: Random House, 1943.

——. *Zoology*. In *Selections*, translated by Phillip Wheelright. New York: Bobbs-Merrill, 1951.

Asher, Richard. "Munchausen's Syndrome." *Lancet* 1 (1951): 339–41.

Bancroft, George. *The Native Races*. 1874.

Baudrillard, Jean. *The Ecstasy of Communication*. New York: Semiotext(e), 1988.

——. *Selected Writings*. Edited by Mark Poster. Stanford, CA: Stanford University Press, 1988.

Biddiss, Michael D. *Father of Racist Ideology: The Social and Political Thought of Count Gobineau*. New York: Weybright and Talley, 1970.

Black, Edwin. *War against the Weak: Eugenics and America's Campaign to Create a Master Race*. New York: Four Walls Eight Windows, 2003.

Blassingame, John W. *The Slave Community: Plantation Life in the Ante-Bellum South*. New York: Oxford University Press, 1972.

Borowski, Tadeusz. *This Way for the Gas, Ladies and Gentlemen*. New York: Penguin Books, 1976.

Bradford, Phillips Verner, and Harvey Blume. *Ota Benga: The Pygmy in the Zoo*. New York: Delta, 1992.

Breggin, Peter. *Toxic Psychiatry*. New York: St. Martin's Press, 1991.

Breggin, Peter R., and Ginger Ross Breggin. *The War against Children of Color: Psychiatry Targets Inner City Youth*. Monroe, ME: Common Courage Press, 1998.

Breitman, Richard. *The Architect of Genocide: Himmler and the Final Solution*. Hanover, NH: University Press of New England, 1991.

Brown, Dee. *Bury My Heart at Wounded Knee: An Indian History of the American West*. New York: Henry Holt, 1970.

Browning, Christopher R. *Nazi Policy, Jewish Workers, German Killers*. Cambridge, UK: Cambridge University Press, 2000.

Burleigh, Michael. *Death and Deliverance: Euthanasia in Germany 1900–1945*. Cambridge, UK: Cambridge University Press, 1994.

Burroughs, Edgar Rice. *Tarzan of the Apes*. Cutchogue, NY: Buccaneer Books, 1914.

Caplan, Paula J. *Don't Blame Mother: Mending the Mother Daughter Relationship*. New York: Harper & Row, 1989.

———. *They Say You're Crazy: How the World's Most Powerful Psychiatrists Decide Who's Normal*. Reading, MA: Addison-Wesley, 1995.

Carroll, Charles. *The Negro a Beast or in the Image of God*. St. Louis: American Book and Bible House, 1900.

Chamberlin, J. Edward, and Sander L. Gilman. *Degeneration: The Dark Side of Progress*. New York: Columbia University Press, 1985.

Channell, David F. *The Vital Machine: A Study of Technology and Organic Life*. New York: Oxford University Press, 1991.

Cournot, Alice. "Le 'devenir-animal' chez Gilles Deleuze." In *Animalitiés: Revue d'Esthetique* 40, no. 1 (2001).

Crevier, Daniel. *AI: The Tumultuous Search for Artificial Intelligence*. New York: Basic Books, 1993.

D'Souza, Dinesh. *The End of Racism*. New York: Free Press, 1995.

Danziger, Kurt. *Constructing the Subject: Historical Origins of Psychological Research*. Cambridge, UK: Cambridge University Press, 1990.

Davidson, Arnold I. "The Horror of Monsters." In *The Boundaries of Humanity: Humans, Animals, Machines*, edited by James J. Sheehan and Morton Sosna. Berkeley: University of California Press, 1991.

De Waal, Frans. *Good Natured: The Origins of Right and Wrong in Humans and Other Animals*. Cambridge, MA: Harvard University Press, 1996.

———. *Peacemaking among Primates*. Cambridge, MA: Harvard University Press, 1989.

Deichmann, Ute. *Biologists under Hitler*. Cambridge, MA: Harvard University Press, 1996.

Deleuze, Giles, and Félix Guattari. *Anti-Oedipus: Capitalism and Schizophrenia*. New York: Viking, 1977.

———. *Kafka: Toward a Minor Literature*. Minneapolis: University of Minnesota Press, 1986.

———. *A Thousand Plateaus: Capitalism and Schizophrenia*. Translated by Brian Massumi. Minneapolis: University of Minnesota Press, 1987.

Dennett, Daniel C. *Darwin's Dangerous Idea*. New York: Touchstone Books, 1996.

Denno, Deborah W. *Biology and Violence: From Birth to Adulthood*. Cambridge, UK: Cambridge University Press, 1990.

Descartes, René. *Discourse on Method*. Translated by John Cottingham et al. Cambridge, UK: Cambridge University Press, 1988.

———. *The Philosophical Writings*, vols. I and II. Translated by John Cottingham, Robert Stoothoff, and Dugald Murdoch. Cambridge, UK: Cambridge University Press, 1984.

———. *Selections*. Edited by Ralph M. Easton. New York: Charles Scribner's Sons, 1955.

———. *Treatise on Man*. Translated by Thomas Steele Hall. Cambridge, MA: Harvard University Press, 1972.

Dippie, Brian W. *The Vanishing American*. Lawrence, KS: University Press of Kansas, 1982.

Dixon, Thomas, Jr. *The Clansman: An Historical Romance of the Ku Klux Klan*. Lexington: University Press of Kentucky, 1970 [1904].

———. *The Leopard's Spots: A Romance of the White Man's Burden—1865–1900*. Ridgewood, NJ: Gregg Press, 1967 [1902].

Doney, Willis, ed. *Descartes: A Collection of Critical Essays*. Notre Dame, IN: Notre Dame University Press, 1968.

Douglass, Frederick. *Narrative of the Life of Frederick Douglass as a Slave*. New York: Modern Library Edition, 2000.

Dow, George Francis. *Slave Ships and Slaving*. Westport, CT: Negro Universities Press, 1970 [1927].

Dreifus, Claudia, ed. *Seizing Our Bodies: The Politics of Women's Health*. New York: Vintage Books, 1977.

Ebling, F. J., ed. *Racial Variation in Man*. New York: John Wiley & Sons, 1975.

The Entrepreneurial City: A How-To Handbook for Urban Innovators. New York: Manhattan Institute for Policy Research, n.d.

Equiano, Olaudah. "The Life of Olaudah Equiano." In *The Classic Slave Narratives*, edited by Henry Louis Gates Jr. New York: Mentor, 1987.

Eyer, Diane E. *Mother-Infant Bonding: A Scientific Fiction.* New Haven, CT: Yale University Press, 1992.

Fanon, Frantz. *The Wretched of the Earth.* New York: Grove Press, 1968.

Feig, Konnilyn G. *Hitler's Death Camps: The Sanity of Madness.* New York: Holmes and Meier, 1979.

Foucault, Michel. *The Birth of the Clinic: An Archaeology of Medical Perception.* New York: Vintage, 1975.

———. *Discipline and Punish: The Birth of the Prison.* New York: Vintage, 1979.

———. *Madness and Civilization: A History of Insanity in the Age of Reason.* Translated by Richard Howard. New York: Vintage Books, 1965.

Frankovits, André, ed. *Seduced and Abandoned: The Baudrillard Scene.* New York: Stonemoss Services and Semiotext(e), 1984.

Fraser, Steven, ed. *The Bell Curve Wars: Race, Intelligence, and the Future of America.* New York: Basic Books, 1995.

Fredrickson, George M. *The Arrogance of Race: Historical Perspectives on Slavery, Racism, and Social Inequality.* Middletown, CT: Wesleyan University Press, 1988.

Freud, Sigmund. "Anal Eroticism and the Castration Complex." In *Standard Edition*, vol. 19.

———. "A Difficulty in the Path of Psychoanalysis." In *Standard Edition*, vol. 17.

———. *The Ego and the Id.* New York: W. W. Norton, 1960.

———. "Inhibitions, Symptoms and Anxiety." In *Standard Edition*, vol. 20.

———. *Sexuality and the Psychology of Love.* New York: Collier Books, 1963.

———. "Some Psychological Consequences of the Anatomical Distinction Between the Sexes" (1925). In *Sexuality and the Psychology of Love.* New York: Collier Books, 1963.

Friedlander, Henry. *The Origins of Nazi Genocide: From Euthanasia to the Final Solution.* Chapel Hill: University of North Carolina Press, 1995.

Fury, David. *Kings of the Jungle.* Jefferson, NC: McFarland, 1994.

Gates, Henry Louis, Jr., ed. *The Classic Slave Narratives.* New York: Mentor, 1987.

Gilman, Sander L. *Difference and Pathology: Stereotypes of Sexuality, Race and Madness.* Ithaca, NY: Cornell University Press, 1985.

Glass, James M. *"Life Unworthy of Life": Racial Phobia and Mass Murder in Hitler's Germany.* New York: Basic Books, 1997.

Gobineau, Arthur Compte de. *The Moral and Intellectual Diversity of Races.* New York: Garland, 1984. First published 1856 by J. B. Lippincott.

Goldhagen, Daniel Jonah. *Hitler's Willing Executioners: Ordinary Germans and the Holocaust.* New York: Knopf, 1996.

Gould, Stephen J. *The Mismeasure of Man.* New York: W. W. Norton, 1996.

Graves, Joseph L., Jr. *The Emperor's New Clothes: Biological Theories of Race at the Millennium.* New Brunswick, NJ: Rutgers University Press, 2001.

Griffin, Donald R. *Animal Minds: Beyond Cognition and Consciousness*. Chicago: University of Chicago Press, 2001.

Hall, Gwendolyn Midlo. *Social Control in Slave Plantations: A Comparison of St. Domingue and Cuba*. Baltimore: Johns Hopkins Press, 1971.

Ham, Jennifer, and Matthew Senior. *Animal Acts: Configuring the Human in Western History*. New York: Routledge, 1997.

Hamel, Frank. *Human Animals: Werewolves and Other Transformations*. New Hyde Park, NY: University Books, 1969.

Hannaford, Ivan. *Race: The History of an Idea in the West*. Baltimore: Johns Hopkins University Press, 1996.

Haraway, Donna J. *Primate Visions: Gender, Race and Nature in the World of Modern Science*. New York: Routledge, 1989.

———. *Simians, Cyborgs, and Women: The Reinvention of Nature*. New York: Routledge, 1991.

Harper, Chancellor. "Harper's Memoir on Slavery." In *The Pro-Slavery Argument*. New York: Negro Universities Press, 1968 [1832].

Herrnstein, Richard J., and Charles Murray. *The Bell Curve: Intelligence and Class Structure in American Life*. New York: Free Press, 1994.

Heyer, Paul. *Nature, Human Nature, and Society: Marx, Darwin, Biology, and the Human Sciences*. Westport, CT: Greenwood Press, 1982.

Hitler, Adolf. *Mein Kampf*. Translated by Ralph Manheim. Boston: Houghton-Mifflin, 1971.

Hobbes, Thomas. *Leviathan*. Edited by C. B. Macpherson. London: Penguin, 1985.

Hochschild, Adam. *King Leopold's Ghost: A Story of Greed, Terror and Heroism in Colonial Africa*. Boston: Houghton Mifflin, 1999.

Horsman, Reginald. *Race and Manifest Destiny: The Origins of American Anglo-Saxonism*. Cambridge, MA: Harvard University Press, 1981.

Hrdy, Sarah Blaffer. "Empathy, Polyandry, and the Myth of the Coy Female." In *Feminist Approaches to Science*, edited by R. Bleier. New York: Pergamon, 1988.

———. *Mother Nature: A History of Mothers, Infants, and Natural Selection*. New York: Pantheon Books, 1999.

Ihde, Don. *Bodies in Technology*. Minneapolis: University of Minnesota Press, 2002.

Ingold, Tim, ed. *What Is an Animal?* London: Unwin Hyman, 1988.

Kachigan, Sam Kash. *The Sexual Matrix: Boy Meets Girl on an Evolutionary Scale*. New York: Radius Press, 1996.

Kant, Immanuel. *Anthropology from a Pragmatic Point of View*. Translated by Victor Lyle Dowdell. Carbondale, IL: Southern Illinois University Press, 1978.

Kay, F. George. *The Shameful Trade*. South Brunswick and New York: A. S. Barnes, 1967.

Kelling, George L., and Catherine M. Coles. *Fixing Broken Windows: Restoring Order and Reducing Crime in Our Communities*. New York: Free Press, 1996.

Kevles, Daniel J. *In the Name of Eugenics: Genetics and the Uses of Human Heredity.* Cambridge, MA: Harvard University Press, 1995.

Laurence, Leslie, and Beth Weinhouse. *Outrageous Practices: The Alarming Truth about How Medicine Mistreats Women.* New York: Fawcett Columbine, 1994.

Le Bras-Chopard, Armelle. *Le Zoo des philosophes: De la bestialisation á l'exclusion.* Paris: Plon, 2000.

Levy, Anita. *Other Women: The Writing of Class, Race, and Gender, 1832–1898.* Princeton, NJ: Princeton University Press, 1991.

Lewin, Rhoda, G. *Witnesses to the Holocaust: An Oral History.* Boston: Twayne Publishers, 1990.

Lewontin, R. C. *Biology as Ideology: The Doctrine of DNA.* New York: HarperPerennial, 1991.

———. *It Ain't Necessarily So: The Dream of the Human Genome and Other Illusions.* New York: New York Review Books, 2000.

Lewontin, R. C., Steven Rose, and Leon J. Kamin. *Not in Our Genes: Biology, Ideology, and Human Nature.* New York: Pantheon, 1984.

Lewy, Guenther. *The Nazi Persecution of the Gypsies.* New York: Oxford University Press, 2000.

Lifton, Robert J. *The Nazi Doctors: Medical Killing and the Psychology of Genocide.* New York: Basic Books, 2000.

Lippit, Akira Mizuta. *Electric Animal: Toward a Rhetoric of Wildlife.* Minneapolis: University of Minnesota Press, 2000.

Lombroso, Cesare. *Crime: Its Causes and Remedies.* Boston: Little, Brown & Co., 1918.

Lombroso, Cesare, and William Ferrero. *The Female Offender.* New York: D. Appleton & Co., 1895.

Loomba, Ania. *Colonialism/Postcolonialism.* London: Routledge, 1998.

Lorenz, Konrad. *On Aggression.* New York: Harcourt, Brace & World, 1966.

Lorenz, Konrad, and Paul Leyhausen. *Motivation of Human and Animal Behavior: An Ethological View.* New York: Van Nostrand Reinhold, 1973.

Loury, Glenn C. *One by One from the Inside Out: Essays and Reviews on Race and Responsibility in America.* New York: Free Press, 1995.

Lyotard, Jean-François. *Heidegger and "the jews."* Translated by Andreas Michel and Mark S. Roberts. Minneapolis: University of Minnesota Press, 1990.

———. *The Inhuman: Reflections on Time.* Stanford, CA: Stanford University Press, 1991.

Magnet, Myron. *The Dream and the Nightmare: The Sixties Legacy to the Underclass.* New York: William Morrow, 1993.

Mallet, Marie-Louise, ed. *L'animal autobiographique: Autour de Jacques Derrida.* Paris: Galilée, 1999.

Mander, Jerry. *Four Arguments for the Elimination of Television.* New York: Quill, 1978.

Marks, Paula Mitchell. *In a Barren Land: American Indian Dispossession and Survival.* New York: William Morrow, 1998.

Masson, Jeffrey Moussaeiff. *A Dark Science: Women, Sexuality and Psychiatry in the Nineteenth Century.* New York: Farrar, Straus & Giroux, 1986.

Masson, Jeffrey Moussaeiff, and Susan McCarthy. *When Elephants Weep: The Emotional Lives of Animals.* New York: Delacorte Press, 1995.

McLuhan, Marshall. *Understanding Media: The Extensions of Man.* New York: Signet, 1964.

McLynn, Frank. *Crime and Punishment in Eighteenth-Century England.* London: Routledge, 1989.

Mednick, Sarnoff E., et al., eds. *The Causes of Crime: New Biological Approaches.* Cambridge, UK: Cambridge University Press, 1987.

Morgan, Lewis Henry. *Ancient Society.* 1877.

Morris, Desmond. *The Human Zoo.* New York: McGraw-Hill, 1969.

———. *The Naked Ape: A Zoologist's Study of the Human Animal.* New York: McGraw-Hill, 1967.

Neihardt, John G. *Black Elk Speaks.* Lincoln/London: University of Nebraska Press, 1979.

Nietzsche, Friedrich. *Beyond Good and Evil.* Translated by Walter Kaufmann. New York: Vintage, 1989.

Nussbaum, Soumerai, and Carol D. Schultz. *Daily Life during the Holocaust.* Westport, CT: Greenwood Press, 1998.

Oakley, Ann. *Woman's Work: The Housewife, Past and Present.* New York: Vintage, 1976.

Olson, Eric T. *The Human Animal: Personal Identity without Psychology.* New York: Oxford University Press, 1997.

Otten, Charlotte F., ed. *A Lycanthropy Reader: Werewolves in Western Culture.* Syracuse, NY: Syracuse University Press, 1986.

Parenti, Christian. *Lockdown America: Police and Prisons in the Age of Crisis.* London: Verso, 1999.

Plato. *The Republic.* Translated by Francis MacDonald Cornford. New York: Oxford University Press, 1971.

Poliakov, Léon. *The Aryan Myth: A History of Racist and Nationalist Ideas in Europe.* New York: Basic Books, 1971.

Pope-Hennessy, James. *Sins of the Fathers: The Atlantic Slave Traders, 1441–1807.* London: Phoenix Press, 1967.

Postman, Neil. *Technopoly: The Surrender of Culture to Technology.* New York: Knopf, 1992.

Priest, Josiah. *Bible Defence of Slavery or the Origin, History, and Fortunes of the Negro Race.* Glasgow, KY: The Rev. W. S. Brown, 1853.

Proctor, Robert N. *Racial Hygiene: Medicine under the Nazis.* Cambridge, MA: Harvard University Press, 1988.

Ritvo, Harriet. "The Animal Connection." In *The Boundaries of Humanity: Humans, Animals, Machines*, edited by James J. Sheehan and Morton Sosna, 68–84. Berkeley: University of California Press, 1991.

Rodis-Lewis, Geneviève. "Limitations of the Mechanical Model in the Cartesian Conception of Organism." In *Descartes: Critical and Interpretive Essays*, edited by Michael Hooker (Baltimore: Johns Hopkins University Press, 1978).

Rosenberg, Alfred. *Race and Race History*. Edited by Robert Pois. New York: Harper & Row, 1970.

Russett, Cynthia Eagle. *Sexual Science: The Victorian Construction of Womanhood*. Cambridge, MA: Harvard University Press, 1989.

Sade, Marquis de. *Juliette*. Translated by Austryn Wainhouse. New York: Grove Press, 1976.

Sax, Boria. *Animals in the Third Reich: Pets, Scapegoats, and the Holocaust*. New York: Continuum, 2000.

Schreier, Herbert A., and Judith A. Libow. *Hurting for Love: Munchausen by Proxy Syndrome*. New York: Guilford, 1993.

Senior, Matthew. "When the Beasts Spoke." In *Animal Acts: Configuring the Human in Western History*, edited by Jennifer Ham and Matthew Senior. New York: Routledge, 1997.

Shelley, Mary. *Frankenstein or, the Modern Prometheus*. New York: Signet/Penguin, 1983.

Shorter, Edward. *A History of Psychiatry: From the Era of the Asylum to the Age of Prozac*. New York: John Wiley & Sons, 1997.

Shufeldt, R. W. *America's Greatest Problem: The Negro*. Philadelphia: F. A. Davis, 1915.

Sim, Stuart. *Lyotard and the Inhuman*. Cambridge, UK: Icon Books, 2001.

Singer, Peter. *Animal Liberation*. New York: HarperCollins, 2002.

———, ed. *In Defense of Animals*. New York: Basil Blackwell, 1985.

Skal, David, J. *The Monster Show: A Cultural History of Horror*. New York: W. W. Norton, 1993.

———. *Screams of Reason: Mad Science and Modern Culture*. New York: W. W. Norton, 1998.

Sofsky, Wolfgang. *The Order of Terror: The Concentration Camp*. Princeton, NJ: Princeton University Press, 1997.

Sorabji, Richard. *Animal Minds and Human Morals: The Origins of the Western Debate*. Ithaca, NY: Cornell University Press, 1993.

Spiegel, Marjorie. *The Dreaded Comparison: Human and Animal Slavery*. Secaucus, NJ: Mirror Books, 1996.

Stone, Gregory B. "The Philosophical Beast: On Boccaccio's Tale of Cimone." In *Animal Acts: Configuring the Human in Western History*, edited by Jennifer Ham and Matthew Senior (New York: Routledge, 1997).

Szasz, Thomas. *The Manufacture of Madness: A Comparative Study of the Inquisition and the Mental Health Movement.* New York: Harper & Row, 1970.

Tavris, Carol. *The Mismeasure of Woman: Why Women Are Not the Better Sex, the Inferior Sex, or the Opposite Sex.* New York: Simon & Schuster, 1992.

Taylor, Jared. *Paved with Good Intentions: The Failure of Race Relations in Contemporary America.* New York: Carroll and Graf, 1992.

Taylor, Telford. "Opening Statement of the Prosecution, Dec. 9, 1946." In *The Nazi Doctors and the Nuremberg Code: Human Rights and Human Experimentation.* New York: Oxford University Press, 1992.

Theweleit, Klaus. *Male Fantasies,* vols. 1 & 2 (Minneapolis: University of Minnesota Press, 1989.

Thiroux, Jacques P. *Ethics: Theory and Practice.* New York: Macmillan, 1990.

Thomas, Hugh. *The Slave Trade: The Story of the Atlantic Slave Trade: 1440–1870.* New York: Touchstone, 1997.

Tiger, Lionel, and Robin Fox. *The Imperial Animal.* New York: Holt, Rinehart & Winston, 1971.

Vallenstein, Elliot S. *Great and Desperate Cures: The Rise and Decline of Psychosurgery and Other Radical Treatments for Mental Illness.* New York: Basic Books, 1986.

Van Evrie, J. H. *Negroes and Negro Slavery: The First an Inferior Race the Latter Its Normal Condition.* New York: Van Evrie, Horton & Co., 1863.

———. *White Supremacy and Negro Subordination or, Negroes a Subordinate Race and (so-called) Slavery Its Normal Condition.* New York: Van Evrie, Horton & Co., 1868.

Walvin, James. *Slavery and the Slave Trade.* Jackson: University of Mississippi Press, 1983.

Whitehead, Alfred North. *Process and Reality: An Essay in Cosmology.* New York: Harper & Row, 1957.

Wiesel, Elie. *Night/Dawn/Day.* Northvale, NJ: Jason Aronson, 1985.

Wilson, E. O. *Sociobiology: The New Synthesis.* Cambridge, MA: Harvard University Press, 1975.

Wilson, James Q., ed. *Crime and Public Policy.* San Francisco: ICS Press, 1983.

Wilson, Margaret D. *Descartes.* London: Routledge/Keegan Paul, 1978.

Wright, Robert. *The Moral Animal: Why We Are the Way We Are: The New Science of Evolutionary Psychology.* New York: Pantheon Books, 1994.

Index

www.ingramcontent.com/pod-product-compliance
Lightning Source LLC
Chambersburg PA
CBHW061017280326
41935CB00009B/999